INTERNATIONAL POLITICAL ECONOMY SERIES

General Editor: Timothy M. Shaw, Professor of Political Science and International Development Studies, and Director of the Centre for Foreign Policy Studies, Dalhousie University, Nova Scotia, Canada

Recent titles include:

Pradeep Agrawal, Subir V. Gokarn, Veena Mishra, Kirit S. Parikh and Kunal Sen
ECONOMIC RESTRUCTURING IN EAST ASIA AND INDIA: Perspectives on Policy Reform

Solon L. Barraclough and Krishna B. Ghimire
FORESTS AND LIVELIHOODS: The Social Dynamics of Deforestation in Developing Countries

Steve Chan (*editor*)
FOREIGN DIRECT INVESTMENT IN A CHANGING GLOBAL POLITICAL ECONOMY

Edward A. Comor (*editor*)
THE GLOBAL POLITICAL ECONOMY OF COMMUNICATION

Paul Cook and Frederick Nixson (*editors*)
THE MOVE TO THE MARKET? Trade and Industry Policy Reform in Transitional Economies

O. P. Dwivedi
DEVELOPMENT ADMINISTRATION: From Underdevelopment to Sustainable Development

George Kent
CHILDREN IN THE INTERNATIONAL POLITICAL ECONOMY

David Kowalewski
GLOBAL ESTABLISHMENT: The Political Economy of North/Asian Networks

Laura Macdonald
SUPPORTING CIVIL SOCIETY: The Political Role of Non-Governmental Organizations in Central America

Gary McMahon (*editor*)
LESSONS IN ECONOMIC POLICY FOR EASTERN EUROPE FROM LATIN AMERICA

Juan Antonio Morales and Gary McMahon (*editors*)
ECONOMIC POLICY AND THE TRANSITION TO DEMOCRACY: The Latin American Experience

Paul J. Nelson
THE WORLD BANK AND NON-GOVERNMENTAL ORGANIZATIONS:
The Limits of Apolitical Development

Ann Seidman and Robert B. Seidman
STATE AND LAW IN THE DEVELOPMENT PROCESS: Problem-Solving and
Institutional Change in the Third World

Tor Skålnes
THE POLITICS OF ECONOMIC REFORM IN ZIMBABWE: Continuity and
Change in Development

Howard Stein (*editor*)
ASIAN INDUSTRIALIZATION AND AFRICA: Studies in Policy Alternatives
to Structural Adjustment

Deborah Stienstra
WOMEN'S MOVEMENTS AND INTERNATIONAL ORGANIZATIONS

Larry A. Swatuk and Timothy M. Shaw (*editors*)
THE SOUTH AT THE END OF THE TWENTIETH CENTURY: Rethinking the
Political Economy of Foreign Policy in Africa, Asia, the Caribbean and Latin
America

Sandra Whitworth
FEMINISM AND INTERNATIONAL RELATIONS

International Political Economy Series
Series Standing Order ISBN 0–333–71110–6
(*outside North America only*)

You can receive future titles in this series as they are published by placing a standing order.
Please contact your bookseller or, in case of difficulty, write to us at the address below with
your name and address, the title of the series and the ISBN quoted above.

Customer Services Department, Macmillan Distribution Ltd
Houndmills, Basingstoke, Hampshire RG21 6XS, England

Globalization and the South

Edited by

Caroline Thomas
Reader in Politics
Southampton University

and

Peter Wilkin
Lecturer in Politics and International Relations
Lancaster University

First published in Great Britain 1997 by
MACMILLAN PRESS LTD
Houndmills, Basingstoke, Hampshire RG21 6XS and London
Companies and representatives throughout the world

A catalogue record for this book is available from the British Library.

ISBN 0–333–65943–0

First published in the United States of America 1997 by
ST. MARTIN'S PRESS, INC.,
Scholarly and Reference Division,
175 Fifth Avenue, New York, N.Y. 10010

ISBN 0–312–17564–7

Library of Congress Cataloging-in-Publication Data
Globalization and the South / edited by Caroline Thomas and Peter
Wilkin.
  p.   cm. — (International political economy series)
Includes bibliographical references and index.
ISBN 0–312–17564–7 (cloth)
1. Southern hemisphere—Foreign economic relations.
2. International economic relations.   3. International relations.
I. Thomas, Caroline.   II. Wilkin, Peter, 1963–   .   III. Series.
HF1359.G584 1997
337.1'1814—dc21   97–12143
                                                                CIP

This book is printed on paper suitable for recycling and made from fully managed and sustained forest sources.

10   9   8   7   6   5   4   3   2   1
06 05 04 03 02 01 00 99 98 97

Printed in Great Britain by
The Ipswich Book Company Ltd
Ipswich, Suffolk

SEVEN DAY LOAN

This book is to be returned on
or before the date stamped below

UNIVERSITY OF PLYMOUTH 13 1-25

PLYMOUTH LIBRARY

Tel: (01752) 232323
This book is subject to recall if required by another reader
Books may be renewed by phone
CHARGES WILL BE MADE FOR OVERDUE BOOKS

Contents

Figures and Tables

Acknowledgements

The editors would like to acknowledge the superb administrative support provided by Anita Catney and Melvyn Reader, both of the Politics Department, Southampton University. The cheerful assistance of these two individuals made the technical side of the editorial task a very happy one.

Contributors

Patricia Adams is the Executive Director of Probe International, a Canadian environmental group. She is the author of *Odious Debts: Loose Lending, Corruption, and the Third World's Environmental Legacy* (London and Toronto: Earthscan, 1991).

Walden Bello is Co-Director of the Bangkok-based organization, Focus on the Global South, and Professor of Sociology and Public Administration at the University of the Philippines. He is the author of *Dragons in Distress: Asia's Miracle in Crisis* (London: Penguin, 1991).

Tony Evans is a Lecturer in International Relations at the University of Southampton. He specializes in the politics of human rights, and has just published *US Hegemony and the Project of Universal Human Rights* (London: Macmillan, 1996).

Frank Furedi lectures at the University of Kent, and is the author of *The New Ideology of Imperialism* (London: Pluto Press, 1994).

Barry Gills is a Lecturer in Politics at the University of Newcastle upon Tyne. He is co-editor with J. Rocamora and R. Wilson of *Low Intensity Democracy: Political Power in the New World Order* (London: Pluto Press, 1993).

Dipak Gyawali is Research Director at Interdisciplinary Analysts, Kathmandu, an adviser to the Nepal Water Conservation Foundation, and a member of Pragya, the Royal Nepal Academy of Science and Technology, Kathmandu. He is a frequent contributor to *Water Nepal* and *Himal*.

Larry Lohmann, formerly of *The Ecologist*, is a researcher and writer on global ecology with a special interest in Thailand. He is co-author of *Whose Common Future?* (London: Earthscan, 1993).

Fahimul Quadir is a doctoral candidate in Political Science at Dalhousie University, Nova Scotia, a lecturer in Political Science at Chittagong University in Bangladesh, and in International Development Studies at Dalhousie University, Nova Scotia.

Mohamed A. Mohamed Salih is a Senior Lecturer at the Institute of Social Studies in the Hague, the Netherlands. His recent publications include *Management of the Crisis in Somalia: The Politics of Reconciliation*, and *Inducing Food Insecurity: Perspectives on Food Policies in Eastern and Southern Africa* (both Uppsala: Scandinavian Institute of African Studies, 1994).

Julian Saurin is a Lecturer in International Relations at the University of Sussex, with a special interest in global hunger. He is the author of *In Search of Sufficiency* (London: Routledge, forthcoming).

Timothy M. Shaw is Professor of Political Science and International Development Studies at Dalhousie University, Nova Scotia. He is the General Editor of the Macmillan/St Martin's Press International Political Economy Series, for which he recently co-edited *The South at the End of the Twentieth-Century*.

Caroline Thomas lectures in International Relations at the University of Southampton. She is the editor of *Rio: Unravelling the Consequences* (London: Frank Cass, 1994).

Peter Wilkin is a Lecturer in Politics at Lancaster University. He is author of *An Introduction to Naom Chomsky* (Edinburgh: AK Press, 1995), and *Noam Chomsky: On Knowledge, Power and Human Nature* (London: Macmillan/St Martin's Press, 1996).

Acronyms

AFTA	ASEAN Free Trade Area
APEC	Asia Pacific Economic Cooperation
ASEAN	Association of South-East Asian Nations
BJP	Bharatiya Janata Party
EAEG	East Asia Economic Group
EPG	Eminent Persons' Group
FAD	Food Availability Decline
FAO	Food and Agricultural Organisation
G7	Group of 7 countries
G77	Group of 77 countries
GATT	General Agreement on Tariffs and Trade
GDP	Gross Domestic Product
GEF	Global Environmental Facility
GNP	Gross National Product
GSP	Generalised System of Preferences
IBRD	International Bank for Reconstruction and Development
IDA	International Development Association
IFI	International Financial Institution
IMF	International Monetary Fund
INGO	International Non-Governmental Organization
JICA	Japanese International Cooperation Agency
KMT	Kuomintang
LDC	Less Developed Country
MDB	Multilateral Development Bank
MITI	Ministry of International Trade of Industry Japan
MNC	Multinational Corporation
NACLA	North American Congress on Latin America
NAFTA	North American Free Trade Area
NEA	Nepal Electricity Authority
NGO	Non-Governmental Organization
NIC	Newly Industrializing Country
OECD	Organisation for Economic Cooperation and Development
RSS	Rastriya Swayamsevak Sangh
SAF	Structural Adjustment Facility
SAL	Structural Adjustment Loan
SAP	Structural Adjustment Program
TNC	Transnational Corporation
TRIMS	Trade Related Investment Measures
TRIPS	Trade Related Intellectual Property Rights
UNCED	United Nations Conference on Environment and Development
UNDP	United Nations Development Program
UNEP	United Nations Environment Program
UNFPA	United Nations Population Fund
UNRISD	United Nations Research Institute for Social Development

Acronyms

USAID	United States Agency for International Development
VHP	Vishwa Hindu Parishad
WCED	World Commission on Environment and Development

1 Globalization and the South

Caroline Thomas

This volume brings together a group of authors who share a common concern with the effects of globalization on the South. Included among these effects is the accelerating erosion of the social, economic and political significance of the territorial distinction on which the terms South and North are founded. Our aim is explicit: to offer a *unique perspective on globalization which places the transformation of the South and the renewed global organization of inequality at the heart of our understanding of the global order.* This chapter outlines some of the main arguments of the book and draws some conclusions for global politics as we enter the twenty-first century.

We identify a liberal philosophy underpinning the process of global economic integration and the accompanying global reorganization of social relations. We illustrate how the practical application of the dominant philosophy of economic and political liberalism is resulting in fundamental changes in the world order which privilege some actors and marginalize others. We show that ideas of universality held by a range of international institutions such as the World Bank and the IMF, and inherent in a range of liberalization processes, serve to undermine the possibility of meaningful self-determination for the majority of people in the South. We conclude that this hegemony brings forth a counter-hegemony, and thus we encounter heterogenous resistance to the process and effects of globalization.

THE PROBLEM

We are faced with a worrying trend. After 50 years of official development policies, the gap between rich and poor is growing, and poverty is widespread.

Even more worrying than the trend itself is the domination of a *neo-liberal* understanding of the problem in the world's major economic institutions. Institutions such as the IMF, the World Bank and the Group of 7 define the discussion of appropriate remedial action (Thomas, 1996). The neo-liberal understanding

1

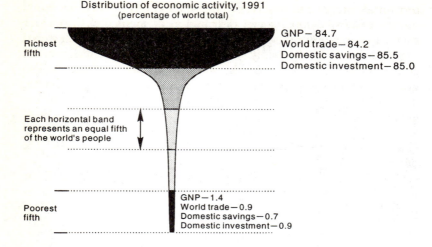

Distribution of economic activity, 1991
(percentage of world total)

Richest fifth

GNP— 84.7
World trade— 84.2
Domestic savings— 85.5
Domestic investment— 85.0

Each horizontal band represents an equal fifth of the world's people

Poorest fifth

GNP— 1.4
World trade— 0.9
Domestic savings— 0.7
Domestic investment— 0.9

Figure 1.1 Global Economic Disparities

Source: UNDP, 1994, p. 63.

informing their policies is rooted in a local, essentially Western, capitalist worldview. Adherents champion this as universal and natural. Yet it privileges the interests of a select group of powerful transnational capitalist actors while purporting to serve the interests of the majority of humankind. It is presented as offering the only 'respectable' knowledge about just economic, social and political organization and practice. Opposing ideas are neutralized, often by the language of incorporation into the dominant view (Marglin and Marglin, 1990; Graf, 1992).

   Growing economic disparities and poverty characterize not simply the state system, but the global social order. In other words, it is no longer enough to think only in terms of rich and poor *states*; we need to consider *groups or classes* of rich and poor people which cross-cut state boundaries. Of course, if we group populations by territorial states, we find that the North/South disparity remains a central facet of the global order. The 23 per cent of the global population living in the North enjoys 85 per cent of the world's income, while the 77 per cent in the South enjoys just 15 per cent (Falk, 1995, pp. 57–8). However these statistics need to be treated with great caution, for they tell us nothing about distribution within the South or within the North. Indeed, such territorial categorization serves to mask, and even mystify, the much more significant global social distribution of inequality. Moreover such categorization refuses to acknowledge the transnational/global organization of inequality. While there is an indisputable concentration of poverty in the geographic South, there is also growing wealth among certain classes in the geographic South, just as there is growing poverty among certain classes in the geographic North. There is a need to map global poverty, wealth and inequality as global social relations and not as territorial characteristics. Thus, for example, Table 1.1 reveals the decreasing share of global income going to the poorest 20 per cent of the global population over the period 1960–90, and the increasing share going to the richest 20 per cent over the same period.

Table 1.1 Global Income Distribution, 1960–90

Year	Share of global income going to richest 20% (%)	Share of global income going to poorest 20% (%)	Ratio of richest to poorest
1960	70.2	2.3	30:1
1970	73.9	2.3	32:1
1980	76.3	1.7	45:1
1990	82.8	1.3	64:1

Source: Brown and Kane, 1995, p. 46.

To understand this situation, we need to liberate our thinking from the constraints imposed by interpretation within a territorially-based state-centric worldview, which concentrates on a North/South gap in terms of *states*. State-centric thinking presents an artificial picture, for even while it may now differentiate between states previously categorized as 'Third World', such as the least developed, the newly industrializing and newly industrialized states (NICS) and the oil-rich states, it fails to tell us anything about internal entitlement and distribution within these societies. Further, it fails to tell us how this relates to and reflects the global construction of entitlement and distribution. Similarly, it fails to highlight the existence of a growing 'South' in the 'North' and to relate this to the global construction of entitlement and distribution. Within the states usually referred to as Northern or developed, there is a growing gap in income and in life-chances which cascades through generations. Table 1.2 reveals the changing distribution of income in the US over the 1980s.

Table 1.2 Changes in US Income Distribution, 1977 and 1988

- 10%	- 3%	+ 4%	+ 9%	+ 34%
Bottom fifth	Next lowest fifth	Middle fifth	Second highest fifth	Top fifth

Source: Falk, 1995; reprinted from *International Herald Tribune*, 25 July 1991.

This table reveals the development of a growing underclass in the US, plus a concentration of wealth in a narrow élite. The trend is evident in many other industrialized states. The growth of the underclass is being accelerated by the process of globalization which transfers production and jobs to parts of the world where labour costs are cheaper, environmental standards less stringent and the potential for profit for the owners of capital greater. Similarly, we are seeing the enrichment of certain classes within the 'Third World' countries, and the increasing marginalization of others. We need to take a critical look at traditional categories and, where appropriate, develop new ones more reflective of this emerging global order. Our traditional understanding of North/South (or 'Third World') is under scrutiny. A more productive focus is one which identifies different life-chances of *groups or classes of people* within a *global framework.*

In March 1995, the UN World Summit for Social Development, more commonly referred to as the Poverty Summit, took place in Copenhagen to address the issues of increasing inequalities and widespread poverty. The sort of concerns which prompted the gathering included: the lack of access to clean water or sanitation for 500–1000 million people; the paradox of increased food production being 'one of the outstanding global achievements of the post-war period', while 800 million people are malnourished and 40,000 die every day from hunger and related diseases (International Commission on Peace and Food, 1994, pp. 104, 106); and the un- or under-employment of 30 per cent of the global labour force.

Clearly something has gone wrong in the development process to date. The model of development in place is unable to meet professed goals. There were some impressive achievements in 'Third World' countries prior to the 1980s when measured by the conventional yardstick of growth in GDP per capita. However, this success was not reflected in the societies at large. Without specific economic and social policies directed towards poverty reduction, growth would not result in overall improvement. Reflecting on the development trajectory of the South in the post-war period, the South Commission has commented that

> Inequalities tended to widen as the economy grew and became more industrialized.... . Increasingly, the rich and powerful in the countries of the South were able to enjoy the life-style and consumption patterns of developed countries of the North. But large segments of the population experienced no significant improvement in their standard of living, while being able to see the growing affluence of the few. The worst sufferers... were usually the most vulnerable of the poor: women, children and other socially disadvantaged groups (South Commission, 1990, p. 38).

With the development of modernity over the past 500 years, we have seen the gradual expansion of *capitalism* across the globe. Socialist experiments, by comparison, have been less successful in terms of expansion and durability. But in fact both have much in common: the transformation of traditional subsistence economies defined as 'backward' into large-scale industrial economies defined as 'modern'; industrialization of agriculture; centralization; top-down decision-making; conceptions of poverty as a material condition; environmental blindness; individuals selling their labour rather than producing to meet their family's needs. The emphasis on selling one's labour, paid employment and commodification has in certain important respects decreased rather than increased an individual's or a community's control and self-determination over their life-chances, and placed more power in the hands of either the market or the government. Neither the market nor the state has served the most vulnerable well; indeed the opposite often seems to be the case (Thomas *et al*, 1994, p. 22).

GLOBALIZATION

The argument of this book is that *globalization, interpreted most importantly but not solely as the latest stage of capitalism, is compounding inequalities already in place and developing new ones.* The process is intensifying economic, social and political inequalities by privileging the private over the public sphere and by marginalizing the actual, as well as the potential, importance of the commons. This is occurring on a *global scale*, even though it is not a uniform process and it does not have homogeneous results. The process is supported by *liberal ideology* which places a premium on individual choice in the market-place.

However, there is a real sense in which both the process and the ideology supporting it are increasing global social divisions. The apparent triumph of the West, of liberal economics and politics, is not nearly so universal as is often suggested. We are witnessing the process by which the ideology of dominant groups, presented as universal, is used to legitimate the marginalization and neutralization of competing visions and values. This is evident across a wide range of issues and areas, encompassing not only the important, obvious and related discourses on finance, trade, development, aid, and economic policy generally, but also those on ecology, human rights, law and so forth. Since the process is not universal or comprehensive, then counter-hegemonic groups or movements are able to continue offering alternative visions or practices.

A few words on our interpretation of globalization are in order here. *Globalization as used in this volume refers broadly to the process whereby power is located in global social formations and expressed through global networks rather than through territorially-based states.* The contributions in this volume see globalization as being driven by capitalism which has entered a stage wherein accumulation is taking place on a global rather than a national scale. Transnational capitalist institutions are speeding up and deepening the realignment of social and class relations within what is already a single world-system. They are setting the global economic, social and political agenda. This process of globalization has been accelerating with the restructuring of the global capitalist economy since the demise of the Bretton Woods system in the early 1970s. Tables 1.1 and 1.2 above reveal the deepening inequalities resulting from this process over the 1970s and 1980s.

In addition to the accumulation of capital, as classically understood, there is the accumulation of power in other forms which has often been ignored, e.g. knowledge, military capability, regulatory capacity. These other accumulations can be identified across a wide spectrum, for example in the universal legitimacy accorded to Western liberal social and political values, and in the human rights discourse. Global accumulation in all its aspects undermines the value of local diversity and legitimizes the dominant liberal agenda.

Globalization erodes the authority of states differentially to set the social, economic and political agenda within their respective political space. It erodes the capacity of states to different degrees to secure the livelihoods of their respective citizens by narrowing the parameters of legitimate state activity. This is part of a wider process of redrawing hierarchical social relations in the world system. With the wide-ranging subversion of the regulatory capacity of the state, other actors influence entitlement. These include intergovernmental bodies such as the World Bank and the IMF, the Group of 7 (G-7), and non-state actors such as transnational corporations (TNCs) and banks.

It appears then that we are in a transition phase where old identities, sites of legitimacy and capacity are being eroded, subverted by new ones arising due to the process of globalization under way. People are developing new political and social identities in response to the globalization process, some contained within the state, and some transcending it. The significance and meaning of terms like development, state and South/Third World are thrown into question.

LIBERAL PHILOSOPHY

The process of economic, political and social accumulation is supported and driven by a liberal ideology. The liberal ideology attributes universal legitimacy to a conception of freedom based on private power. This has served to mystify its practical impact, and given the appearance of increasing an individual's control over or consumption of the products which capitalism is generating (Wilkin, Chapter 2, this volume). In fact, those without the necessary economic, social or political power are excluded from the benefits. Therefore the *liberal ideology is legitimizing global inequalities of life-chance;*

it is legitimizing a situation where inequalities are greater than at any period in history.

In recent years a series of international forums have lent legitimacy to economic liberalization by neutralizing opposition via the incorporation of the language of criticism into mainstream free-market formulations. The Brundtland Report of 1987 stressed the importance of further growth for sustainability; UNCED and Agenda 21 in 1992 promoted free-market principles for sustainable development; then at Copenhagen in 1995, the Poverty Summit legitimated further application of economic liberalization as the best economic policy to counter poverty.

Hand in hand with the promotion of liberal economics has gone the promotion of liberal political ideology. In the post- Cold-War era, there were optimistic assumptions about the possibility of 'Western-style' democratization across the world. Indeed one writer even remarked that 'What we may be witnessing is . . . the end of history as such: that is, the end point of mankind's ideological evolution and the universalization of Western liberal democracy as the final form of human government' (Fukuyama, 1989, p. 4). Latin America and Africa enjoyed some successes, and in other parts of the world, such as China, there were democratic challenges, albeit unsuccessful.

Important questions arise about the progress of *substantive* rather than *formal* democracy (Gills, Rocamora and Wilson, 1994). The latter, demonstrated through periodic elections, for example, do not tell us whether there has been any significant change in empowerment of the general population. We should not assume that liberal democracy is socially progressive. Moreover, the widening inequalities resulting from economic liberalization cast doubt on the ability of the economically powerless to organize and exercise their democratic rights in a meaningful way within the liberal democratic model. Liberal democracy therefore hides growing inequalities.

The liberal political discourse is related directly to rights discourse. In the post-Second World War period the US has attempted the philosophical and legal legitimation of a set of internationally recognized human rights norms (Evans, Chapter 6, this volume). Yet underlying this position are clear economic and political interests which result in the highlighting of civil and political over economic and social rights.

The South has tried to resist the promotion of these interests, and championed social and economic as well as civil and political rights preferred by the US. It is doubtful whether the limited success of the past on this front can be sustained under the existing conditions of increasing globalization. Evans argues that international law is a legal code operating between states. This applies equally to the international law of human rights. Yet the institutions of globalization which are intimately involved in eroding social and economic rights, such as the multinational banks and transnational corporations, can operate largely outside national regulation, and outside international law pertaining to rights. The state is no longer able (if indeed it ever was) to secure such rights for its citizens, even assuming that it wants to.

Pervading the liberal economic and political rights discourse is the belief that a set of essentially local, Western norms are universal. The expansion of liberal values across the globe is not seen as hegemonic but rather as a natural development toward the endpoint of human political, social and economic history. With the demise of the socialist experiment in Eastern Europe and the USSR, the West is presented as triumphal. 'The triumph of the West...is evident first of all in the total exhaustion of viable systematic alternatives to western liberalism' (Fukuyama, 1989, p. 3). There is no recognition of any other possible form of social, political or economic organization. Indeed where other views surface, they are rejected out of hand as inferior and inconsequential. The only alternative as perceived from the liberal viewpoint has been discredited. The global power structure favours a Western knowledge and a Western understanding of events and processes.

This position is arrogant at best, and racist at worst. It is a continuation of the 500 years of history of capitalist expansion across the globe. Empires were justified in the cause of civilizing the natives and bringing them into a state of knowledge of the Christian God. In the post-war period, neo-colonialism has been presented as helping 'them' achieve economic development. Now we have entered a phase whereby a liberal–humanitarian discourse is legitimating attempts to 'save the Third World from itself' (Furedi, Chapter 5, this volume). Such representations ignore the crucial role of the global political economy now and over the past 500 years in the present difficulties facing the non-Western, non-white world.

A recurrent theme in the liberal agenda has been to present a picture of a unified globe which necessitates and legitimizes a common response in terms of management. Thus we have heard UN-inspired think-tanks in the 1980s talk of 'Our Common Future', 'Common Security', and so forth. One of the latest additions to this tradition is in the environmental area, where it is fashionable to discuss a *global ecological crisis requiring global management*. This raises various important points such as: whose globe and whose environment are we talking about; who is to manage it; and in whose interests? The notion of global environmental management assumes that there is a common understanding of the problem and thus agreement about how it is to be addressed. This, however, is not true.

The South has perceived this global ecologism as an exclusionist ideology, one which prevents the mass of humanity from enjoying the benefits of development and deprives the South of the opportunity to utilize their natural resources for their own benefit (see Salih, Chapter 8, this volume; national ownership and the right to indigenous resources are also identified by Evans's Chapter 6 in this volume as a significant part of the struggle by the South to establish economic human rights). Talk of a global environmental crisis and the need for global management hints at something new but in reality masks the perpetuation of the old order and presents a crisis precipitated by development of a particular sector of the world as a global problem, effectively removing responsibility from the perpetrators to all humanity. The crisis results from the economic prosperity enjoyed historically by the North, evident in high-consumption life-styles.

PRACTICAL APPLICATIONS

Most of the chapters in this collection bear witness to the process of neutralization of competing ideas and values which bolsters the dominant worldview and lends it false legitimacy. Particularly important is the equation of freedom and democracy with liberal economics and liberal politics. The effects are evident across many sectors and issues.

Liberal economic ideology informed the decision by the Group of 7 to push a free-market approach to development via structural adjustment in the late 1970s (Ould-Mey, 1994). In the 1980s this approach was institutionalized by the IMF and the World Bank as a debt-management strategy, bringing with it a range of problems for the international financial institutions (Adams, Chapter 10, this volume). They applied structural adjustment packages with increased vigour throughout much of the rest of the world. They oversaw the opening up of national economies to foreign investment; the cutting of bureaucracies and of subsidies for food, health and transport; and the promotion of exports. However, the contradictions inherent in the ensuing patterns of entitlement strain political systems (Shaw and Quadir, Chapter 3, this volume).

The resilience of the dominant liberal economic ideology even in the face of contrary evidence is surprising. A good example is provided by orthodox explanations of the remarkable growth of East Asian economies. The IMF and the World Bank emphasize that growth is dependent on further liberalization, and that the free market is the global panacea. However, there is evidence to suggest not only that the state played a leading economic role in the East Asian Tigers, but that it has been 'the central factor in the take-off of these economies' (Bello, Chapter 9, this volume). Despite the evidence, the myth is perpetuated that the market is the key to growth, and this model has been imposed throughout the South and former Eastern Bloc in the 1980s and 1990s via the structural adjustment policies aforementioned.

Japan's Ministry of International Trade and Industry (MITI), concerned at the continued blind acceptance of the free-market model in the face of contrary evidence, provided most of the funding for a World Bank study on 'The East Asian Miracle'. The Bank study identified the important role of *state intervention*, as Japan had anticipated, but it then argued that this model would not be applicable elsewhere! (Bello, Chapter 9, this volume).

Economic liberalization and the interests it supports received a further boost with the conclusion of the *Uruguay Round* of trade negotiations. Areas previously excluded from GATT rules, such as trade-related intellectual property rights and trade-related investment measures, now came under its remit. This amounted to the *further opening of Southern economies to transnationals, financial and insurance industries based mainly in the North*. This of course represented an increase in the power of the already powerful, and a further weakening of those already disadvantaged.

The role of transnational corporations in the globalization process is particularly worrying given that their constituency is their shareholders and it is to them that they are accountable. While their activities fundamentally affect life-chances, they have no formal responsibility towards people in the way that governments do. They have no mechanisms such as public policy of governments to address people's needs, even if they felt they had a responsibility and the authority to do so. The idea that basic needs can be met in the market-place without the resources and authority of governments is fanciful.

This is clear in relation to the continued existence of hunger amidst plentiful global food supplies. The state, which throughout the twentieth century has increasingly protected and industrialized national agriculture, has been displaced by *agribusiness* as the primary source of resources, ideas and authority in this area (Friedmann and McMichael, cited in Saurin, Chapter 7, this volume). An examination of existing social structures or named agents is necessary to understand the crucial global role of transnationals which are superseding states in the production and marketing of food. Agribusiness is instrumental in and responsible for the development of new social relations and new food insecurities. It is eroding the responsiveness and responsibility of the public domain (Saurin, Chapter 7, this volume).

Since the early 1980s structural adjustment policies have given a boost to the undermining of the national organization of agriculture and food production already under way. So too has the *aggressive pursuit of unilateralist trade policies by the US*, such as the invocation of free trade to legitimize prising open the Korean agricultural market which had traditionally been protected by the government (Bello, Chapter 9, this volume). The result is an increasingly global organization of food provision and of access to food. Transnational corporations play the major role here.

The power of transnational corporations in global agenda-setting was evident at the UNCED in June 1992. Most glaringly absent from the Rio output were guidelines – let alone regulatory policies – for transnationals. It is possible that transnationals played a formative role in shaping the Rio agenda, aided by their financial support for the conference, and the high-profile role and the access given to the Business Council for Sustainable Development by Conference Chairperson Maurice Strong (Chatterjee and Finger, 1994). At the behest of the US, all references to transnational corporations were removed from Agenda 21. Yet these actors are responsible for 70 per cent of world trade, and of course their production and transportation activities have important environmental effects. Prior to UNCED, as part of Boutros Ghali's UN reforms, the UN Center on Transnational Corporations had been dismantled. This body, under the lead of Sweden and the Group of 77 (G-77), had been urging the formulation of internationally recognized guidelines to make transnationals more open and accountable. Thus the way was left open for these corporations to plead their own case for self-regulation. In this, they were successful. The idea that self-regulating transnational corporations will be environmentally responsible, when such behaviour will conflict with the profit motive and their responsibility to their shareholders in the short term, is hard to sustain when one considers their history.

Agenda-setting gives great power. The UNCED provides an interesting example of the neutralization of views which do not concur with the dominant orthodoxy. This is evident in the content of the Rio agenda. In the run-up to the Rio Conference in 1992, there was a clear split between the governments of the North and business interests, and Southern governments, and to a lesser extent even between Northern and Southern NGOs, even over identification of the problem. For the South, the environmental problem cannot be separated from the problem of development; for the older industrialized states, development and environment were two separate issues. While the full name of the Rio conference – the UN Conference on Environment and Development – suggested that the interpretation of the South held sway, in practice all the critical developmental questions that really mattered were swept aside. These included identification of, and action to curb, unsustainable development, which would have necessitated a critical evaluation of the dominant model of development and action on the massive levels of consumption of the world's resources by a small proportion of its people. It would also have necessitated action on debt and trade.

COUNTER-HEGEMONY: RESISTANCE TO GLOBALIZATION

Globalization is not occurring evenly across the globe, and likewise it is not resulting in a common response. We can detect a variety of responses in different localities. The globalization of a particular set of values does not continue without resistance.

While resistance is generally assumed to take place at grassroots level, for example Indian peasant protest against Cargill seed factories, in fact it sometimes occurs at state level. In the East Asian region there is significant resistance by state-élites to continued liberalization, in favour of state-assisted capitalism. Essentially we are witnessing resistance to the basic values of Western liberal economic ideology, which raises the importance of individuals and companies and diminishes the importance of communities and nations or states. This is clear in Bello's account here of the response of the Southeast Asian governments to the US push for an Asia Pacific Economic Cooperation (APEC) Free Trade Area Initiative. Resisting further integration into a free-market system, which the US had been working for hitherto in its bilateral dealings with these states, they opted for a faster timetable for their own ASEAN Free Trade Area (AFTA). An even firmer statement is evident in the Malaysian proposal to create the East Asia Economic Group, a regional trade bloc that would exclude Australia, Canada, the US and the Latin American countries.

Resistance is also occurring at grassroots level in the East Asian region, with opposition to both free-market and state-assisted capitalism (Bello, Chapter 9, this volume). Both are regarded as environmentally destructive and socially iniquitous, failing to tackle redistribution issues. In place of both these models, grassroots organizations in East Asia are articulating sustainable development based not on private property or public ownership, but rather on the commons, on equity, environmental sensitivity, community participation in transparent decision-making, and small-scale and labour intensive projects using appropriate technology.

The dominant model of development based on massive capital investment, expatriate expert advice, and the exploitation and domination of nature is increasingly a focal point for grassroots mobilization and NGO activity. There have been some notable success stories. A recent case was the withdrawal of World Bank funding for the Arun-3 dam in Nepal following a campaign by Nepalese and other NGOs. This has sounded a death knell for the project in the near future (Gyawali, Chapter 11, this volume).

The World Bank has previously admitted publicly that it has 'greened' itself largely in response to NGO pressure. In the 1980s NGOs targeted their anti-Bank activities around Congressional hearings in the US. They campaigned to have US funding for the Bank made conditional on greening up the Bank's act. Given the pivotal role of the US in funding the Bank, this proved to be an effective strategy. However, while every example of non-state pressure effecting changes in major international organizations is important and indicative of the potential role of non-state actors in bringing about change, fundamental structures still remain in place.

It is important to remember that in assessing responses to globalization from the 'outside' we often miss significant insights about the local response. Acknowledging that different actors contend with and influence globalization, we need to recognize the existence of other discourses which are in fact challenging the apparent universality. In this volume (chapter 12) Lohmann describes an exchange between a mother and daughter in Thailand which reveals a direct incidence of resistance to globalization at an individual level. Responses to the globalization process thus take various forms, not immediately apparent to the external analyst.

CONCLUSION

Globalization, understood as the latest stage in capital accumulation, is resulting in fundamental changes in the global order. First, inequalities are widening as some classes and actors benefit while others are marginalized, thus affecting global social formations. Secondly, a local, Western neo-liberal ideology equating freedom with private power is being presented as universal. Thirdly, the authority and capacity of the state are being eroded differentially, and various other transnational capitalist actors (such as agribusiness or the IMF/World Bank) are superseding the state in determining entitlement on a now global scale. Fourth, the possibility of meaningful self-determination by the majority of the world's people is being undermined while on the face of it they are being given the chance to benefit from control over or consumption of the wealth generated in this latest phase of capitalism.

While the outlook is not particularly optimistic, the varied resistance to globalization reveals that the universalizing mission is far from complete. Alternative understandings of our current global predicament are being articulated by a wide variety of groups and movements.

It is instructive to close with a short reference to the *'New World Order'*. This phrase is usually attributed to President Bush who, in the context of the Gulf War and Operation Desert Storm, spoke in 1991 of the possibility of a global security system based on international law, shared norms, and international institutions. In fact the phrase had been coined earlier by the South Commission which identified the passing of the Cold War as an opportunity to develop a global order based on justice, equity and democracy. The legitimation of the dominant knowledge means that few in or outside the 'West' realise that this phrase has an older vintage than 1991. While Bush's version has come to dominate, this apparent universal moral consensus has been challenged following attempts to operationalize it. Such challenges suggest that it would be wise neither to forget nor to dismiss alternative and competing conceptualizations of a future global order. Despite liberal universalist rhetoric to the contrary, justice is, after all, a contested concept.

REFERENCES

Adams, N. (1993) *Worlds Apart: The North–South Divide and the International System* (London: Zed).
Bennis, P. and Mouchabeck, M. (eds) (1993) *Altered States: A Reader in the New World Order* (New York: Olive Branch).
Brown, L. and Kane, H. (1995) *Full House: Reassessing the Earth's Population Carrying Capacity* (London: Earthscan).
Chatterjee, P. and Finger, M. (1994) *The Earth Brokers* (London: Routledge).
Falk, R. (1995) *On Humane Governance* (Cambridge: Polity).
Fukuyama, F. (1989) 'The End of History?', *The National Interest*, Summer, pp. 3–18.
Gills, B., Rocamora, J. and Wilson, R. (eds) (1994) *Low Intensity Democracy* (London: Pluto).
Graf, W. (1992) 'Sustainable Development Ideology and Interests: Beyond Brundtland', *Third World Quarterly*, 13, 3, pp. 553–9.
International Commission on Peace and Food (1994) *Uncommon Opportunities: An Agenda for Peace and Equitable Development* (London: Zed).
Kneen, B. (1995) *Invisible Giant: Cargill and its Transnational Strategies* (London: Pluto).
Marglin, F.A. and Marglin, S.A. (eds) (1990) *Dominating Knowledge: Development, Culture and Resistance* (Oxford: Clarendon).

Ould-Mey, M. (1994) 'Global Adjustment: Implications for Peripheral States', *Third World Quarterly*, 15, 2, pp. 319–36.

Sen, A. (1982) *Poverty and Famines* (Oxford: Clarendon).

South Commission (1990) *The Challenge to the South* (Oxford: University Press).

Thomas, A. *et al* (1994) *Third World Atlas* (Milton Keynes: Open University Press, second edition).

Thomas, C. (1996) 'Poverty, Development and Hunger', in J. Baylis and S. Smith (eds) (1996) *The Globalisation of World Politics* (Oxford: Oxford University Press).

Thomas, C. (ed) (1994) *Rio: Unravelling the Consequences* (London: Cass).

UNDP (1994) *Human Development Report, 1994* (Oxford: Oxford University Press).

UNDP (1995) *Human Development Report, 1995* (Oxford: Oxford University Press).

World Bank (1995) *World Development Report 1995: Workers in an Integrating World* (Oxford: Oxford University Press).

2 New Myths for the South: Globalization and the Conflict between Private Power and Freedom

Peter Wilkin[1]

> The history of the world is one of a constant series of revolts against inequality (Wallerstein, 1979, p. 49).

INTRODUCTION

This chapter is concerned with the way broad changes in the global economy since the decline of the Bretton Woods system in the late 1960s and early 1970s have helped to generate a range of '*new myths*' about the world-system. The most important of these is the way in which freedom and its possibilities have become synonymous with the transcendence and extension of a particular conception of private power.

The reach of these ideas, underpinned as they are by important structural changes in the global economy, represents one aspect of the qualitative transformation in the power of a capitalist world-system to produce, reproduce and transform itself over time and space (Wallerstein, 1979, pp. xi-xii). As has frequently been observed in the literature on globalization, the compression of global time and space that has been facilitated by technological developments in the post-war period has intensified the transmission of diverse ideas, practices and forms of social, economic and political organization (Dicken, 1992, pp. 1–4; Robertson, 1992, p. 8). None the less, we need to be clear here that this does not mean that there is any simple or linear relationship between the transmission of these ideas and practices and either how they are received or whether they are even seen as legitimate by the world's population. As we will see later, it is reasonably clear that they do not have anything like universal legitimacy.

The revival of liberal conceptions of freedom has coincided with
the restructuring of the global economy that has taken place since
the mid–1970s and has led to a widening of inequality across a
whole range of indices, from wealth and income to mortality and
morbidity ratios (Mihill, 1995; *NACLA*, 1993; Boutros Ghali, 1995;
Roxborough, 1992; *Third World Resurgence*, 1994a, 1994b and 1994c;
World Bank, 1994). This fact raises an initial contradiction for the
new mythology of private power and freedom as this deepening
inequality excludes those without the necessary social, economic
and political power from either control over or consumption of the
very products that capitalism is able to generate (Wallerstein, 1991,
pp. 38–41).

My main contention is that this *restructuring of the world economy and
its attendant ideological entrenchment have served to bring about two substantive
changes in the world-system:* First, it has reinforced and sought to
legitimize the diverse forms of exploitation and inequality in the
world-system, the aforementioned inequalities of health, income,
wealth and mortality, and so on. These inequalities, in turn,
reflect the inequalities of social power felt by conflicting social
forces and are essentially concerned with questions of class
relations (Murphy, 1994, pp. 1–31; Sklair, 1991, p. 68). Second, if
we are to understand the social forces that have helped to generate
these changes then we need to recognize that prevailing ideas as to
what we mean by the terms '*North*' and '*South*' must be seriously
revised.

By this I mean that the type of objective indices by which we
attempt to measure inequality in its diverse social, political and
economic forms have become increasingly synonymous with parts
of what has conventionally been described as the North *as well as*
the South (Sen, 1992, ch. 7; Walker, 1995; Chomsky, 1993, ch. 11).
Conversely, specific parts of the South have become significantly
wealthy and powerful and seem set to increase this power in the
years ahead (*The Economist*, 1994; Wood, 1994, ch. 1; Amsden,
1989; Helleiner 1990).[2]

If we map these inequalities globally, as well as nationally, we find
that there are substantive grounds for re-defining our
understanding of North–South in the world-system (Dicken,
1992, p. 45). Most crucial here is that these transformations
reflect the ongoing production and realignment of class relations
in the world-system, as transnational capitalist institutions, actors
and social and economic structures help to intensify the speed and

dynamism of what is already a world-system. Having established the boundaries of this chapter's concern with globalization, we can briefly set out what I take to be its general dynamic and its broad implications for the world-system, before turning to the powerful claims and contradictions of liberal conceptions of freedom and private power.

GLOBALIZATION AS A PROCESS: TWO HISTORICAL APPROACHES

Globalization can best be seen as a process of transformation in the capitalist world-system, one that intensifies an array of structural and ideological tendencies as all aspects of the world-system come increasingly into the orbit of what we can see as a single and continuous circulation of ideas, commodities, social relations and, most important, sites of conflict.[3] Much as it brings transformation and social change, we must not lose sight of the fact that globalization has also generated resistance that cuts across national boundaries through such issues as religion, cultural autonomy, the environment, and workers' rights (Beyer, 1994; Vilas, 1993; Ekins, 1992; Shiva, 1989).

While the debate about globalization is diverse and expanding, there is one question that we need to set out here with regard to the way in which *these processes confront the world-system*. This question does not exhaust the debate over globalization by any means: it merely serves to offer a framework within which we can constrain our analysis to those aspects of the process that are most important for our focus upon the meaning of private power and freedom in this new era of rampant global capitalism. We need to ask, then: *What are the mechanisms that drive this process of globalization and how (if appropriate) should we order them?*

Open Pluralism

I must immediately concede that this is a debate that requires far more detailed attention than I can pay it here. However, what I can do is set out what I take to be the dominant approaches to this process, approaches that reflect long-established understandings of how we might explain historical change (Callinicos, 1995; Mann, 1988). There are *two main approaches to globalization* as a theory of history which we can set out here, accepting that I am presenting this as a general overview within which there is both overlap and significant degrees of diversity. There are, though, coherent and important differences between these two approaches that we can focus upon.

First, we have the approach that is broadly influenced by what we can see as a *Weberian* theory of history, which sees globalization as a process that is contingent and multi-centred in such a way that there is no *single* site of power and transformation that serves as a mechanism to drive it. Historical transformation is seen as a contingent phenomenon. In this category of theorists, globalization represents a qualitative shift in international society as various autonomous forms and sites of political, ideological, cultural, economic and military power conflict and transform the world-system with no form of social power possessing primary importance (Mann, Giddens, Runcimann, Robertson, Feather-stone, Scholte, and, I would argue, various postmodern and poststructuralist writers).

Under this view of history and globalization changes are contingent upon the interaction of discrete spheres of human action and social forces. As a consequence there is no central mechanism by which we might understand globalization or social change under capitalism, merely a shifting and transitory series of hierarchical relationships. Necessary relationships and causal mechanisms are not features of this conception of globalization (Sayer, 1990, pp. 111–12).

Structured Pluralism

The second approach to globalization that I want to introduce very briefly here is that which is usually termed historical materialism, which in the context of globalization we might more specifically call '*structured pluralism*'. I take it that while these approaches to globalization are varied, they generally agree that the driving mechanisms of globalization are to be found in the structure of capitalism as a world-system and its logic which drives it towards both increased exploitation and the appropriation of capital (for example, see Cox, 1988; Gill and Law, 1990; Wallerstein, 1984). Thus there is no straightforward determination of culture, society, politics and ideology by economic transformations as such a simple-minded understanding of structure and agency is untenable in the face of the diversity of historical norms and practices (Wallerstein, 1979, p. 189; Wood, 1995).

Instead, globalization is an historical process which requires us to view it as a *structured totality* within which the various levels of human practice (politics, ideology, culture) are produced, reproduced and transformed in history as competing social forces assert their power over each other. While the capitalist world-system provides the structural framework within which society, culture, ideology and politics are established, the process is dynamic and evolving rather than a linear transmission of ideas from the dominant source of social power to its related parts. The key to our understanding here is to view the world-system as a totality of social relations rather than a series of autonomous spheres that have become interdependent.

As a consequence, globalization can be best understood as the *necessary relations that exist between a series of mechanisms that are capable of generating a range of cultural, social and ideological responses which, in turn, reflect the prevailing power of conflictual social groups.* For example, the weakness of labour forces in the past 25 years has been mirrored by the ascendance of neo-liberal ideas about individualism, anti-collectivism and anti-trade unionism. As one social force retreats, the social space it once occupied is taken by another emergent and antagonistic social force.

The idea of a *structured pluralism* refers to the fact that while historical materialism recognizes that different mechanisms in society generate and reflect contrasting social relations, forces and structures, it is the capitalist world economy that is the driving force that enables and constrains these developments.[4] However, this is not a reductive understanding of the world-system. As Gramsci observed, an economic system requires a conducive political and cultural environment in which to develop. Thus politics, culture and ideology have an independent existence and force within a framework that is the capitalist world-system (Thompson, 1978, p. 254).

As I have already mentioned, this is a very broad and general overview of what I see as the two dominant approaches to globalization and the mechanisms that drive it. It serves us here as a heuristic device by which we can examine our main concern, which is an account of what I take to be one of the most significant trends in this process, the ideological reconstruction of freedom as being *essentially* and *naturally* about the deepening and widening of private power.[5] It is my contention that the structural pluralist approach to understanding historical processes is the most fruitful. It presents us with an understanding of class, exploitation, social power and the generation of inequalities as the *necessary* outcome of social relations in a capitalist world-system, as opposed to the understanding of them as *contingent* outcomes that is representative of the '*open pluralism*' of the Weberian approach to history.[6]

We can now examine some of the main claims of the neo- liberal agenda with regard to the issues of private power and freedom before looking at the relationship between inequality and freedom. Finally we can return to the theme we mentioned earlier about the need to re-draw the way in which we map our understanding of North–South relations on to the capitalist world-system. This final point will illustrate most clearly why it is that the *structured pluralist* approach is the most satisfactory explanation of globalization thus far. A note of caution here is necessary. This emphasis upon social relations, structures and forces does not mean that state structures are unimportant to our analysis of the world-system. On the contrary, they are extremely important mechanisms for securing specific social, economic and political orders in particular geographic domains.

What we do need to stress is that states are best seen as a site of conflict between these conflicting social forces rather than the coherent and homogenous representatives of nations as collective entities. States are never that. Rather, they are the most significant mechanisms for the representation and defence of the unequal social relations that define the world-system. However, as Benedict Anderson has persuasively argued, nation–states are also the source of identity that offers the most enduring ground for popular movements in modernity. This has proven to be both a strength and a weakness for these oppositional forces, at once galvanizing popular resistance to oppression and exploitation around a series of potent symbols and ideas about the nation, while at the same time separating opposition forces along national lines. How this dilemma can be overcome remains the key, I would suggest, to future progressive transformations in the capitalist world-system. What is clear is that national identity, for good or ill, is liable to play a significant part in these struggles (Anderson, 1991).

LIBERALISM REVISITED: THE SOUTH, PRIVATE POWER AND FREEDOM

The neo-liberal international economic restructuring that has coincided with the emergence of the debates over globalization provides us with fairly clear clues as to the real meaning of globalization as a process within the capitalist world-system. As Walden Bello observes, these changes serve to intensify inequality and the exploitation of the worst-off in the world-system (Bello, 1994). Retreating slightly, we can view the developments that have taken place in the capitalist world-system since the early 1970s as signifying three main shifts in social power:

(1) The dominant social forces in the Northern or core nation–states have, in conjunction with major corporate institutions, sought to *overturn the limited gains made by working people* throughout the world-system in the post-war period (Bello, 1994; Furedi, 1994).

(2) The *technological changes* in the production and investment processes of the capitalist world-system have served to help intensify the integration of production, distribution and the social division of labour (Sayer and Walker, 1992). As a consequence this has massively increased the power of corporations and governments to undermine the post-war Corporatist structures that have proven instrumental in integrating the state, capital and parts of labour in the core Northern states (Albert, 1993; Murphy, 1994; Bello, 1994, pp. 2–3). The liberalization of financial controls and the return to the myth of the self-regulating market (Polanyi, 1944, p. 3) have created a structural imperative to the capitalist world-system that sees all governments coming under the disciplinary power of global capital movements. Thus, governments are disciplined into curbing public expenditure, giving priority to the control of inflation and enhancing the strength of private power. We would do well to remember that these changes in the capitalist world-system have been brought about by the power of governments and corporations and so, far from being the apparently inevitable or uncontrollable outcome of market forces, they reflect concrete social forces pursuing specific goals and interests. The idea that all governments are necessarily powerless to control the forces of capitalism serves only to mystify and mythologize the workings of the capitalist world-

system and to reify the restructuring that has taken place. As is well recognized, it is the people of the South that have suffered most severely from this global discipline (Bello, 1994).

(3) Finally, I would argue that we are seeing the creation of a *new historic bloc*, to borrow Gramsci's phrase, that incorporates more clearly transnational class interests.[7] This bloc depends upon integrating not only transnational capital but also significant parts of the world's workforce which are able to maintain and help legitimize the hierarchical division of labour by performing tasks that are not only productive but also concerned with order and control (Gill and Law, 1990, pp. 365–72). This historic bloc is far from stable, as it has to contain not only transnational class interests between élites who wish to curb production costs and intensify capital accumulation. It has also to constrain intra-class conflict which sees nation–states pitched against each other as they seek to export their unemployment and inflation while dominating the agenda of. international trade agreements. This is illustrated by friction in the final GATT round, the NAFTA treaty and the continuing conflict within Europe over its future integration.[8] At the same time the possibility of an alternate historic bloc being formed by those excluded or opposed to these transformations is always there, and is capable of manifesting itself both nationally and, potentially, transnationally.

These three aspects of globalization have been reinforced by an *ideological assault upon ideas of collectivism, society and the public realm* in which freedom is a social good rather than a private one. Liberalism has set out its agenda very clearly and, as we have argued, with devastating consequences for parts of the world-system. The neo-liberal idea of freedom as the extension of private power and activity at the expense of the public realm serves to underpin the changes that have taken place in the world-system. In so doing, this conception of freedom acts to constrain and narrow the public space within which political action can take place, excluding those who do not have the necessary forms of private power to take part and reinforcing the power of those who ultimately dominate. It is the claims and difficulties for significant sections of the world-system that these understandings of freedom raise that we can elaborate upon here.

I take it that the *main ideas about freedom put forward by the neo-liberals have been threefold*. First, that market economies are the only alternative to Stalinist command economies and that the freer the market is from state interference the more effectively it will function, perhaps even attaining the ideal of a perfectly functioning market system (Rothbard, 1978; Friedman, 1978). Second, that inequality is, in itself, a good thing as it generates progress and creates wealth which we will all benefit from. And third, that we need a neutral state that provides us with the means to maximize our individual and private freedoms through legal and contractual arrangements and transactions.

These neo-liberal limits to freedom set the legitimate boundaries to the freest possible form of social organization. These are new myths for the world-system as it is being reshaped, that serve to obscure and legitimize the real nature of the social relations that are being *reinforced* through the transformation and globalization of the capitalist world-system. Crucially, they all hinge upon the belief that the extension of private power is the way in which freedom is maximized, a claim that is susceptible to empirical evaluation.[9]

The mythical nature of these claims needs to be understood in relation to the *real* interests and goals of the dominant social forces that have generated them. They may be mythical in their ability to distort the nature of social relations and to reify and mystify existing conditions, but they do reflect the interests of social forces who have tried to reassert their primacy both nationally and now transnationally. The appeal of these myths is strengthened by an array of coercive and persuasive factors: from the dismantling, harassment, criminalization and murder of a variety of opponents, including trade unions, human rights activists, church activists and similar groups; through to the slow but steady strangulation, co-optation and division of political parties[10] whose ideology, at least in theory, was in opposition to a return to a political–economic ideology that never, in truth, existed in practice (Lazonick, 1992, pp. 8–14; Robinson, 1970; Lang and Hines, 1993).

Conversely, the impact of global mass communications to promote and disseminate the material commodities produced under capitalism and the ways of life that are said to ensue are significant persuasive components that help to secure, however fragile the coalition might be, the hegemonic bloc that hopes to gain from these practices, while also helping to disable the claims of its opponents.

This latter realm of what Sklair calls the '*ideology of consumption*' (Sklair, 1991, pp. 129–30) does not mean that people are simply duped into fetishizing a particular life-style. Indeed, there is an important contradiction here between the promotion and dissemination of ideas of abundance, wealth and luxury and the reality which sees one in five people in the world living in absolute poverty, global inequality greater than at any other period in history, and economic security of the world's workforce seriously undermined by the liberalization of the workplace. It is one thing for capitalist industries to transmit symbols, ideas and images to the general populace; it is quite another to say how people actually interpret or decode these symbols. People are not simply blank slates waiting for messages and ideas to be transcribed upon them, and as a consequence will interpret these messages in diverse ways, and as a result of the myriad factors that help establish their sense of social and political identity.

What is important about the propagandistic role of mass communications in promoting the ideology of consumption is the way in which this diverse field promotes and reinforces a view of the world that serves to mystify social relations. As Cohen and Rogers have pointed out, it is very difficult for people to organize themselves collectively or even to begin to imagine the possibilities of alternate forms of social and economic organization when they are faced with the psychological and material pressures of the insecurities generated in a capitalist world-system (Cohen and Rogers, 1983). The appeal of authoritarian political ideologies that offer order, security and simple answers to what appear to be intractable problems may well be reflected in these conditions.

What, then, of the liberal claims about private power and freedom and what they mean, in turn, for the way in which we describe the world-system? The first claim that market economies are the only alternative to Stalinist command economies promotes two myths: it tells us that market economies and their attendant liberal social and political relations are really the end of history (Fukuyama, 1992; Sachs, 1995). We can go no further than this, having reached the teleological summit of human existence. This kind of *naturalization* of existing society serves the ideological purpose of reinforcing inequalities which are at the centre of social conflict and act as a motor for social change. At the same time it also forecloses the possibility of alternative forms of social and economic organization that might seek to promote both liberty and equality.

The ideal of the perfectly functioning free market, uninhibited by state interference and optimally meeting demand with supply, is a myth that few capitalists have believed in and for very good reasons. Karl Polanyi noted the way in which pure capitalist markets were anti-social and liable to destroy existing society rather than preserve it. This is a claim that is being met in many parts of the world-system where the neo-liberal aims of minimal state provision of welfare to the poor are being imposed far more severely than has proven to be politically possible within the core Northern states (Polanyi, 1944, p. 3; Bello, 1994). Equally significant here is the fact that, contrary to their apparent promotion of individualism and the entrepreneurial spirit, corporations actually *are* in favour of state intervention in the economy and always have been (Dicken, 1992, pp. 169–75). So long as the state intervenes to primarily preserve the interests of powerful actors (the dominant historic bloc) at the expense of the general populace then it is quite legitimate for such intervention to take place. From the state enforcement of trade agreements and the forcing open of closed economies to Northern exports, through to the public subsidies for private profit through tax incentives, enterprise zones, state investment in corporate research and development, it is clear that the state has a huge role to play in the preservation of market economies and the private power of élite actors and institutions.

The second liberal myth seeks to counter the conflict over inequality, by arguing that such inequalities are good for us as individuals and as a society in that inequality is the mechanism that drives historical change by encouraging us to achieve more by striving ever harder to improve our social position. If you remove inequality, rather than ending conflict, you bring progress to a halt and the economy will stagnate. Under the conditions of a liberal capitalist economy wealth will be created and will '*trickle down*' to the rest of society, dragging us up on the heels of innovative entrepreneurs. Contrary to liberal claims, twenty years of liberalization of the world economy has not led to the general trickle-down that they have predicted, either in absolute or in relative terms. Global inequality is greater now than at any period in history, as is absolute poverty (Boutros Ghali, 1995).

The redistribution of resources that has taken place since the mid–1970s has taken two related directions. In conventional state-centric terms we can see it as having moved from the Southern states to the North. More specifically, if we see it in terms of social forces we can see this redistribution of resources as moving from the weaker social forces to the dominant ones. This latter perspective is not geographically bound and illustrates the patterns and commonalities that connect different peoples throughout the world-system. Thus this distribution of resources is massively skewed both within and across state boundaries (Clairmonte, 1993, pp. 16–22; Wood, 1994, ch. 1; Roxborough, 1992, pp. 425–6; Hamilton and Hirszowicz, 1993, pp. 278–9; *Third World Resurgence*, 1994a, 1994b, 1994c).[11]

Rather than accepting the evidence as it stands, neo- liberals of a more puritanical bent tend to respond by saying that this is a result of market imperfections. What we actually need is a *freer* market system, one which really removes state intervention from the economy (remembering always that *state intervention* is a code-phrase for the redistribution of resources to the worse-off in society: it most definitely does not refer to the earlier mentioned public subsidies for private power and profit). It should be reasonably clear by now that there is very little that is actually liberal about neo-liberalism if we take liberalism to be concerned with the restriction of state power to interfere with citizens' lives. Neo-liberalism within the Northern core states has seen massive state intervention through the previously mentioned public subsidies for private profit and through the increased powers of states to control workforce organization, pressure groups, curb civil liberties, and so on.

The final liberal myth concerns the idea of our *equality before the neutral state* which enables us to enter into contractual arrangements with each other so that we might exercise our freedoms most effectively. This idea reflects the ahistoricism and abstract quality of neo-liberal theory, as it has no conception of the way in which the dominant social forces in society are able to reinforce their position both nationally and internationally through the wealth that is needed to influence market transactions and the legal framework that underpins it. This is illustrated by the recent GATT round which saw the inclusion of Trade Related Intellectual Property Rights (TRIPS) and Trade Related Investment Measures (TRIMS) – both of which met with severe opposition from significant actors in Southern states. The reason for this opposition was that TRIMS meant that Southern states had to open up their economies to the core Northern financial and insurance industries who possess the economic power to dominate these sectors in Southern states. Similarly, TRIPS enabled Northern transnational corporations (TNCs) to take out patents on a range of genetic, agricultural and pharmaceutical materials that have their origins in the historical practices of Southern farmers, communities, and so on. Having secured the patent, Northern-based TNCs will then be free to sell these commodities back to Southern states at profitable prices (Peng, 1990; Raghavan, 1990).

Thus, what was once a *public good* becomes an instrument for *private profit* and *exploitation*. The liberal state does not provide us with an equality before the law as different actors, institutions and ultimately, historic blocs, have radically uneven social power with which to influence and constrain these legal outcomes. There are, though, clear reasons why these ideas of liberal equality, meritocracy and justice as entitlement have to be promoted if the powerful are to defend their position successfully. The fact that the evidence shows that these principles are nothing but myths presents the capitalist world-system with one of its most destabilizing problems.

As we noted at the beginning of this chapter, many people continue to struggle against social inequality, however fragmented and weak this opposition might seem. Again, it is worth emphasizing that the South as a homogeneous bloc did not lose out from these liberal changes in world trade: only specific social forces that stretch across the South (including the vast majority of people) stand to suffer as a consequence in terms of security, wages, welfare provision, and so on. Sections of the Southern élites will no doubt gain substantially from the increased integration of their states within the workings of the capitalist world-system.

RETHINKING THE NORTH–SOUTH DIVIDE

Concluding this chapter, we can see that the neo-liberal conception of private power and freedom that has been a central ideological tenet of globalization, thus far, leads us towards two main positions. The first relates to how we should understand the mechanisms that drive globalization and the second relates to what the implications of this are for how we conceptualize the world-system.

I have argued that if we wish to understand the central (though clearly, not the only) process of globalization then we have to focus upon the dynamics of the capitalist world-system. The central principles of capitalist organizations that seek to accumulate capital and control costs have underpinned the intensification of global transactions with regard to technology, politics and culture. Far from being the mystical process that seems to leave us in its thrall, as some adherents of globalization imply, we can focus on the mechanisms of accumulation, the ideology and motives that support it, and the consequences of these developments for the world's population. Globalization and the liberal agenda of freedom as private power offer us a a coherent explanation of one aspect of the process, an aspect that appears to be crucial. While open pluralists point to contingent and frequently inexplicable social processes, we do not have to accept the limitations of such analyses.[12]

The global redistribution of resources that has taken place in the past 25 years leads us finally to the issue that is central to this chapter, *how we should conceptualize the meaning of the North–South divide in the current period of globalization in the world-system*. The analysis I have presented here leads me to conclude that the traditional meanings attached to these terms are of limited use and are frequently distorting of our understanding of social relations in the world-system. The world-system is an integrated totality of social relations that is illustrated by the range of exploitation and social inequalities that we have already touched upon: the increased integration of production processes across time and space, the resurgence of infectious disease in all parts of the world, the massive increase in inequality in the world-system, homelessness, mass migration, hunger and poverty, the spread of hyper-rich global cities in which the heights of wealth and power rest alongside the new hyper-exploited (Castells, 1989; Walker, 1995; Sen, 1992).[13]

How are we to explain this new map of the world-system? The most appropriate means is to adhere to the notion of class that is inherent within the *structured pluralist* approach to globalization that I have attempted to outline here, and which has to take on board the way in which transnational class alliances and interests have been formed through a range of formal and informal institutional mechanisms, ranging from the G7 to the IMF–World Bank axis of the United Nations.[14] As I argued earlier, this represents an attempt to establish a new historic bloc which incorporates transnational interests that include capitalists, sections of the managerial and skilled labour force, and the military and cultural elites. Such an alliance is unstable and contradictory, containing, as it does, groups that are liable to be pulled in different directions as they pursue conflicting interests. None the less it has had the social power necessary to take us thus far along the path of globalization, and with dire consequences for a great many people in the world system. This shared exploitation does not automatically make them an alternate historic bloc, of course, but it at least suggests that the possibility is there that they might become so. It would not be an overstatement to say that a very great deal depends upon them becoming so.

NOTES

1. The author wishes to thank the following for their comments: John Roberts and Dr Kate Currie, Department of Sociology at Lancaster University; Dr Julian Saurin, School of African and Asian Studies, Sussex University; John Glenn and Simon Eagle, Department of Politics, Southampton University.
2. Peter Dicken notes that 13 major Third World countries have historically dominated both foreign direct investment and GDP growth (Dicken, 1992, p. 26).
3. For an account of the significance of tendencies as opposed to laws in natural science see Bhaskar (1979).
4. Bhaskar (1979) gives the best overview of this 'Critical Realist' perspective.
5. Margaret Thatcher is remembered for the phrase, 'there is no alternative', which nicely sums up the neo-liberal attempt to represent capitalism as an inevitable outcome and end of human history and nature.
6. Ellen Wood, in *Democracy Against Capitalism* (1995), deals with this issue very clearly in chapter 3 where she looks at the meaning of class as both a process and a relationship.
7. Murphy (1994) describes this clearly, when he says, 'Moreover, Gramsci believed that no economic system can fully develop – not even the contradiction within its inner logic can fully develop – outside of a conducive political and cultural environment. A historical bloc is the dialectical unity of base and superstructure, theory and practice, of intellectuals and masses that makes all such development possible' (p. 27).
8. Gill and Law (1990, pp. 210–25) stress the importance of avoiding generalizations about the relationship between Third World élites and TNCs while recognizing that capitalism in its globalized phase is a transnational phenomenon.
9. For an assessment of the fact–value relationship see Bhaskar (1979) and Sayer (1990).
10. For example, socialist or social democratic parties in Spain, New Zealand, Australia, the United Kingdom, France, and Italy, have all moved to

incorporate significant aspects of the neo-liberal agenda in the face of a range of threats, from capital disinvestment to demonization of socialism, in a media that is global and overwhelmingly capitalist (see Bagdikian, 1992).

11. See also 'Table 30: Income distribution' in the *World Development Report, 1994* (World Bank, 1994, pp. 220–1). This table reveals the massively skewed distribution of income throughout the world-system.

12. I am thinking here of writers such as Anthony Giddens, who has argued in his more recent work, *Beyond Left and Right* (1994), that globalization leaves us with 'the insuperable complexity of society and nature' (p. 27). Such views present us with an image of society as being out of control and beyond our explanation, an argument that seems to be leading us towards either Nietzschean gloom or grand metaphysical speculation.

13. Table 27, 'Health and Nutrition', in the *World Development Report 1994* (World Bank, 1994, pp. 214–15), illustrates the wide differentials in health and nutrition between different areas of the world-system (although it does not give us a breakdown of this distribution *within* nation–states, only between them). Table 29, 'Gender Comparisons' (pp. 218–19), illustrates the complexities of gender inequality in the world-system in terms of life expectancy, employment – and so on, although again this does not indicate the distribution within nation–states.

14. Murphy's *International Organisation and Industrial Change* (1994) focuses upon the way in which these diverse international regimes have emerged and the way in which they serve to secure a range of interests that are transnational as well as national. Similarly Gill, in *American Hegemony and the Trilateral Commission* (1990), is concerned with the part played by international regimes in promoting what he sees as a consciousness-raising role among the world's élites.

REFERENCES

Albert, M. (1993) *Capitalism Against Capitalism* (Paris: Whurr).

Amsden, A. K. (1989) *Asia's Next Giant: South Korea and Late Industrialisation* (Oxford: Oxford University Press).

Anderson, B. (1991) *Imagined Communities* (London: Verso).

Bagdikian, B. (1992) *The Media Monopoly* (Boston, MA: Beacon).

Bello, W. (1994) *Dark Victory: The United States, Structural Adjustment and Global Poverty* (London: Pluto).

Beyer, P. (1994) *Globalization and Religion* (London: Sage).

Bhaskar, R. (1979) *The Possibility of Naturalism* (Hemel Hempstead: Harvester Wheatsheaf).

Boutros Ghali, B. (1995) 'A New Departure on Development', *Foreign Policy*, Spring.

Callinicos, A. (1995) *Theories and Narratives: Reflections on the Philosophy of History* (Cambridge: Polity).

Castells, M. (1989) *The Informational City* (Oxford: Blackwell).

Chomsky, N. (1993) *Year 501: The Conquest Continues* (London: Verso).

Clairmonte, F. (1993) 'China: Enter the Dragon', *Third World Resurgence*, 32, pp. 16–22.

Cohen, J. and Rogers, J. (1983) *On Democracy* (Harmondsworth: Penguin).

Cox, R. W. (1988) *Production, Power and World Order: Social Forces in the Making of History* (Boston, MA: Columbia University Press).

Dicken, P. (1992) *Global Shift: The Internationalisation of Economic Activity* (London: Paul Chapman).

The Economist (1994) 'A Survey of the Global Economy', 1 October.

Ekins, P. (1992) *A New World Order: Grassroots Movements for Global Change* (London: Routledge).

Friedman, D. (1978) *The Machinery of Freedom: Guide to Radical Capitalism* (Lexington, KY: Arlington House).

Fukuyama, F. (1992) *The End of History and the Last Man* (London: Penguin).

Furedi, F. (1994) *The New Ideology of Imperialism* (London: Pluto).

Giddens, A. (1994) *Beyond Left and Right: The Future of Radical Politics* (Cambridge: Polity).

Gill, S. (1990) *American Hegemony and the Trilateral Commission* (Cambridge: Cambridge University Press).

Gill, S. and Law, D. (1990) *The Global Economy: Perspectives, Problems and Policies* (Hemel Hempstead: Harvester Wheatsheaf).

Hamilton, M. and Hirszowicz, M. (1993) *Class and Inequality: Comparative Perspectives* (Hemel Hempstead: Harvester Wheatsheaf).

Helleiner, G. K. (1990) *The New Global Economy and the Developing Countries: Essays in International Economics and Development* (Aldershot: Edward Elgar).

Lang, T. and Hines, C. (1993) *The New Protectionism: Protecting the Future Against Free Trade* (London: Earthscan).

Lazonick, W. (1992) *Business Organisation and The Myth of the Market Economy* (Cambridge: Cambridge University Press).

Mann, M. (1988) *States, War and Capitalism* (Oxford: Blackwell).

Mihill, C. (1995) 'Public Enemy Number One', The *Guardian* (London), 2 May.

Murphy, C. N. (1994) *International Organisation and Industrial Change: Global Governance Since 1850* (Cambridge: Polity).

NACLA (North American Congress on Latin America) (1993) 'A Market Solution For The Americas? The Rise Of Wealth And Hunger', special issue, February.

Peng, M. K. (1990) *The Uruguay Round and Third World Sovereignty* (Penang: Third World Network).

Polanyi, K. (1944) *The Great Transformation* (Boston, MA: Beacon).

Raghavan, C. (1990) *Recolonisation: GATT, The Uruguay Round and the Third World* (Penang: Third World Network).

Robertson, R. (1992) *Globalization: Social Theory and Social Culture* (London: Sage).

Robinson, J. (1970) 'The New Mercantilism', in *Freedom and Necessity: An Introduction to the Study of Society* (London: George Allen and Unwin).

Rothbard, M. (1978) *For A New Liberty* (New York: Collier Macmillan).

Roxborough, I. (1992) 'Neo-liberalism in Latin America: Limits and Alternatives', *Third World Quarterly*, 13, 3, pp. 421–40.

Sachs, J. (1995) 'Consolidating Capitalism', *Foreign Policy*, Spring.

Sayer, A. (1990) *Method in Social Science* (London: Routledge).

Sayer, A. and Walker, R. (1992) *The New Social Economy: Reworking the Division of Labour* (Oxford: Blackwell).

Sen, A. (1992) *Inequality Re-Examined* (Oxford: Clarendon).

Shiva, V. (1989) *Staying Alive: Women, Ecology and Development* (London: Zed).

Sklair, L. (1991) *Sociology of the Global System* (Hemel Hempstead: Harvester Wheatsheaf).

Third World Resurgence (1994a) 'Workless: Mass Unemployment in the New World Order', 44, special issue, April.

Third World Resurgence (1994b) 'The Drain From the South', 46, special issue, June.

Third World Resurgence (1994c) 'A World in Social Crisis', 52, special issue, December.

Thompson, E. P. (1978) *The Poverty of Theory* (London: Merlin)

Vilas, C. V. (1993) 'The Hour of Civil Society', *North American Congress on Latin America (NACLA)*, September–October.

Walker, R. (1995) 'California Rages Against the Dying of the Light', *New Left Review*, January–February, pp. 42–71.

Wallerstein, I. (1979) *The Capitalist World-Economy* (Cambridge: Cambridge University Press).

Wallerstein, I. (1984) *The Politics of the World-Economy* (Cambridge: Cambridge University Press).

Wallerstein, I. (1991) *Geopolitics and Geoculture* (Cambridge: Cambridge University Press.

Wood, A. (1994) *North-South Trade, Employment and Inequality*, (Oxford: Clarendon).

Wood, E. M. (1995) *Democracy Against Capitalism* (Cambridge: Cambridge University Press).

World Bank (1994) *World Development Report, 1994* (Oxford: Oxford University Press).

3 Democratic Development in the South in the Next Millennium: What Prospects for Avoiding Anarchy and Authoritarianism?

Timothy M. Shaw and Fahimul Quadir

> Democracy had come to be seen as the only legitimate and viable alternative to an authoritarian regime of any type (Huntington, 1991, p. 58).

> Instead of more democratic policy-making processes, electoral systems have become more nonrepresentative, more divorced from popular needs. Authoritarianism is on the rise everywhere and repression has become a routine feature of civilian rule (Petras and Morley, 1992, p. 7).

> We live in a corporatist society with soft pretensions to democracy. More power is slipping every day over towards the groups. That is the meaning of the marketplace ideology and of our passive acceptance of whatever form globalization happens to take (Saul, 1995, p. 32).

> Larger and larger numbers of people are no longer willing to accept, fatalistically, exploitative or repressive regimes and state structures, or a development paradigm that excludes them. They may not be concerned with the capture of state power and 'big bang' revolutions. Yet they may in reality be building, consciously or unconsciously a countervailing power to the dominant state power (Wignaraja, 1993, pp. 18, 19).

INTRODUCTION

Dramatic changes in the global political economy in the 1990s have encouraged a widespread enthusiasm among liberal scholars to

36

engage in debates/ideas such as 'the end of history' (Fukuyama, 1992) and 'the clash of civilizations' (Huntington, 1993). These suggest that the future of the world lies in: (1) the construction of liberal democracy; (2) the promotion of market capitalism; and (3) the linear movement towards modernity. Continuing transformations in the global political economy also pose major challenges to established theories, assumptions, prescriptions, frameworks and concepts in several interrelated fields such as political economy, development studies, comparative foreign policy and security studies. These create new opportunities, indeed imperatives, to define and redefine many dominant theories and notions. More importantly, these changes motivate academics and activists, policy-makers and politicians to search for alternatives to established as well as emerging neo-liberal dogma: to expand the agenda beyond structural adjustment and political democracy. (For example, see Gills, Chapter 4, this volume).

Given the ongoing process of globalization of production, finance and distribution, this chapter seeks to identify the futures of the South in the world of democratization: how sustainable are new democracies? Contrary to the optimistic liberal view, this study casts profound doubt as to the prospect for constitutional democracy in the South, and goes beyond the simplistic stereotypes of both anarchic and developmental orthodoxies. In addition to challenging neo-liberal hegemony, this revisionist analysis provides a critical understanding of the prospect for sustainable democratic development in the South in the twenty-first century.

Focusing on the role of emerging civil societies across the South – local, national, regional and continental – this chapter will argue that, while a considerable number of Southern countries will witness a general breakdown of democracy (reversion to authoritarianism or corporatism), an erosion of consensus, a rise in religious fanaticism and/or ethno- nationalist movements, the prospect for sustainable development and democracy is not so bleak. The proliferation of new social movements and the empowerment of vulnerable groups are expected to provide a structural basis for alternative developmental and democratic changes in the South.

The chapter comprises five main sections. The first section outlines the process of globalization and its implications for democratic development in the South. A review of recent literature on democratization is presented in Section 2. Section 3 looks at the state of democratization and development across the South. In addition to exploring the framework of democratic development, Section 4 evaluates the prospect of corporatism in the next millennium.

GLOBALIZATION AND ITS IMPLICATIONS FOR DEMOCRACY AND DEVELOPMENT

Any plausible explanation of development and democracy at the end of the twentieth century has to begin by recognizing and evaluating transformations in the global political economy, especially in the South itself. Central to any understanding of unprecedented structural changes at the global level (and also at the regional, national and local levels) is the ongoing process of globalization of production, finance and distribution. Thus, this section proceeds with several meanings of globalization and analyses its implications for democracy and development in the South.

Globalization can be defined as a process of expanding market capitalism across the globe (Glyn and Sutcliffe, 1992, p. 76). In the past 15 years or so, the world in general, and the South in particular, has witnessed the replacement of all types of interventionist development models including state socialism, state capitalism and the non-capitalist path of development with market economies. Structural Adjustment Programmes designed by the two most powerful macro-economic strategists – the World Bank and the International Monetary Fund (IMF) – have been instrumental in the entire process of expanding capitalist relations of production in the South.

With mounting debt burdens, many countries in Asia, Africa and Latin America have been forced by the international donor community to constantly engage in restructuring their economies, creating a global environment for the 'triumph' of market capitalism (UNRISD, 1995, pp. 36–56). Naturally, the South's transitions towards free markets have eventually led to the process of what is called the 'commodification of social life', in which everything becomes nothing but a commodity (Moufee, 1988, pp. 93–4).

The globalization of production and finance is, more importantly, creating a highly interconnected world order (Held,

1991, p. 206) which demands a new definition of state sovereignty. With the liberalization of trade, commerce and monetary policy, integration of the global political economy has gained unprecedented momentum. Cross-national investment, trade and the flows of money are growing faster than ever before, thus transnationalizing national economic structures. Not only does such a process of internationalization give rise to transnational forces of production and finance as powerful entities *vis-à-vis* any state; it also enables them to limit the traditional economic space controlled or regulated by the state (Underhill, 1994, p. 36). Also, the growth of a variety of global and regional organizations, mainly inter-governmental, has developed a 'transnational process of consensus formation among the official caretakers of the global economy' (Cox, 1987, p. 254). In other words, the recent transformation of the global economic system creates a new form of transnational structure in which the state is constantly engaged in sharing its decision-making power with the global forces of production and finance.

In addition, tremendous advancements in science and technology – particularly in the fields of communication and computer technologies – are expanding the networks of transnational linkages both at the formal and informal levels. The world is also experiencing the emergence of non-business non-state actors with transnational linkages, many of which have enormous influence over national decision-making (Stanley Foundation, 1992, p. 9). In brief, the proliferation of transnational socio-economic functions - and the intensified power of global forces of production are rapidly changing the post-war international order in which state sovereignty used to be the central feature and issue (Cerny, 1995). It is increasingly becoming evident that traditional patterns of state activity are assuming a global character and the autonomy of states in regard to national decision-making is shrinking.

More importantly, by implementing stabilization programmes, Southern regimes and countries are witnessing a general breakdown of social services (Bratton, 1989, p. 410). Under intense pressure from the international financial community, governments in the South are rapidly abandoning their role as service providers. Given growing balance-of-payments problems, these countries are simply unable to maintain their post-colonial standard of public service provision (UNRISD, 1995, pp. 36–8). Their immediate priority is quickly shifting from fulfilling popular demands to the removal of market 'barriers', which results in a significant loss of states' distributive capability. With growing inability to meet public expectations, state–society relations have become highly confrontational, thus clouding the future of democracy and development in the South.

Globalization is not only eroding the state but is also internationalizing 'domestic' politics, economy and society. In particular, it is increasingly becoming problematic to analyse domestic politics without giving adequate emphasis to the socio-political changes that are taking place outside the boundary of nation–states. Remmer provides an engaging explanation of why one should pay particular attention to the international system when analysing domestic politics:

> The globalization of productive processes and capital markets, the liberalization of trade barriers, the rising influence of international financial institutions and nongovernmental organizations, and other related phenomena have all but obliterated the capacity of state or subject populations to act in isolation from the international system.
>
> Any account of democratization in Africa, for example, needs to address ... the growing pressures of the international financial community, and the related ability of Western states ... and nongovernmental organisations to exercise leverage over domestic political choice and outcomes (Remmer, 1995, p. 106).

This statement not only outlines the changing concept of sovereignty, but also highlights the diminishing analytical distinction[1] between national and international politics.

THEORIES OF DEMOCRATIZATION: WHAT DO THEY EXPLAIN?

While the contemporary literature on democratization offers a variety of frameworks for analysis, it rarely deals with changes in the external environment in order to comprehend the recent global movement towards democracy. With a clear focus on domestic factors, the literature, which is dominated by the liberal perspective, develops its perceptions about political and economic reforms in the South. A brief review of the literature reveals how mainstream scholarship has largely ignored the entire aspect of globalization and its consequences for democratization. More importantly, although the literature finds a positive link between economic and political liberalization, it fails to understand the underlying tensions between structural economic reforms and political democracy in the South. Also, by offering an ambivalent attitude towards popular struggles for democracy and development, the liberal perspective often neglects the role of popular organization in greater socio-political change.

Many of the writings on democratization centre primarily around questions of consolidating democracy and the promotion of democratic culture in the South. Key questions include the prerequisites for institutionalizing democracy in developing countries, and the possible contribution of the Western world to global transitions toward democracy. Also, central to the understanding of democratization is the link between democracy and the creation of market economies.

In most cases, discussions on democratization begin with a procedural definition of democracy. For example, drawing on the ideas of Robert Dahl, democracy is referred to as a system in which, as Przeworski suggests, 'multiple forces compete inside an institutional framework'. For him, the primary purpose of democracy is to create a conflict resolution mechanism for 'subjecting all interests to competition' (Przeworski, 1991, pp. 10–12). Within a similar paradigm, Diamond *et al.* emphasize the construction of a system that: (1) allows political organizations to freely compete with each other; (2) ensures political participation of all members of a society in their effort to choose leaders and policies; and (3) provides a structure for the maintenance of extensive civil liberties (Diamond *et al.*, 1990, pp. 6–7).

Democracy is therefore defined as a process of creating the formal institutions of governance. It generates competition among rival political groups and develops a mechanism to reduce the likelihood of a breakdown of the social contract. In particular, democracy ensures that the status quo will be maintained through the preservation of stability. It is no wonder that such an understanding of democracy offers the majority nothing but the right to vote in local and national elections. Clearly, it does not provide the people with a tool for effective control of the environment in which they live. Neither does it explain how the right to vote will improve the standard of living of ordinary people, nor how it will put an end to the structural deprivation and powerlessness of the majority.

Much of the dominant literature on democratization sees the current global movement towards democratization as a process of creating political systems which are open to broad competition for political office. This process is believed to be the beginning of a construction of alternative sources of power and structures to the existing state institutions. That is, the idea that an expansion of civil society poses the most effective challenge to the hegemony of the state. Focusing on the notion 'state versus civil society', the literature defines *civil society* as a political space outside the state (Gellner, 1994, p. 5). In order to protect people from the institutional oppression of the state, it emphasizes the creation of adequate political space in which non-state actors organize themselves freely and promote diverse socio-political interests. Thus, not only will civil society play a key role in promoting democratic political culture but it is also expected to defend individual rights against governmental violation (Harbeson, 1993, p. 1).

The role of *'autonomous' civil society* is particularly important due to the increasing emphasis placed upon the linkage between economic liberalization and political democratization. Both policy-makers and mainstream academics began to share the idea that market-oriented economic reforms and political liberalization towards constitutional democracy are mutually reinforcing. It is believed that 'modern democracies are normally oriented toward market economies' (Ardito-Barletta, 1990, p. 167). Indeed, political democracy is considered, according to Diamond, as 'the form of government most conductive to the spirited flow of ideas, people and resources, which enhances the dynamism of market economies' (Diamond, 1993, p. 6). Economic liberalization, on the other hand, creates the demand for broader political participation in decision-making, which eventually leads to democratization.

While it is not clear whether economic liberalization contributes to democratization or vice versa, an autonomous, if not vibrant, *civil society is a prerequisite for the promotion of both market capitalism and democratization since civil society is instrumental in protecting individual rights and private ownership* (Fukuyama, 1992, p. 117). More interestingly, the literature usually assumes that both economic reforms and political liberalization reduce the traditional domain of state activity and therefore facilitate the growth of civil society.

Thus, the literature's focus on the expansion of political space for civil society rests on the assumption that *political liberalization and market-oriented economic reforms are complementary.*

This is exactly the same logic that 'inspires' key donor agencies and countries including USAID, Germany, the Netherlands, OECD and International Financial Institutions (IFIs), especially the World bank and the IMF, to use *foreign aid as a tool for the promotion of democracy and strengthening civil society* (Robinson, 1995, pp. 70–80). Since the mid-1980s, bilateral aid donors have been pushing Southern governments to introduce political and economic liberalization programmes. Channelling a considerable amount of aid money through non-governmental organizations, the international actors are actively involved in both initiating political reform and accelerating the formation of an autonomous civil society, hoping to inculcate a democratic political culture (Harbeson, 1993, p. 3). Such a process of *'democratization from above'*, as Gibbon suggests, helps the external actors to overthrow state socialism and subsequently reduce popular resistance to the expansion of market-oriented economic reforms (Gibbon, 1992).

With growing criticism about the failure of structural economic reforms, *the World Bank introduced the concept called 'good governance' as the political conditionality for foreign aid.* Putting aside its traditional exclusively economic agenda, the Bank began advocating the need for developing countries to practice democratic norms and values in order to resolve the crisis of development in the South. In its 1989 document entitled *Sub-Saharan Africa: From Crisis to Sustainable Growth, the Bank identified the lack 'of good governance' as the primary cause of continued underdevelopment and growing poverty in Africa.* The document stated:

> History suggests that political legitimacy and consensus are a precondition for sustainable development . . . . By governance is meant the exercise of political power to manage a nation's affairs . . . dedicated leadership can produce a quite different outcome. It requires a systematic effort to build a pluralistic institutional structure, a determination to respect the rule of law, and vigorous protection of the freedom of the press and human rights (World Bank, 1989, pp. 60–1).

Thus *democratization becomes what Leftwich calls 'a new orthodoxy' in 'official Western aid policy and development thinking'* (Leftwich, 1993, p. 60).

The process of democratization typically starts, according to Linz, with a dramatic political event that prompts the authoritarian regime to hold national elections and to transfer power to a democratically elected civilian group within a stipulated period of time. And the transition towards democracy ends largely with the departure of an authoritarian regime and the subsequent assumption of power by a democratically elected authority. Also, in order for transition to be complete, it is important to promulgate a new constitution that provides a framework for governance in the country (Linz, 1990, p. 156).

Such *a transition from authoritarianism to democracy, however, does not automatically lead to the consolidation of democracy.* Holding free and fair elections, the installation of a democratic authority and the creation of a new constitution are simply the preliminary steps towards democratic consolidation. It is argued that the consolidation of democracy depends upon the success of institutionalizing democracy, meaning the development of a conflict resolution mechanism. The process of institutionalization requires an élite consensus on the rules of the game.

For Bratton and Van de Walle, the central question in *consolidation* is 'the commitments of elites to open a responsive politics' (Bratton and Van de Walle, 1992, p. 29). Given the decline of states, it is, however, not clear how responsive politics can be constructed. Linz, on the other hand, defines the process of consolidation as:

> one in which none of the major political actors, parties or organized interests, forces or institutions consider that there is any alternative to democratic processes to gain power, and that no political institution or group has a claim to veto the action of democratically elected decision makers .... To put it simply, democracy must be seen as the 'only game in town' (Linz, 1990, p. 158).

The central questions in consolidation are the ways through which democracies are sustained and/or are made. The contemporary literature on democratization usually suggests that transitions should emerge from negotiation since this enhances the possibility of constructing a viable political democracy (O'Donnell and Schmitter, 1986, p. 36). According to Przeworski, negotiation is essential for the consolidation of democracy. He writes:

All transitions to democracy are negotiated: some with representatives of the old regime and some only among the pro-democratic forces seeking to form a new system. Negotiations are not always needed to extricate the society from the authoritarian regimes, but they are necessary to constitute democratic institutions. Democracy cannot be dictated; it emerges from bargaining (Przeworski, 1991, p. 80).

What is even more important in Przeworski's analysis is the emphasis that the reformers and moderates must be in full control of the entire negotiation process. He suggests that, in order to enhance the possibility of consolidation, the hard-liners should either be excluded from negotiations or be assigned an insignificant role in any transition towards democracy. In a similar tone, Huntington regards negotiation and/or agreements as the methods of democracy (Huntington, 1991, p. 164).

Therefore, *the dominant liberal literature does not view civil society as the domain of any real change in terms of democracy or development. In order to prevent political space from becoming too radical, liberal scholarship seems to put a limit on popular participation. It encourages the participation of civil society groups only when the latter agrees to work within the constitutional framework to promote democracy and market capitalism.* This is exactly why scholars such as Diamond, Linz and Przeworski have begun to argue that the revolutionary spirits of ordinary people might prove to be dysfunctional for democratic consolidation, while some others have emphasized the ethics of tolerance in successful democratization (Al-Sayyid, 1993, pp. 228–42). Harik, for instance, suggests that 'too much emphasis on the concept of civil society seems to distract one from focusing on democratization' (Harik, 1994, p.56).

THE SOUTH IN THE MIDDLE OF THE 1990S: A RISING TIDE OF ANARCHY

Contrary to prevailing liberal expectations, then, much of the South in the middle of the 1990s confronts a contradictory predicament: democratization and rising anarchy in the form of ethnic tensions, religious fundamentalisms, regional secessionism and renewed authoritarianism. The primary tension emerging is economic contraction and concentration with political liberalization. This paradox is all too easily overlooked by the prevailing optimistic, adjustment paradigm, especially with its emphasis on 'good governance' (Nyang'oro and Shaw, 1992). Despite the apparent hegemony of the ideology of democracy, there is a continuing counter-tendency: the threat of authoritarian and corporatist reactions, including military rule and descent into anarchy. In many cases, some of the consequences of ubiquitous *structural adjustment programmes have already led to the breakdown of socio-political consensus, necessitating political centralization, coercion or exclusion rather than popular participation.*

The future of *democratic consolidation in the South has largely been threatened by the contradictions generated by structural economic reforms.* As by-products of economic conditionalities, much of the South has witnessed cuts in government services, growing poverty and social impoverishment of the majority. Also, people have experienced the mounting inability of their governments to deliver what their communities want, leading to violent resistance to adjustment programmes. Elsewhere, from Venezuela, the Dominican Republic, Tunisia, Jordan and Sudan to Bangladesh, cutbacks in public services and/or the withdrawal of subsidies from consumer goods not only met severe criticism but, more importantly, sparked bloody riots that led to the killings of many civilian protesters. In the midst of these 'IMF riots', many Southern countries found it increasingly difficult to institutionalize their newly achieved democracies. Following the eruption of riots and violent demonstrations, several Southern leaders expressed their anger and frustration with 'adjustments' and openly blamed the IMF for undermining their democratic futures. The outraged Venezuelan President Carlos Andrés Pérez, for example, publicly denounced the IMF's economic adjustments programmes in his 1988 election campaign, comparing 'Fund policies to a neutron bomb that kills only people' (Chua-Eouan, 1989).

In addition, *structural adjustment policies have detrimental effects on ethnic relations.* Disappointing socio-economic relations have pushed different ethnic groups to the wall. Throughout the South, rival ethnic groups have begun to mobilize people along ethnic identities, creating volatile political landscapes in which 'statelessness' (Adekanye, 1995, pp. 362–3) increasingly becomes the ultimate fate of many so-called 'sovereign' countries. Things have got out of control where ethnic tensions had already existed. For instance, Karachi – the port city of Pakistan – has become a 'city of death' with rising ethnic strife. The city is literally 'taken over by the bands of armed youths who took on their political rivals and let loose their fury against the state on law-enforcing agencies and government property' (Hanif, 1995, p. 35). The entire country is waiting for an explosion to take place, similar to the one in 1971 that led to the emergence of Bangladesh. No wonder the crisis has put the future of Benazir Bhutto's democratic regime on the line; another military take-over is not unlikely.

Likewise, on the eve of severe ethnic tensions, many African countries are virtually on the brink of total breakdown. The *proliferation of light weapons and the 'privatisation of security' in much of the African continent illustrate a simple fact that people are increasingly losing 'confidence in the capacity of the state to protect them'* (Cock, 1996, p. 1). Gradually losing all hope, people are exercising measures that are not legally acceptable. Primarily motivated by ethnic identities, more and more people have begun to rely on guns and private security plans, thus creating chaotic environments in countries such as Angola, Burundi, Liberia, Mozambique, Sierra Leone, Rwanda, Somalia and Sudan.

Similarly, criminal groups are taking advantage of declining states in the continent. Organized crimes including robbery, murder, illegal arms trading and drugs trafficking are on the rise. Is anarchy an inevitable fate for them? Kalpin warns the world by sketching a frightening scenario within the context of West Africa. In his words:

> West Africa is becoming *the* symbol of worldwide demographic, environmental, and societal stress, in which criminal anarchy emerges as the real 'strategic' danger. Disease, overpopulation, unprovoked crime, scarcity of resources, refugee migrations, the increasing erosion of nation–states and international borders, and the empowerment of private armies, security firms, and international drug cartels are now most tellingly demonstrated through a West Africa prism (Kaplan, 1994, p. 46).

Such an anarchic situation is not confined only to West or East Africa, however; many other countries in the South, particularly Central American and South Asian states, are confronting similar, if not the same, socio-political circumstances.

The decline as well as redesign of the state has also been largely responsible for the resurgence of religious fundamentalism across the South. Frustrated with the diminished ability of the state to both recognize and satisfy the needs of different communities, people are turning to religion-based organizations, both political and voluntary, for a better alternative (Sullivan, 1992, p. 34). In the Muslim world, given the persistent crisis of legitimacy, Islamic organizations are clearly gaining momentum, leading to the emergence of 'Islam' as a powerful political idlology. Manipulating the failure of economic liberalization programmes, these political forces are mobilizing people by arguing that neither Western democracy nor capitalism can solve the socio-economic problems of the needy; only Islam can build a better world. Such a populist approach has already earned electoral victories for a few radical Islamic parties in some places, notably Algeria and Turkey. Not only has the rising tide of Islamic fundamentalism appeared as an effective challenge to modernity; but it has also emerged as a threat to both secularism and constitutional democracy in the Muslim world.

Likewise, India, known as the world's largest democracy, has witnessed the rise of Hindu fundamentalism over the past few years. With the uneven and disappointing outcomes of economic reforms, a number of Hindu communal parties including the Bharatiya Janata Party (BJP), Rastriya Swayamsevak Sangh (RSS), Vishwa Hindu Parishad (VHP) and Shiv Sena are constantly engaged in restoring *Ram-rajya*, the rule of Lord Rama, in India. The growing popularity of Hindu fundamentalism has been reflected in the amazing success of the BJP in the national elections of 1991 and the provincial elections in 1995 (Ghimire, 1995, pp. 35–7). The BJP emerged as the single largest party in the national election in May 1996. Clearly, the rise of Hindu communalism not only poses a threat to India's secular state (Hargrave and Kochanek, 1993, p. 178) but also appears as a serious challenge to the country's democratic governance.

In brief, then, *with widening tensions between economic and political liberalization, much of the South has already entered a precarious stage where emerging anarchy is increasingly shattering the future of democratic consolidation.* Contrary to what dominant liberal scholarship widely anticipated, many Southern countries have witnessed the erosion of democratic institutions over the past few years. In the wake of massive social unrest, insurgencies and a deteriorating law and order situation, a number of countries have either returned to miliary authoritarianism (Algeria, Nigeria, Sudan) or have experienced the rise of repressive state structures (Egypt, Peru, Russia – the list goes on) (Monshipouri, 1995, p. 5). Also, democratic consolidation has been constrained in a number of countries (Argentina, Chile, Guatemala, Uruguay) by the fact that the military continues to maintain its 'veto' power over civilian institutions, making democratic transitions nothing but a big joke (Petras and Morley, 1992, pp. 8–12).

Such breakdowns of democracies cast profound doubt upon the validity and hegemony of both the governance 'paradigm' and liberal theories of democratization. It is increasingly becoming evident that neither a North–South approach nor any analysis that relies excessively on domestic factors (especially on the role of key political actors) can adequately explain the problems of democratic consolidation in the South.

THE SOUTH IN THE NEXT MILLENNIUM: CORPORATISM OR DEMOCRATIC DEVELOPMENT?

In order to avoid social unrest, political chaos and authoritarianism, some parts of the South might again be forced to move towards corporatist frameworks, whilst others would still find it worthwhile to take risks to attain the goals of democratic development. The following discussion outlines the reasons and ways in which the South might witness such a contradictory process of constructing corporatism and democracy simultaneously.

Corporatist Coalitions

In the 1990s, there have been renewed prospects of various forms of 'corporatism' emerging in the South, given the ongoing tension between economic contraction and political liberalization. With growing stress in state–society relations, many regimes' natural inclination is to look for arrangements with different social groups, which ensure both their longevity and the aversion of anarchy. Everywhere the adjustment process is permissive, even supportive, of the rise of a 'national' bourgeoisie alongside more bureaucratic, comprador, military, political and technocratic factions. Therefore, incumbent leaders have sought, in a period of declining economies, to replace the corruptive tendencies of co-optation with those of 'corporatism'. They can no longer afford the expansive (and expensive!) gestures of patronage. Instead, they have begun to rely on the less predictable but also less expensive arrangements of corporatism, primarily because it gives them a political framework that seeks to maintain social cohesion through the avoidance of conflict in the state–society domain.

Central to the understanding of corporatism is a relationship, somewhat reciprocal, between the state and major organized interests (Cawson, 1986, pp. 20–2). It revolves around the understanding of different groups about state and economy, particularly between labour and both national and international capital. Unlike pluralist democracy or governance debates, corporatism often supports the idea that the state will play a key role in decision-making (Schmitter, 1979). None the less, it offers a political structure to establish connections with other major social institutions in the political culture, such as religious groups and universities, media and interest groups, professional associations and NGOs, women's and youth groups.

Indeed, corporatism at the level of the 'state' may not be incompatible with limited political pluralism at the level of 'society' or market forces at the level of the 'economy' – particularly in a period of adjustment, when the national level has become less salient than the global. More formal national-level arrangements amongst state, capital and labour may be compatible, then, with more informal supra- and sub-national activities of co-operatives, ethnic communities, interest groups, religions, NGOs etc; that is, compatible forms of post-adjustment 'self-reliance'.

With growing demands for democracy and human rights, it is therefore likely that NICs and near-NICs in Southeast Asia will come to replace their established 'developmental(ist) states' with some relevant form of corporatism appropriate to the Pacific Rim at the dawn of the twenty-first century (Saul, 1995, pp. 142–3). Likewise, some African and many Latin American countries continue to find it beneficial to maintain their corporatist structures. It is, however, unlikely that the state will allow any such popular organizations to play a meaningful role in decision-making. While, within an exclusive and hierarchical structure, the state might grant key business and political groups a certain level of autonomy, it is probable that less organized and/or less important groups would be placed in the corner, living at the mercy of both the state and key socio-political actors. Thus, the growth of civil society is severely constrained, which in turn places heavy limitations on prospects of democratic consolidation.

Prospects for Democratic Development

The current global experiments of political democracy – notably formal multi-party constitutions, elections and governance – will not be sustained unless they are supported and complemented by the concept of *'democratic development'; that is, reinforcement of dynamic civil societies at the local and national and global levels.* Thus it is important to recognize the fact that a transition towards constitutional democracy only gives people the right to vote in an election. The conventional notion of democracy hardly appreciates the importance of creating political space for the majority to control in a protracted manner the 'material and institutional conditions under which they exist' (Bratton, 1990, p. 89). There has been a growing consensus that democracy can only be a meaningful concept if it provides an environment in which marginalized groups can exercise their right to be empowered.

In other words, democracy must encourage people to raise their voices against all kinds of deprivation and exploitation, structural as well as informal. Democracy will also allow people to 'participate in and to determine together those decisions that profoundly affect their lives' (Johansen, 1991, p. 210). Clearly, this indicates that the conventional notion of democracy needs to be redefined.

The concept of sustainable democratic development takes the agenda beyond popular participation in elections. Linking democracy and development, it offers a framework that focuses on the sustainable livelihoods of people, on the one hand, and on the other, it emphasizes the need to bring vulnerable and disadvantaged groups such as the rural poor, peasants, women and the old into the process of development.[2] It seeks to ensure people's participation 'in conceptualising their development needs and in development decision-making with regards to the control and use of scarce resources' (Heyzer, 1995, p. 2) (see Gyawali, Chapter 11, this volume for an illustration from the Nepali hydro sector).

Central to the argument of sustainable democratic development is the need to strengthen civil society (Macdonald, 1995, p. 2). Unlike mainstream theories of democratization, it focuses on the role of a strong and determined civil society. Without depending on state institutions and/or market forces, *democratic development initiates a search for a more focused role for popular organizations, notably (I)NGOs.*

While NGOs differ from one another in terms of political ideology, social objectives and their specific place in the global political economy, NGO networks have shown tremendous potential for both greater socio-political change and democratization. In addition to their traditional engagement in delivering welfare services and in community development programmes, NGOs (especially 'third generation NGOs', which are largely involved in advancing socio-political change towards sustainable development) (Korten, 1987, pp. 145–60) attempt to reorient public policies in favour of vulnerable groups. The NGO sector can effectively organize underprivileged people and give them a voice against all sorts of socio-economic injustice imposed on them. For instance, the *Grameen Bank*, a leading and well-known development institution in Bangladesh, has successfully changed the traditional place and role of women in rural Bangladesh over the past two decades. By supporting income-generating enterprises of marginalized groups, especially rural women, the Bank has enabled them to break out of stereotyped female occupations in a traditional society which is still dominated by religious and patriarchal values (Wahid, 1994, pp. 1–15).

In order to put an end to structural deprivation and discrimination, some NGO networks have begun to challenge the institutions of both states and markets, focusing on the importance of developing an alternative basis for democratic development. They are making efforts to generate popular power, to give people the right to control the institutions which shape their lives. By successfully motivating and organizing disempowered socio-economic groups, voluntary organizations are initiating what are called 'new social movements' (NSMs) for the empowerment of the poor and oppressed (Wignaraja, 1993, pp. 10–12). Such movements in many parts of the South have helped people to change, if not destroy, exploitative social structures. They have encouraged people to develop solid resistance against the current global trend towards the commodification of socio-cultural life. Elsewhere, NSMs have forced governments and the international financial community to devise concrete plans for both the preservation of the environment and the promotion of popular interests. Also, they have 'brought the rights of the indigenous people into the limelight' (Clark, 1991, p. 14).

Apart from developmental and democratizing activities, NGOs can make a big difference in peace-building operations (Pugh, 1995, pp. 1–32). Long before a conflict takes place, NGO networks can successfully promote confidence and mutual trust between rival groups and prevent them from descending into violent conflict. In particular, NGOs with a grassroots base have the ability to remove potential causes of conflict and to resolve differences between contending groups through political negotiations. Not only do they have a better understanding about the psychological and cultural aspects of conflicts, but they also have the 'know-how for conflict resolution based on traditional culture and wisdom' (Kunugi, 1995, p. 2). However, in some cases NGO efforts may be insufficient to promote co-operation between hostile groups because of the serious nature of their disputes. Nevertheless, they can still prevent a disaster by sending early warnings to the government, international organizations, the media and other concerned parties.

Interestingly enough, in part encouraged by the new global acceptability of democracy, the international community has had to come to accept the legitimacy and activity of several types of non-state actors. These have historically included multinational corporations (MNCs) and major religions, but now they extend to international and local NGOs such as ethnic, environmental, indigenous peoples', women's and youth groups. Together with the media, as well as 'old-fashioned' co-operative and labour groups, these constitute a 'civil society', which increasingly exists at global and regional as well as national and local levels.

If *the contemporary process of constructing regional and global civil societies can be continued, it is quite likely that the South will find a firm route to democratic development.* The emergence of transnational networks of civil society groups has brought together a wide range of NGOs working in the fields of peace, security and development across national boundaries. Against both the interests and exploitation of the global forces of production and finance, these transnational NGO networks began to ensure meaningful participation of civil society associations in international decision-making. In addition to advancing resistance to the current orthodoxy of neo-liberalism, these emerging transnational networks of voluntary organizations are actively involved in creating alternative routes for development.

With the proliferation of such strong and committed civil societies, the prospect of sustainable democratic development in the South has become a reality. Indeed, the mid-1990s constitute an unexpectedly promising period for the South's redirection and renaissance as the hegemonic position of neo-conservative policies is under challenge everywhere. The 'lost' or 'adjustment' decade, in Africa, the Caribbean, Latin America and South Asia especially, was one of neo-classical ascendancy in most of the North. Yet both the adjustment and monetarist projects of the 1980s, with their mutual preoccupation with debt, have been confronted with seemingly insuperable problems in the 1990s.

The 'triumphalism' attendant on the ending of both the Cold and Gulf Wars has rapidly yielded to pessimism and defeatism as liberalization in the East has gone awry and in the South is stagnant. The combination of prolonged recession in the West with protracted depression in the East has even begun to give pause to the IFIs – as they celebrated their fiftieth anniversaries! – about the appropriateness of structural adjustment. With a renewed focus on jobs, rather than deficits, some form of social democracy is likely again to become more acceptable (as well as imperative) in the North.

In short, the mid-1990s constitute an unanticipated conjuncture for much of the South to either escape from the dictates of the adjustment 'paradigm' or to reduce the growing tension between political and economic liberalization. It can begin to escape from interventive conditionalities and redefine its own development direction, with profound global implications. This is particularly feasible in those states where civil society has already been revived and rehabilitated, thus constituting an energetic source of alternative policy innovation and programme implementation. This prospect has been widened further by the construction of regional and global development coalitions outside the purview of inter-state organizations.

CONCLUSION

Neither orthodox governance conditionalities nor idealistic prerequisites (such as a negotiated transition, élite consensus or the exclusion of the popular sector) for democratic consolidation may be enough to sustain democracy in the twenty-first century. The neo-liberal logic that market capitalism and political democracy are mutually indispensable will continue to create tension in state–society relations unless the entire process of democratization is both supported and reinforced by spirited civil societies. Without effective involvement of local and global civil society in sustainable democratic development, it is unlikely that the renewed possibility of anarchy and different forms of authoritarianism and corporatism would be contained and/or challenged. However, the success of global civil society will largely depend on its capability to recognize and prioritize emerging development issues such as the environment, gender, the informal sector, justice, equality and empowerment in any framework of democratic development. Otherwise, sustainable, let alone consolidated democratic development, will continue to be elusive because the adjustment paradigm will remain as hegemonic as it did throughout the lost decade of the 1980s.

NOTES

1. For a general discussion of the anarchical nature of the state system and the traditional distinction between international and domestic politics, see Waltz (1979).
2. For a discussion of the concept 'people-centred development' see Korten and Klauss (1994).

REFERENCES

Adekanye, B.J. (1995) 'Structural Adjustment, Democratization and Rising Ethnic Tensions in Africa', *Development and Change*, 26, 2, April.

Agha, Z. (1995) 'Congress (I): Battle for the Party', *India Today*, 15 June.

Al-Sayyid, M.K. (1993) 'A Civil Society in Egypt?', *Middle East Journal*, 47, 2, Spring.

Archibugi, D. and Held, D. (1995) *Cosmopolitan Democracy: An Agenda for a New World Order* (Cambridge: Polity).

Ardito-Barletta, N. (1990) 'Democracy and Development', *The Washington Quarterly*, 13, 3, Summer.

Bailey, S.D. (1994), 'Non-official Mediation in Disputes: Reflections on Quaker Experience', *International Affairs*, 61, 2, March.

Barnet, R.J. and Cavanagh, J. (1994) *Global Dreams: imperial corporations and the New World Order* (New York: Simon & Schuster).

Bratton, M. (1989) 'Beyond the State: Civil Society and Associational Life in Africa', *World Politics*, 41, 3, April.

Bratton, M. (1990) 'Non-governmental Organizations in Africa: Can They Influence Public Policy?', *Development and Change*, 21, 1, January.

56   *Democratic Development in the South in the Next Millennium*

Bratton, M. and Van de Walle, N. (1992) 'Towards Governance in Africa: popular demands and state responses', in G. Hyden and M. Bratton (eds) (1992) *Governance and Politics in Africa* (Boulder, CO: Lynne Rienner).

Brecher, J. *et al.* (1993) *Global Visions: Beyond the New World Order* (New York and Boston, MA: South End).

Cawson, A. (1986) *Corporatism and Political Theory* (New York: Blackwell).

Cerny, P. G. (1995) 'Globalization and the Changing Logic of Collective Action', *International Organisation*, 49, 4, Autumn, pp. 595–625.

Chaing, P. (1981) *Non-Governmental Organizations: Identity, Role and Function* (New York: Praeger).

Chomsky, N. (1994) *World Orders: Old and New* (New York: Columbia University Press).

Chua-Eouan, H. G. (1989) 'The Debt Police', *Time*, 134, 5, 31 July.

Clark, J. (1991) *Democratizing Development: The Role of Voluntary Organizations* (Hartford, CT: Kumarian).

Cock, J. (1996) 'The Link Between Security and Development: The Problem of Light Weapons Proliferation on Southern Africa', paper presented at the ACDESS Conference on South Africa and Africa: Emerging Policy Frameworks, Berea, Johannesburg, January.

Cox, R.W. (1983) 'Gramsci, Hegemony and International Relations', *Millennium*, 12, 2, Summer, pp. 162–75.

Cox, R.W. (1987) *Production, Power and World Order* (New York: Columbia University Press).

Denham, M. and Lombardi, M. (eds) (1986) *Problems Without Borders: Perspectives on Third World Sovereignty* (London: Macmillan).

Diamond, L. (1993) 'Economic Liberalization and Democracy', unpublished manuscript (Stanford, CA: Hoover Institution), June.

Diamond, L. *et al.* (eds) (1990) *Politics in Developing Countries: Comparing Experiences with Democracy* (Boulder, CO: Lynne Rienner).

Drache, D. and Gertler, M.S. (eds) (1991) *The New Era of Global Competition: State Policy and Market Power* (Montréal and Kingston: McGill-Queen's).

Ekins, Paul (1992) *A New World Order: Grassroots Movements for Global Change* (London: Routledge).

Farrington, J. and Bebbington, A. *et al.* (1993) *Reluctant Partners?: NGOs, the State and Sustainable Agricultural Development* (London: Routledge for ODI).

Fukuyama, F. (1992) *The End of the History and the Last Man* (New York: Free Press).

Gellner, E. (1994) *Conditions of Liberty: Civil Society and Its Rivals* (New York: Penguin).

Ghai, D. (ed.) (1991) *The IMF and the South: Social Impact of Crisis and Adjustment* (London: Zed).

Ghimire, Y. (1995) 'The Saffron Resurgence', *India Today*, 31 March, pp. 35–7.

Gibbon, P. (1992) 'Structural Adjustment and Pressures towards Multipartyism in Sub-Saharan Africa', in P. Gibbon *et al.* (eds) (1992) *Authoritarianism, Democracy and Adjustment: The Politics of Economic Reform* (Uppsala: Scandinavian Institute of African Studies), pp. 127–68.

Gibbon, P. (ed.) (1993) *Social Change and Economic Reform in Africa* (Uppsala: SIAS).

Glyn, A. and Sutcliffe, B. (1992) 'Global but Leaderless?: The New Capitalist Order', in R. Miliband and L. Panitch (eds) (1992) *The Socialist Register 1992* (London: Merlin).

Gurtov, M. (1991) *Global Politics in the Human Interest* (Boulder, CO: Lynne Rienner).

Hanif, M. (1995) 'City of Death', *India Today*, 15 July.

Harbeson, J. W. (1993) 'Civil Society and Democratization in Africa: Some Preliminary Notes from the Field', *Africa Voices*, 2, 3, Fall/Winter.

Hargrave, R. L. and Kochanek, S. A. (1993) *India: Government and Politics in a Developing Nation* (New York: Harcourt Brace Jovanovich College).

Harik, I. (1994) 'Pluralism in the Arab World', *Journal of Democracy*, 5, 3, July.

Held, D. (1991) 'Democracy, the Nation-State and the Global System', in D. Held (ed.) (1991) *Political Theory Today* (Stanford, CT: Stanford University Press).

Held, D. (1992) 'Democracy: From City-States to a Cosmopolitan Order?', *Political Studies*, 40, special issue.

Held, D. and McGrew, A. (1993) 'Globalization and the Liberal Democratic State', *Government and Opposition*, 28, 2, Spring.

Hellinger, D. (1987) 'NGOs and the Large Aid Donors: Changing the Terms of Engagement', *World Development*, 15, Supplement, Autumn.

Heyzer, N. (1995) 'Toward New Government–NGO Relations for Sustainable and People-Centred Development', in N. Hayzer, J. V. Riker and A. B. Quizon (eds) (1995) *Government–NGO Relations in Asia: Prospects and Challenges for People-centred Development* (London: Macmillan).

Huntington, S. P. (1991) *The Third Wave: Democratization in the Late Twentieth Century* (Norman, OK: Oklahoma University Press.

Huntington, S. P. (1993) 'The Clash of Civilizations?', *Foreign Affairs*, 72, 3, Summer.

Johansen, R. C. (1991) 'Real Security is Democratic Security', *Alternatives*, 16, 2, Spring.

Kaplan, R. D. (1994) 'The Coming Anarchy', *Atlantic Monthly*, 273, 2, February.

Kasfir, N. (1992) 'Popular Sovereignty and Popular Participation: Mixed Constitutional Democracy in the Third World', *Third World Quarterly*, 13, 4, December.

Korten, D. C. (1987) 'Third Generation Strategies: A Key to People-Centred Development', *World Development*, 15, special supplement, Autumn.

Korten, D. C. and Klauss, R. (eds) (1994) *People-Centred Development: Contributions Towards Theory and Planning Frameworks* (West Hartford, CT: Kumarian).

Kunugi, T. (1995) 'The Role of NGOs in the Peace Process', paper presented at the Academic Council on the United Nations System (ACUNS) annual meeting, New York, June.

Leftwich, A. (1993) 'Governance, Democracy and Development in the Third World', *Third World Quarterly*, 14, 3, June.

Lindberg, S. and Sverrisson, A. (eds.) (1996) *Social Movements in Development: The Challenge of Globalization and Democratisation* (London: Macmillan).

Linz, J. (1990) 'Transitions to Democracy', *The Washington Quarterly*, 13, 3, Summer.

McCarthy, K. D. *et al.* (1992) *The Nonprofit Factor in the Global Community: Voices from Many Nations* (San Francisco, CA: Jossey-Bass).

Macdonald, L. (1995) *Supporting Civil Society: The Political Role of NGOs in Central America* (London: Macmillan).

Macdonald, L. (1994) 'Globalising Civil Society: Interpreting International NGOs in Central America', *Millennium*, 23, 2, Summer.

Mawlawi, F. (1993) 'New Conflicts, New Challenges: The Evolving Role for Non-Governmental Actors', *Journal of International Affairs*, 46, 2, Winter.

Mittelman, J. H. (ed.) (1996) *Globalization* (Boulder, CO: Lynne Rienner, IPE Yearbook no. 10).

Monshipouri, M. (1995), *Democratization, Liberalization and Human Rights in the Third World* (Boulder, CO: Lynne Rienner).

Moore, D. and Schmitz, G. J. (eds) (1995) *Debating Development Discourses: Institutional and Popular Perspectives* (London: Macmillan).

Moufee, C. (1988) 'Hegemony and New Political Subjects: Towards New Concept of Democracy', in C. Nelson and L. Grossberg (eds) (1988) *Marxism and the Interpretation of Culture* (Chicago, IL: University of Illinois Press).

Munck, R. and Waterman, P. (eds) (1996) *Labour Worldwide in the Era of Globalisation* (London: Macmillan).

Nelson, P. J. (1995) *The World Bank and NGOs: The Limits of Apolitical Development* (London: Macmillan).

Nyang'oro, J. E. and Shaw, T. M. (eds) (1989) *Corporatism in Africa: Comparative Analysis and Practice* (Boulder, CO: Westview).

Nyang'oro, J. E. and Shaw, T. M. (eds) (1992) *Beyond Structural Adjustment in Africa: The Political Economy of Sustainable and Democratic Development* (New York: Praeger).

O'Donnell, G. and Schmitter, P. C. (1986) *Transitions from Authoritarian Rule: Tentative Conclusions for Uncertain Democracies* (Baltimore, MD: Johns Hopkins University Press).

Petras, J. and Morley, M. (1992) *Latin American in the Time of Cholera: Electoral Politics Market Economics and Permanent Crisis* (London: Routledge).

Przeworski, A. (1991) *Democracy and the Market: Political and Economic Reforms in Eastern Europe and Latin American* (Cambridge: Cambridge University Press).

Pugh, M. (1995) *The Challenge of Peacebuilding: The Disaster Relief Model* (Halifax, Nova Scotia: Centre for Foreign Policy Studies).

Remmer, K. L. (1995) 'New Theoretical Perspectives on Democratization', *Comparative Politics*, 28, 1, October.

Robinson, M. (1995) 'Strengthening Civil Society in Africa: The Role of Foreign Political Aid', *IDS Bulletin*, 26, 2, April.

Saul, R. J. (1995) *The Unconscious Civilization* (Concord, Ontario: Anansi).

Schmitter, P. C. (1979) 'Still the Century of Corporatism?', in P. C. Schmitter and G. Lembruch (eds) (1979) *Trends towards Corporatist Intermediation* (Beverley Hills, CA: Sage), pp. 6–52.

Shaw, M. (1994) 'Civil Society and Global Politics: Beyond a Social Movements Approach', *Millennium*, 23, 3, Winter.

Shaw, T. M. (1994) 'The South in the 'New World (Dis)Order': Towards a Political Economy of Third World Foreign Policy in the 1990s' and 'Beyond any New World Order: The South in the 21st Century', *Third World Quarterly* 15, 1, March.

Stanley Foundation (1992) *Changing Concepts of Sovereignty: Can the United Nations Keep Pace?* (Muscantine, IA: Stanley Foundation).

Steiner, H. (1991) *Non-Governmental Organizations in Human Rights Movement* (Cambridge, MA: Harvard Law School Human Rights Program).

Stubbs, R. and Underhill, G. R. D. (eds) (1994) *Political Economy in the Changing World Order* (Toronto, Ontario: McClelland and Stewart).

Sullivan, D. J. (1992) 'Extra-State Actors and Privatization in Egypt', in I. Harik and D. J. Sullivan (eds) (1992) *Privatization and Liberalization in the Middle East* (Bloomington, IN: Indiana University Press).

Thomas, C. P. (1992) *Intermediary NGOs: The Supporting Link in Grassroots Development* (West Hartford, CT: Kumarian).

Underhill, G. R. D. (1994) 'Conceptualising the Changing Global Order', in R. Stubbs and G. R. D. Underhill (eds.) (1994) *Political Economy and the Changing Global Order* (Toronto, Ontario: McClelland and Stewart).

UNRISD (United Nations Research Institute for Social Development) (1995) *States of Disarray: The Social Effect of Globalization* (London: UNRISD).

Wahid, A. N. M. A. (1994) 'The Grameen Bank and Poverty Alleviation in Bangladesh: Theory, Evidence and Limitations', *The American Journal of Economics and Sociology*, 53, 1.

Waltz, K. N. (1979) *Theory of International Politics* (New York: Random House).

Wignaraja, P. (1993) 'Rethinking Development and Democracy', in Wignaraja, P. (ed.) (1993) *New Social Movements in the South: Empowering the People* (London: Zed).

World Bank (1989) *Sub-Saharan Africa: From Crisis to Sustainable Growth* (Washington, DC: World Bank).

4 Whither Democracy?: Globalization and the 'New Hellenism'
Barry Gills

INTRODUCTION

There is a strong assumption in the current intellectual and political atmosphere that we are witnessing an historical global advance of both capitalism and liberal democracy. If this were true, it could be argued that we are entering into a new golden age of human progress. However, there is evidence to suggest that this already conventional proposition is quite wrong on both counts, and that in fact what *we are witnessing is an 'historical reversal' of capitalism and a worrying 'crisis of democracy'*. Globalization is producing what I will call the *'New Hellenism'*.

This chapter explores the relationship between the evolving world economy and the new processes of democratization we see today. Following the basic premise of all political economy – i.e. that the political and economic are not separate realms – my first proposition is that the causes of recent political trends in the world are inextricably related to recent economic trends, and vice versa. The next proposition concerns the character of this relationship, i.e. the one between so-called economic 'globalization' and the current extension of *formal* democratic political practices in many parts of the world. In short, the accelerating liberalization of the world economy, driven by powerful structural imperatives as well as by political agency, is a central force behind the extension of formal neo-democratic practices. However, this liberalism–democratism is not necessarily socially progressive. In fact, it may serve primarily to mask deeper and growing social inequalities, increasing economic exploitation, and popular disempowerment.[1] (See Shaw and Quadir, Chapter 3, this volume.)

While the nature of the ongoing liberalization, or globalization processes, constitutes a stimulus to the extension of *formal* democratic practices, the very structure of the world economy and these same economic processes also represent significant obstacles to the extension of *substantive* democratization. Substantive democratization is concerned not merely with the appearances or procedures of competitive or 'open' political processes *per se*, but more fundamentally, with their social outcomes, discussed broadly under the headings of social justice, reform, the reduction of inequality, and popular empowerment.

A brief reference to my general philosophical perspective on historical processes of social change is in order. In preference to either a stage theory or a cycles theory approach, I now find it more useful to see recurrent themes and 'tensions' in political economy. I call this the 'perennial political economy' approach. This approach can subsume certain elements of the other two without necessarily succumbing to the limitations of either. It is through such a 'perennial' perspective that contemporary events can perhaps best be subjected to the litmus test of historical analogy.

GLOBAL DEMOCRACY AND THE 'NEW HELLENISM'

In keeping with the belief that a historical perspective can be instructive, *the experience of Hellenism is offered as an interesting analogy*. In the wake of the destruction of the Persian Empire (assumed to be a fetter on the freedom of economic and political activity) by Alexander the Great, the conquering Greeks founded numerous cities and greatly stimulated economic activity, including international commerce. At the same time, they exported Greek-style democratic constitutions to the cities, both old and new, in preference over either oligarchies or tyrannies. Thus to all appearances, it was a golden age of prosperity and democracy.

But things are not always as they seem. The paradox of the Hellenistic period was that whilst these cities often proudly sported 'democratic' constitutions, the dominant political reality of the age was the increasing power and opulence of the oligarchic classes and the monarchies, and the rapid expansion of the institution of slavery, accompanied by a general increase in economic exploitation and popular disempowerment. In international relations, the period was no longer as racked by ideological antagonism, but far more so by competition and rivalry among the quite similar states of the system. Culturally, Hellenism was founded on the chauvinist Aristotelian doctrine of Greek superiority (as opposed to Alexander's apostate cosmopolitanism), which justified exclusive Greek political dominance and validated Greek institutions.

Indeed, one historian of the Hellenistic period has remarked on the similarity between this pattern and modern (European) colonialism (Price, 1991, p. 316).

> Even more significantly, while democracy was accepted by all as the ideal civic constitution, in practice real popular participation in government declined in the Hellenistic age and dominance by the wealthy increased.... The kings could pose as democrats while being indirectly responsible for the growing power of the rich.

Furthermore, the relationship between rich and poor classes was fundamentally altered. The rich captured the magistracies and used them to control the popular assemblies. Pointedly, this produced 'a decline in real democracy, that is, genuine popular control over public life' (Price, 1991, p. 333). The extravagant growth of public munificence by the wealthy (as advised in Aristotle's *Politics*) likewise led to a greater public reliance on them and on their prestige, and the deterioration of indiscriminate law in favour of very discriminate privilege.

Historically speaking, these trends led to even worse things for 'democracy'. Much as G. E. M. de Ste Croix argues (de Ste Croix, 1981), Hellenism's perversion of the functions of democratic institutions was a prelude to the débâcle of democracy under the auspices of the Roman Empire. Rome consolidated what the Hellenistic monarchs and oligarchies had initiated. The long denouement to the class struggles of the Greek world was the Roman consolidation of the legal basis for power monopoly by the wealthy classes; achieved primarily through wealth qualifications for office-holding and through the final and brutal political defeat of the revolutionary impetus of the lower classes. The two great revolutionary demands of the preceding age of class struggle, i.e. redistribution of land and cancellation of debt, which had politically destabilized so many cities over the centuries, were systematically quelled under the *pax romanica* and in the name of 'Roman freedom'. Roman freedom, however, ruthlessly excluded the option to re-establish truly popular democracies within the empire or in any way threaten the new oligarchic/monarchic status quo. The inevitable renewal of tension between rich and poor classes was met by further repression and popular disempowerment.

Taken altogether, the upshot of these trends was eventually nothing less than a full-scale civilizational crisis. According to de Ste Croix, 'the great and growing concentration of wealth in the hands of the upper classes' was the primary cause of the system's historical undoing. Moreover,

> the Roman political system (especially when Greek democracy had been wiped out) facilitated a most intense and ultimately destructive economic exploitation of the great mass of the people, whether slave or free, and it made radical reform impossible. The result was that the propertied classes, the men of real wealth, who had deliberately created this system for their own benefit, drained the life-blood from their world and thus destroyed Graeco-Roman civilisation over a large part of the empire (de Ste Croix, 1971, p. 503).

Or as Peter Brown pithily expresses it, 'Altogether, the prosperity of the Mediterranean world seems to have drained to the top' (Brown, cited in de Ste Croix, 1971, p. 34).

This particular historical analogy is not intended to suggest an immediate apocalyptic situation. The processes briefly described above took place over several centuries and under different historical conditions. Nevertheless, certain key historical tensions in political economy appear to be both instructive and relevant. Is the problem of tension between wealth concentration, growing inequality and social polarization, and the deteriorating character of democratic political life no less a legitimate worry in the present historical circumstances?

John Kenneth Galbraith recently echoed a similar prophetic fear for the future of Western liberal democratic capitalist societies: 'The present and devastated position of the socially assisted underclass has been identified as the most serious social problem of the time, as it is also the greatest threat to long-run peace and civility' (Galbraith, 1992, p. 180). The obverse side of the same debased coin is of course a perceived increase in concentration of wealth among the wealthy classes and their growing indifference (or even hostility) to the fate of those 'beneath' them. This trend towards greater social polarization and inequality undermines the progressive direction of democratic societies over the past several decades, and threatens the viability of those transitions to democracy still only tentatively embarked on the long and arduous voyage.

This tendency towards greater social polarization is not only a domestic situation germane to a few rich societies, but is in my view far more general. The 'affluent society' seems to be socially unravelling due to ever-threatening increases in inequality, both within and between rich and poor nations (see Wilkin, Chapter 2, this volume). It is thus appropriate to return to the provocative theses outlined earlier, i.e. that *we are entering a retrogressive period of 'historical reversal' and face a 'crisis of democracy' in the future.* Before proceeding further on these issues however, it is necessary first to address the general question of the role of *politics* in the changing economic circumstances currently being referred to under the catch-all rubric of 'globalization'.

GLOBALIZATION AND THE CHANGING ROLE OF THE STATE: IS THERE A POLITICS OF GLOBALIZATION?

The focus of much recent writing on the state under the conditions of so-called 'globalization' has been its techno-rational or functional role in facilitating capital accumulation, under conditions of rapid and profound technological change. While much of this literature, in my view, therefore suffers from a techno-determinist subtext, i.e. privileging structural forces at the cost of political agency, some of the most sophisticated material makes very clear statements indeed about the general causal relationship between the world economy and changing domestic policy.

For example, Strange and Stopford argued

> that the U-turns we observed in so many developing countries in the late 1980s and early 1990s from protected home markets, state ownership, and import substitution to liberalization, privatization, and export promotion, and from antipathetic exclusion or restriction of the operations of foreign firms to an altogether more welcoming and accommodating posture, were no accident. All these changes came about through the control exercised by those foreign firms over the means to the end of earning foreign exchange which governments desperately needed and were unable to achieve any other way than by negotiation and bargaining with the foreign firms (Strange, 1995, p. 68).

Furthermore, according to Strange, this 'new diplomacy' entails

> the increase in the political, as opposed to the purely economic, activities and responsibilities of transnational enterprises... the responsibility for the location of production; and the assumption of judicial and welfare responsibilities within the community.... Firms, responding to markets, effect more change in less time in the distribution of wealth in the global economy than all the international organizations and bilateral aid programs have done in nearly half a century. Firms are... assuming a much greater political role in the provision of welfare (Strange, 1995, p. 69).

Strange rightly understands these trends – i.e. to the privatization of welfare provision, and the capitulation of the Third World to neo-liberal prescriptions – within the larger context of the monumental shift of production from the developed countries to the less developed. Their phenomenon was first analysed as the 'new international division of labour', then as the 'transnationalization of production' and more recently the somewhat glib term 'globalization'. As indicated above, the backdrop to the 'U-turn' by developing countries was of course the Debt Crisis and its incipient 'disciplinary' effects on governments. As a direct consequence, the militancy of the preceding era rapidly gave way to the resignation and pragmatism of the 1980s among many Third World governments. Rather than commitment to using the state as the alternative to market-dominated development, the new slogan of Third World state managers was 'there is no alternative' (TINA).

Such policies were not necessarily 'the peoples' choice'. Enormous external pressure was brought to bear during the 1980s to persuade governments to convert to the new góspel. The IMF and World Bank were converted into the standard-bearers of the new orthodoxy and were probably the world's most powerful *political* agencies of the decade, given the amount of influence they wielded over the domestic policies of supposedly sovereign governments. Such multilateral pressure was further extended into the GATT negotiations, to open whole sectors previously outside the remit of the global free-trade agreement. Bilateral pressure to open markets was deployed vigorously by powerful governments such as the United States.

The increasing privatization of the functions of the state, as a result of galloping globalization, surely has important implications for the political processes *within* states, as well as between states, and between states and firms. The anticipated 'diffusion of authority' away from the centralized state and towards the eponymous 'new medievalism' implies potentially far-reaching changes in the nature of democratic political processes, not all of which will be progressive in terms of social outcomes. The tone of techno-rational determinism in much of the recent literature on globalization and the state is most disturbing precisely from a *political* point of view. It gives rise to a sort of 'inevitabilism' that may prove to be politically immobilizing.

For example, many on the left have already succumbed to the view that Keynesian methods of dealing with unemployment are now impossibly antiquated due to the globalization of finance. Others believe that deregulation of global finance is irreversible due to technological determinants of the process, ignoring the fact that re-regulation of global capital movements is seriously under consideration both by governments and the upper echelons of the global financial establishment. This *new economic determinism, therefore, breeds defeatism,* glamorized to some extent by the intellectual sophistication of the new arguments surrounding globalization.

However, no argument that depoliticizes the processes of globalization should be politically or intellectually acceptable. On the contrary, globalization should actually serve to focus our attention precisely on the type of political responses it sets in motion, rather than feed the idea that politics is becoming the predictable epiphenomena of technological processes. In reality, the politics of globalization is all around us, and like all politics, it is a fairly fluid and open situation, the outcomes of which will be determined by 'struggle' or contest, and by the balance of forces on each question. It is dangerous to assume that any of these particular political outcomes are already techno-rationally predetermined. Above all, *no account of globalization should 'write out' the response to these processes by popular forces and social movements, including traditional labour movements and 'opposition' political parties. It is by no means certain that politics will follow a pre-written neo-liberal script in the future.*

THE 'HISTORICAL REVERSAL' OF CAPITALISM AND THE 'NEW MALAISE'

This brings us back to the proffered notion of a 'historical reversal' of capitalism.[2] The general political and economic effects of globalization of production and finance seem to be setting a trend for norms to move slowly back to those resembling *pre-unionized* capitalism. This can be seen, for instance, in the slow but inexorable retrenchment of the old welfare state in the Western societies. Moreover, as global over-capacity in many established industries weeds out weaker firms and causes wide-scale restructuring among the survivors, pressure mounts for further concentration in the global corporate structure. This structural tendency intensifies the pressure to 'flexibilize' labour, thus further undermining the political position of traditional union organization and exacerbating the extent of structural unemployment. Firms seeking relocation of production in the new global factory normally have a preference for weaker or non-existent unions, even if they do create employment.

Global (*haute*) finance, coupled to a globalized production system, can increasingly disengage from centralized domestic political processes and re-engage with local or regional political processes more freely than in the more state-regulated environment of the recent past. According to the very well-known scenario of transnationally mobile capital, if unions, taxes, or environmental regulations threaten profits in one country, production sites can be relocated to another with less costs or weaker or non-existent unions. The upshot is a potentially global increase in the rate of exploitation of labour; the 'race to the bottom' as politically weakened states and workers both compete for the favours of multinational firms. This prediction/trend is nothing new and certainly no new discovery. It is only that it seems to be accelerating and its consequences must now be considered globally. Among these consequences I would suggest that economically the 'underconsumptionist' effects are potentially very serious, while politically the trend is toward formal democracy at the expense of progress on substantive democracy.

There has long been an 'underconsumptionist' motif in political economy, stretching right back to the classical political economists and reappearing periodically in various Marxist, neo-Marxist, or Keynesian guises. Underconsumptionist perspectives, which imply an inherent tendency to structural imbalance in the economy, are the antithesis to the liberal tenet of natural 'equilibrium' in the world economic system. The particular Marxist version of 'crisis' brought on by extreme underconsumption, based on the putative tendency for the rate of profit to fall and immiseration of the proletariat to increase, was superseded in practice by the

Keynesian art of 'crisis management', thus leading to the institutions of the liberal post-war international political economy. These institutions combined domestic budgetary stimulus and state welfare provision with international regulation of capital movements and a liberalized international trade system, to produce Galbraith's 'Affluent Society' in the advanced countries during the historically unprecedented post-war boom. Needless to say, the Affluent Society never existed in the colonial and post-colonial Third World, which constituted most of the world's population.

By the historical analogy above, a period characterized by greater social polarization, increasing inequality, growing concentration of wealth, intensifying industrial over-capacity and international competition for market shares, crippling debt servicing burdens for weaker economies, and an unstable balance of power, will be a period in which general prosperity (as opposed to the wealth of a privileged few) slowly ebbs away as exploitation increases and redistributive alternatives are dulled or defeated. The gains of substantive democracy undergo a gradual historical reversal, despite the appearance of the extension of formal democratic practices.

Nevertheless, contrary to old-style Marxist expectations, mounting underconsumptionist pressures in the world economy will not necessarily bring about the cessation of aggregate world economic growth or bring the capitalist system itself into acute crisis. Rather, in today's conditions, and especially given the residual efficacy of the post-war Keynesian, welfare, and liberal international institutions, *underconsumption will contribute to a creeping entropy that undermines the substantive achievements of democracy in both rich and poor societies alike.* Meanwhile, the world economy will rumble on indefinitely, and regional growth may even be markedly high, such as has been the case in East Asia for the past several decades. Such regional variations are not the issue, however. The real question is the state of the global political economy as a whole and the interpretation of the general political character of its development.

As is well known, the post-war liberal–Keynesian institutions weakened considerably during the 1970s. This weakening was met by a vigorous onslaught from the right, calling for monetarist and neo-liberal prescriptions as the solution to the supposed 'failure' of Keynesian or social democratic policies. Internationally, key liberal institutions were allowed to atrophy or drift, or were redeployed to implement the new conservative policy agenda. In the intellectual world, primarily on the left, a plethora of new 'crisis' theories emerged to analyse the short-term manifestations of the breakdown of the previous set of liberal–Keynesian institutions. Perhaps the main shortcoming of these theories of crisis was their 'near- sightedness', i.e. the relative lack of long-term historical perspective.[3] In their obsession to understand an immediate or impending 'crisis', they were unwilling to contemplate what I regard to be the larger truth, i.e. the onset of a very long historical era of *malaise*, as opposed to a revolutionary transformation or a system-transforming breakdown crisis. Such periods of malaise can be understood by an analogy to the concept of entropy (or the winding down of a previous high level of stable and effective organization). They are a recurrent feature of world history, and may in fact have similar social causes behind them.

Every age and every intellectual class suffers from an errant tendency to exaggerate the uniqueness of its own period. I am suggesting that a more historical and long-term perspective would be very useful in clarifying the key issues of the contemporary period and the probable trends of the near and farther future. For instance, is it merely ironic, coincidental, or structurally determined that it was precisely in the wake of the serious breakdown of the previous liberal–Keynesian domestic and international institutions – i.e. during the 1980s – that many 'socialist' and 'nationalist' alternatives suffered collapse and that 'democracy' and the 'open' economy were suddenly the new wave? If not mere coincidence, which I find highly unlikely, then surely the causes are structural, as are their effects, both political and economic. The real question therefore is whether these structural tendencies are truly compatible with the further extension of substantive democratic goals.

PERENNIAL POLITICAL ECONOMY AND 'STATES VERSUS MARKETS'

The developing malaise of the liberal–democratic capitalist world economy has everything to do with the perennial tension in political economy we can refer to as 'states versus markets'. *I take 'state' and 'market' to be abstractions representing two contending forms of socio-economic regulation. A common misconception is that they are necessarily opposites.* On the contrary, the actual historical agencies of either 'state' or 'market' can be quite effectively symbiotic. Indeed, to a certain extent this is always the case. Thus, the 'tension' between these forms of regulation implies a dialectic of perpetual coexistence, not a final victory by one principle over the other. This being said, in the history of the world economy some periods are characterized more by the impact or prevalence of one principle as opposed to the other, at least in some critical respects. The politics of such periods can be markedly different indeed.

Political economy itself, as a science and not necessarily as a practice, began in the seventeenth century as the *statecraft* of wealth creation. Towards the eighteenth century, mercantilism, being based on a doctrine of systematic state intervention in economic pursuits, was developed into something approximating a full-blown international system encompassing the companies, colonies, intense naval arms races, and frequent commercial wars of rival states and firms. State intervention was primarily aimed at enhancing the wealth of élites and of the power and capabilities of the state itself.

The antitheses to this elitist-statism came in the shape of the new liberal political economy, and the rise of nationalism and the industrial proletariat. The counter-tendency to mercantilism emphasized the efficacy of the market in wealth creation, wealth being redefined as the national product distributed over the entire nation. Every increase in production would however make the system ultimately more dependent on increased aggregate consumption. The tenets of liberalism were not entirely or easily reconcilable with the power of the new industrialism. Throughout the nineteenth century, the capitalist world economy was increasingly characterized by a profound tension between the impetus towards economic liberalization on the one hand and that towards monopoly and imperialism on the other. Politically, the counterpart of these tensions expressed itself in tumultuous class struggles in the industrializing nations and colonial wars between 'advanced' and 'less advanced' nations. These tensions culminated in an intense civilizational crisis, encompassing the First and Second World Wars, and the global economic depression between them.

In the aftermath of that holocaust, state intervention again came to the fore as the antidote to structural crisis, responding to the failure of both liberal dogmatism and the naked aggression of raw imperialism. Drawing on Polanyi's critique of that same liberal/ imperialist edifice of capitalist civilization, the crucial point was the perceived efficacy of the state, representing the interests of 'society', to discipline economic forces so as to protect society itself from the vagaries of the unregulated market. The liberal 'self-regulating market society' and its dogma of the natural tendency to equilibrium was brutally exposed in the mid-twentieth century as a great myth, or an ideology, not a condition of nature. Therefore, the state was again called in to stabilize the domestic and international political economy. This took a variety of ideological forms, including liberal-democratic, social-democratic, communist, and nationalist.

This historic post-war trend to redeploy reformist-statist responses probably reached its apogee precisely in the early and mid-1970s, a point in modern history that is still in my view underestimated for the deep-seatedness of the transition it represents. Whereas for three decades preceding, the global trend had been for more and more scope for state intervention or statist solutions to economic and social problems, after the mid-1970s there occurred a 'historic reversal', the gist of which is to gradually reduce the functions of the state and to reduce the political capacity of labour or popular forces, in favour of more 'freedom' for the 'market', i.e. private capital. The previous era was characterized by the expansion of socialism and communism, national liberation movements, nationalization, unionization, and internationally co-ordinated challenges to the liberal international economic status quo, whether revolutionary or reformist.

From the vantage point of the mid-1970s it looked to some as though the 'state' was about to overwhelm the 'market' and a new, post-capitalist era would be dawning. The supreme irony in this history is that precisely the opposite happened. Suddenly the statist or reformist alternative was everywhere defeated or in retreat and the new era's leitmotif was 'liberalization, privatization, and marketization', accompanied, however, by the popular clamour for democratization in many societies. Ideologists of the new right immediately proclaimed the progressiveness of their victory and its benefit to all humanity. Indeed, the popular impetus towards democracy, partly a revolutionary impulse and naturally allied with the cause of reform, was just as quickly 'hijacked' into the service of legitimating the new global neo-liberal economic order.

CONCLUSION

It is already apparent that *the new era is far from utopian.* Those old scourges of economics and of humanity, namely poverty, unemployment, debt, insecurity, and disempowerment, still haunt the world economy, and economists, and nowhere more so than in the Third World/South. Alfred Marshall was quite right to say that there is 'no moral justification for extreme poverty side by side with great wealth'.[4] But what is the place of democracy in a world so economically conceived ? The 'competition process' becomes increasingly unstable and destructive, threatening social cohesion, political stability, and human welfare (Bienefeld, 1994). In this context, the democratic gains of the past become a fetter on the capital accumulation process.[5] Therefore, a new logic is set in train whereby a global undermining of social progress is abetted in the name of restoring growth (read profits). Neo-liberal ideology serves to defend this deepening exploitation of workers and the widening social inequalities in the South and North alike and between the two (Wilkin, Chapter 2, this volume).[6]

The most telling aspect of the new economic liberalization qua *'globalization' and its parallel process of formal democratization is therefore the relatively limited nature of the progressive reform these processes now allow.* History seems to have moved full circle again, as the overriding goal of capital accumulation drowns out the voice of reform. 'Wealth creation first – reform later!' is the slogan of the ascendant market over the moribund state. Writing in the late 1950s, J. K. Galbraith already noted the implications of that same doctrine for the South:

> The people of the so-called backward countries have frequently heard from their presumptively more advanced mentors in the economically more advanced lands that they should be patient about social reform, with all its disturbing and even revolutionary implications, and concentrate on increasing production. It can be remarkably inappropriate advice. Reform is not something that can be made to wait on productive advance. It may be a prerequisite to such advance. In the advanced country, in contrast, increased production is an alternative to redistribution. And, as indicated, it has been the great solvent to the tensions associated with inequality (Galbraith, 1958, p. 86).

Precisely. In this light, the 'new international division of labour' and now 'globalization', when viewed in one global economic context, is also a *device by which the rich and powerful states deflect the burdens of otherwise necessary and/or painful economic and social adjustment on to weaker societies.* That is, increasing global production by relocating production to the less developed and therefore less costly countries allows profits to be sustained and redistributive alternatives to be deferred. Forcing liberalization on the entire world over the dead body of the protective state is yet another string to the same bow of advancing the profit of the already powerful and already wealthy. The interests of global financial and corporate institutions are privileged over those of popular, national, or redistributive goals, whether in the 'first' or the residual 'third' worlds.[7]

This 'New Hellenism' goes forward under the guise of democracy, but its social outcomes are probably already more negative than positive, and we may reasonably expect this trend to worsen over the long term. Paradoxically, it is precisely where democracy is structurally weakest, for instance in East Asia, that economic growth is most dynamic. Conversely, the areas of previously highest substantive democratic achievement, such as Northern or Western Europe, find themselves deeply embedded in the malaise of low growth and high structural unemployment. Democratization without reform is, however, the natural and logical accompaniment of the rise of market forces over the statist alternative, and characteristic of a socially and politically regressive period.

The market and its claim for 'freedom' are of course mere abstractions, masking the deeper reality that 'market forces' are in fact a form of historical agency, representing real interests and bearing very concrete political implications. Since the mid-1970s therefore, the inchoate malaise of which I speak was taking manifestation in the general tendency to unleash private interests via so-called market forces and gradually strip away from workers and 'society' the buffer of state protection. At a certain point these tendencies will extend themselves sufficiently so that a full accounting of their impact on society becomes an urgent political necessity. I believe that point is already being reached. Whether or not a new political counter-tendency will be set in train in response to the rise of the 'market' is the central question of the current historical era. *To succumb completely to the market at this stage will ensure that the New Hellenism will be consolidated. History teaches us that social movements will resist this tendency.* The outcome of this struggle will be decided politically, not by any presumed economic inevitabilities. The time for a response is now. There can be no progress without reform, and no meaningful democracy either.

NOTES

1. This argument is made at more length in Gills *et al.* (1993).
2. I am indebted to Makotoh Itoh for the notion of a 'historic reversal of capitalism', from his seminar on the economic situation in Japan, Department of Politics, University of Newcastle upon Tyne, 7 July 1995.
3. This historical near-sightedness on the left has recently been somewhat ameliorated by two prominent attempts to summarize the twentieth century: Arrighi (1994) and Hobsbawm (1994).
4. Alfred Marshall, *Principles of Economics*, p. 714, cited in Galbraith (1958), p. 42.
5. For further discussion see John Toye (1993) and John Brohman (1995). Brohman contends that in neo-liberalism 'The sphere of market exchange is abstracted from the realm of production and relations of power. In the end, an ideological conception of the market is offered as a substitute for particular, historically constituted markets in different countries. Likewise, a highly ideological conception of the state is offered in place of a careful analysis of variations in state intervention, institutional structures, and power relations' (p. 314).
6. See World Bank (1994).
7. For a different account of the transition between the 'new international division of labour' and 'globalization' see Mittleman (1995).

REFERENCES

Arrighi, G. (1994) *The Long Twentieth Century* (London and New York: Verso).
Bienefeld, M. (1994) 'Capitalism and the Nation State in the dog days of the 20th century', in M. Bienefeld (1994) *The Socialist Register* (London: Merlin), pp. 94–125.
Brohman, J. (1995) 'Economism and critical silences in development studies: a theoretical critique of neoliberalism', *Third World Quarterly*, 16, 2, pp. 297–318.
de Ste Croix, G. E. M. (1971) *The Class Struggle in the Ancient Greek World* (London: Duckworth).
Galbraith, J. K. (1958) *The Affluent Society* (Harmondsworth: Penguin).
Galbraith, J. K. (1992) *The Culture of Contentment* (London: Sinclair-Stevenson).
Gills, B., Rocamora, J. and Wilson, R. (eds) (1993) *Low Intensity Democracy: Political Power in the New World Order* (London: Pluto).

Hobsbawm, W. (1994) *Age of Extremes: The Short Twentieth Century, 1914–1991* (London: Michael Joseph).

Mittleman, J. H. (1995) 'Rethinking the international division of labour in the context of globalisation', *Third World Quarterly*, 16, 2, pp. 273–96.

Polanyi, K. (1944) *The Great Transformation* (Boston, MA: Beacon).

Price, S. (1991) 'The History of the Hellenistic Period', in J. Boardman, J. Griffin and O. Murray (eds) (1991) *The Oxford History of the Classical World* (Oxford: Oxford University Press), pp. 316–37.

Strange, S. (1995) 'The Defective State', *Daedalus*, 124, 2, Spring, pp. 55–74.

Toye, J. (1993) 'Is there a New Political Economy of Development?', in C. Colclough and J. Manor (eds) (1993) *State or Markets? Neo-liberalism and the Development Policy Debate* (Oxford: Oxford University Press).

World Bank (1994) *World Development Report* (Oxford: Oxford University Press).

5 The Moral Condemnation of the South

Frank Furedi

In mainstream international literature and in the media it is generally assumed that *the South has replaced the Soviet Bloc as the main threat to global stability* (Fukuyama, 1992; Lukács, 1993; Macrare, 1990; and Mearsheimer, 1990). *The demonization of the South has become one of the central motifs of the post-Cold War international system.* Many observers have drawn attention to the more explicit racial and cultural dimensions of this process. The argument of this contribution is that *such an emphasis may distract from a far more important development, which is the emergence of a liberal–humanitarian discourse whose mission is to 'save the Third World from itself'. This new discourse is vividly illustrated through the concept and representation of fundamentalism.*

THE STRUGGLE FOR THE MORAL HIGH GROUND

The past decade has seen a dramatic shift in the presentation of the so-called Third World in the West. Today, it is difficult to recall that until the late 1980s, the movements of the South exercised considerable authority. Not so long ago the Non-Aligned Movement occupied the moral high ground. Its demands were debated in international institutions and neither side in the Cold War divide could ignore its aspirations.

During much of the post-war period, especially the 1950s and the 1960s, the momentum of anti-colonial protest helped establish the moral authority of Third World movements. This process coincided with the discrediting of Western imperialism. For the first time, there was a recognition, even in the West, that the social, economic and political problems of the Third World were integrally connected to colonial domination.

The consolidation of the moral authority of what used to be called Third Worldism was intensely resented by the Western political élite. During the 1960s and the 1970s, Western leaders were perturbed by the attraction which Third Worldism exercised over their own youth (Furedi, 1992, pp. 116–19). Many leading Anglo-American Cold War ideologists were sensitive to the vulnerability of the 'Free World' to the charge of imperialism. When Western youth opposed military adventures, like the American invasion of Vietnam, and identified with Third World figures such as Che Guevara, many leaders in London and Washington felt vulnerable. This heroic moment of Third Worldism was experienced as the rejection of the West's imperial past.

The fact that Third World causes could command moral authority struck a direct blow against the old coherence of the superior Western self-image. The sensitivity of Western liberal and conservative intellectuals was demonstrated by their obsessive concern with this problem. During the 1960s and 1970s, books and articles on a variety of subjects lashed out against the Third World. Liberals and student radicals were denounced for their gullibility as regards Third World causes. For example, the leading American sociologist, Daniel Bell, sought to limit the damage by attacking those who sought to play on 'liberal guilt about racism and exploitation'. Bell's attempt to lighten the burden of American foreign policy through pointing to the 'savageries' of 'Rwanda, Burundi, or Uganda' anticipated by more then a decade a central theme in North–South relations (Bell, 1980, pp. 150, 206).[1]

By the mid–1970s, periodicals such as *Foreign Affairs* and even more liberal publications were depicting the Third World as a frightening threat to global peace. Increasingly, the West was represented as the new victim of Third World guerillas and terrorists. This genre of anti-Third World sentiment was well captured by an article in *Foreign Affairs* in July 1975:

> The generations that have come to maturity in Europe and America since the end of the Second World War have asked only to bask in the sunshine of a summertime world; but they have been forced instead to live in the fearful shadow of other people's deadly quarrels. Gangs of politically motivated gunmen have disrupted everyday life, intruding and forcing their parochial feuds upon the unwilling attention of everybody else (Fromkin, 1975, p. 683).

Arguments such as this were mobilized to reverse the moral equation between the North and the South. Increasingly, the former was depicted as the victim of some unimaginable horror emanating from the South.

It was not until the late 1980s that the moral equation between the North and the South was finally reversed. The collapse of the Soviet Union and the new global climate of conservatism had provided the West with an unexpected opportunity to demonize the Third World, and at the same time rehabilitate its imperial past. The failure of the various radical experiments in the South helped to contain the anti-colonial challenge to Western hegemony.

In comparison to the triumphalist anti-Third World rhetoric of the 1990s, Bell sounded positively restrained. The publications of the 1990s, which proclaimed the 'Death of the Third World' or asked 'Who Killed the Third World?', reflected the sentiment that its moral authority has 'disintegrated' (Bissell, 1990, p. 23). This triumphalist tone, most eloquently captured in Francis Fukuyama's well-known essay 'The End of History', expressed the conviction that the moral authority of the West had been regained. With the reversal of the moral equation, the very idea that the West bore responsibility for problems facing the societies of the South was effectively negated.

In contemporary Western publications, the moral condemnation of the South, especially of Africa, is linked to a retrospective vindication of colonialism. *Many societies of the South, especially those of Africa, are treated in pathological terms.* Africans 'are divided by hysterical tribalisms and suffer anarchical social upheavals' stated William Pfaff in his call for the recolonization of the continent (Pfaff, 1995, p. 6). Africans in particular are routinely represented as devoid of any moral qualities. Many accounts of the conflict in Rwanda have pointedly argued that its people simply do not know right from wrong. A major review of the conflict, in the *Sunday Times*, reported that in Rwanda 'deceit and the nurturing of hatred is far more institutionalised and sophisticated than in Europe', and added that 'the process of dehumanisation begins at birth'. According to this report, Rwanda is a society where deception and dishonesty are the most highly esteemed values. The reader was confidently informed that Rwandans 'found it more natural to tell lies than tell the truth' (*Sunday Times*, 31 July 1994).

The image of Africa as a moral wasteland was the central theme of Robert Kaplan's influential article 'The Coming Anarchy'. Kaplan introduced his social pathology of Africa with the comments of a West African minister, 'we did not manage ourselves well after the British departed' (Kaplan, 1994, p. 44). The spectre of primordial bestiality invited nostalgia for the good old colonial days. Just as the old caricatures of African barbarism are recycled as the problem of the 1990s, so the demand goes up for a revamped version of the old imperial solution. *Newsweek* is only one of many influential voices to have talked about how 'the world is groping for an acceptable form of what might be called "The New Colonialism"' (*Newsweek*, 1 August 1994).

Newsweek's advocacy of a New Colonialism is symptomatic of the reversal of the moral equation between North and South. Since the late 1980s, there has been a significant sea-change in the climate of discussion. Instead of merely discrediting Third World societies, there is now a new attempt to celebrate the record of the West, and in the process, to morally rehabilitate imperialism. It is worth noting that, for example, during the aftermath of the Gulf War against Iraq, there was a tendency to celebrate imperial conquest in Britain and the United States (see Furedi, 1994, chapter 5). During the past three years, Western discussions of its colonial past have been more and more upbeat (Beloff, cited in Gough, 1990, p. 169; Casey, 1991; and Elton, 1991, p. 45).

The emergence of a new, unashamed Western imperial rhetoric is not just motivated by the desire to settle accounts with the past. It is also motivated by domestic considerations. Its objective is not merely to morally discredit the Third World – that has already been accomplished. The emphasis of imperial rhetoric is focused towards the establishment of a coherent Western identity. Western societies find it difficult to generate a positive vision on their own account. There are few obvious sources of legitimacy that can be tapped by Western governments. Economic depression, political stagnation and social malaise mean that there is no dynamic towards the creation of a positive national identity in the industrial West.

In these circumstances, Western politicians seek to gain moral authority through highlighting their relationship with other morally 'inferior' societies. That is why failed politicians who are unable to solve the problems of inner-city London or downtown New York feel much more comfortable with handling the situation in Mogadishu with a few helicopter gunships. This sentiment inspired the *Wall Street Journal* to remark that what 'Desert Storm did for America's military credibility, Somalia may do for its moral credibility' (7 December 1992). This preoccupation with 'moral credibility' is driven by a sense of unease about the state of American society. So we are told that in Somalia, 'we assume the US security forces won't have to read teenage thugs their Miranda rights, as they must for the Crips and Bloods in south central Los Angeles'. It is as if the *Wall Street Journal* has relocated the problems raised by the Los Angeles riots to Somalia, where they can be resolved to a satisfactory conclusion with a kick up the backside from the humanitarian marines.

A THREAT TO US – AND A THREAT TO THEMSELVES

The representation of the Third World as a threat to everyone is not a particularly novel theme. Images of Muslim terrorists and Asian expansionism were widely peddled in the post-war period. However, since the end of the Cold War the quality of this threat has been tremendously inflated. A variety of new and more formidable dangers have emerged to excite the Western imagination. It is often predicted that the threats of the twenty-first century will be that of Third World nuclear proliferation, environmental terrorism, an explosion of the drug trade, the spread of fundamentalism, or the peril of overpopulation and migration.

According to the new perspective it is not merely Third World terrorism and military conflict which threaten the West. The inflation of 'their' threat means that the people of the South, by their very existence, represent a danger to the Western way of life. These sentiments often come to the surface in debates about the so-called demographic explosion of Third World societies. In the recent period, it has been suggested that population growth in the Third World would inexorably lead to the rise of mass migration. The migration of millions of desperate and hungry economic migrants is now treated as one of the major threats facing the West in the future (see Kennedy, 1993). The logic of these Malthusian arguments is that the very act of reproduction of ordinary people in the South constitutes a security risk.

During the 1990s, the image of the demographic time-bomb has been linked to the danger of environmental destruction. This synthesis of environment with population has had a major impact on the popular imagination. Unlike conventional Malthusian dangers, which only affect those directly concerned, the environment–population synthesis is evocatively represented as a threat to everyone. As Christa Wichterich pointed out:

> where people in the Third World allegedly bring about their own hunger by their increase, they only injure themselves: but where they allegedly use up the resources that we want to consume, and disturb the ecological balance, they are also injuring us (Wichterich, 1988, p. 24).

According to this schema, population pressure in one part of the world leads to environmental degradation, which in turn threatens the rest of the globe.

This new biological nightmare scenario is all the more frightening since the West can not insulate itself from its consequences. The South, by its very existence, signifies a danger to the North. What is at stake is the very air that we breathe and the water that we drink. As Kaplan argued:

> It is time to understand 'the environment' for what it is: *the* national security issue of the early twenty-first century. The political and strategic impact of surging populations, spreading disease, deforestation and soil erosion, water depletion, air pollution, and, possibly, rising sea levels in critical overcrowded regions like the Nile delta and Bangladesh – developments that will prompt mass migrations and, in turn, incite group conflicts – will be the core foreign policy challenge from which others will ultimately emanate (Kaplan, 1994, p. 58).

With such grotesque caricatures, the dehumanization of the South is completed. Those in the West experience the people of the South, not as fellow human beings, but as polluters.

But the Third World is not merely a threat to us – it is also a threat to itself. It is widely assumed that many societies in the South have failed their people and that therefore in some sense they are morally inferior to those of the West. *Newsweek* wrote of 'failing nations' which are ripped apart by conflict and tension (1 August 1994). According to Western observers, such failed societies have caused immense suffering to their people. Invariably, it is concluded that only the West can save these societies from themselves. At various times this argument has been used to call for Western intervention in Iraq, Somalia, Rwanda, Cambodia, Bosnia, Angola and Haiti.

The widespread acceptance in the West of its right to military intervention in other parts of the world is a testimony to the effectiveness of the moral denigration of the Third World. This widely accepted sentiment is based on the premise that sees the South as the problem and the North as the solution. In terms of international relations, this leads to the acceptance of a two-tiered global system, where the West has an unquestioned authority to intervene where it sees fit.

The theme of saving the Third World from itself is promoted in a variety of forms. In the first instance, right-wing thinkers have recycled the old arguments about how the 'natives cannot look after themselves'. 'Africa will never enjoy the blessings of peace and prosperity and escape the curses of civil war, famine, pestilence and genocide, until the white man once again takes over political control', was the verdict of Peregrine Worsthorne in the *Sunday Telegraph* (31 July 1994). Such old-fashioned colonial sentiments represent the extreme end of the new imperialist spectrum. It is far more common to advance a more limited agenda – one that targets a particular society facing moral disintegration. Such arguments take the form of demanding intervention to prevent chaos and save ordinary people from the terrible predicament in which their leaders have placed them. For example Robert Rotberg, an American specialist in African politics, warned that 'Somalia cannot soon be left to itself' and observed that 'we should have ended the clan warfare earlier' (Rotberg, 1993, p. 194).

The emphasis on political and moral collapse in the failed societies of the South is also expressed in a number of surprisingly curious ways. In the past, Western intrusion into the affairs of Third World societies was pursued through making an issue of their human rights abuses. (For more on the politics of universal human rights, see Evans, Chapter 6, this volume). This tactic, which seeks to win concessions from a particular Third World regime, is still extensively used. In July 1995, representatives of the Kenyan Government were hauled in front of a meeting of its aid donors in Paris, and given a lecture on its human rights record. Commentators in the media reported this meeting as a routine event. Organizations like Amnesty International welcomed the encounter. The right of a group of Western politicians to interfere in the domestic affairs of an African society and to lay down the law about how to manage its economic and political life, was presented as an initiative which was long overdue.[2]

In the 1990s, human rights abuses have been joined by a variety of other 'abuses', which legitimize Western intrusion into the internal affairs of Third World societies. Increasingly it is argued that people of the South have to be saved not only from their governments but also from each other. In addition, the West must save the environment from their pollution. Such apparently non-political and non-military crusades have dominated the agenda in North and South relations in the 1990s. Moral lessons, oriented towards cultural practices and intimate individual behaviour, have been propagated through Western Non-Governmental Organisations (NGOs) and international institutions. High-profile international conferences are routinely held – Rio, Cairo, Beijing – which lecture representatives of the South about their responsibilities for maintaining their environment, how to reduce their rate of population growth and how to treat their women.

In this new climate of Northern moral intrusion, all forms of Southern cultural practices become subject to scrutiny. Western aid agencies, including the World Bank, have emerged as champions of Third World children and women. Campaigns, such as those against female genital mutilation and child labour in India, have been harnessed to the perennial crusade against Third World fertility.[3] Such sensitive subjects often acquire a voyeuristic obsession with exotic sexuality. 'Regarding Muslim societies, perhaps the most distinguishing feature of the Islamist discourse is its excessive (almost obsessive) emphasis on matters of sex, the family, and social morals', observed one account of radical Islamism (Ayubi, 1995, p. 81).

Since many of the campaigns around the issues of fertility, women and children are presented in the vocabulary of rights, they often enjoy the endorsement of Western liberal, left-wing and feminist circles. And yet it can be argued that such *campaigns of moral intrusion represent a form of cultural warfare against societies of the South.* This tendency is particularly evident around the issue of *population control.* Western population policies are not merely about the provision of services but the transformation of cultural practices and individual attitudes. For example, Bongaarts and Bruce, two leading experts working with the Population Council, argue that 'an effective programme is frequently one that goes beyond the provision of family planning and contraceptive services by addressing social or familial disapproval' (Bongaarts and Bruce, 1995, p. 57). Bongaarts and Bruce are so convinced of their cause that they never pause to ask 'who gave them the right' to undermine what they euphemistically refer to as the 'psychological and cultural barriers' to contraception in an African or Asian society.

For family planners the cultural norms and values of target societies are obstacles that need to be overcome through a variety of techniques. A central emphasis is placed on encouraging women to adopt aspirations, life-styles and identities which are at variance with the prevailing norm. 'To reduce unwanted sexual contact and pregnancy, we must assist girls to envision future identities apart from sexual, marital and mothering roles', argue Bongaarts and Bruce (1995, p. 72). The far-reaching implications of this perspective of social engineering are rarely spelled out. This project, designed to foster new aspirations and identities, would systematically undermine the moral foundation of the target society. Whether such societies have a capacity to absorb the effects of such changes, is an issue that is simply evaded by the proponents of the new morality.

Population control literature contains an implicit – sometimes explicit – moral condemnation of the culture of fertility that prevails in target societies. It contains a clear assumption of moral superiority, which is expressed routinely in the moral condemnation of practices deemed to be unacceptable. The United Nations Fund for Population Activities' (UNFPA) *The State of World Population* contains a variable catalogue of practices and beliefs which are confidently dismissed as unacceptable. The report sometimes assumes the tone of a sermon, which runs through a list of practices that should be abolished and which ought to be adopted. Female circumcision is represented as a 'major public health issue'. The need for later marriages is stressed because of its beneficial effect on the rate of population growth. The report advocates Western-type male participation in pregnancy and sex education for young people. Adopting the tone of moral superiority, it lists a series of practices in a manner which invites the reader to react with obvious horror. For example, it notes:

> For the women of the Bariba tribe in Benin, having babies is a test of will. Enduring labour and childbirth alone and in silence is a sure route to social respect. Asking for help is considered a sign of weakness and shameful. As a result, many women who could have easily been saved die of complications during delivery (UNFPA, 1995, p. 45).

The idea that concepts of shame and respect are bound up with a sense of dignity and integrity of a people is not even entertained. From the tone of the report, there is the expectation that all concerned and civilized readers will demand that the Bariba change their standards about respect and shame in the interest of health.

That many of these practices have existed for hundreds of years, that they are integral to the moral and social code of the societies concerned and that these societies ought to have an opportunity to determine their life-style is paradoxically ignored by a publication which continually advertises the importance of human rights. The right of people to live according to the custom and practices that they have evolved over hundreds of years, is one right which population activists can casually reject.

The issue at stake in not whether one approves of a particular idea or practice. There are many practices in *all* parts of the world which offend different groups of people. The issue worth considering is: from where do a group of Western population professionals get the authority to decide what is in the best interest of people in societies around the world? The casual manner with which they condemn other peoples' social practices is only matched by the uncritical way in which they project their own values on people living under very different circumstances.

Regardless of their intentions, such campaigns of moral intrusion reinforce the notion that the West knows best. Such campaigns help construct a consensus about North–South relations, which embraces virtually the entire political spectrum in the West. That there are two kinds of societies – problem ones and those that provide solutions – is now an 'accepted fact' in international relations. In fact, this mood is so pervasive that acts which would have been condemned in the past as oppressive are now not even worthy of comment. For example, whether or not an election in Asia or Africa is democratic is these days determined not by the indigenous electorate, but by a commission of Western election monitors. It seems that only Western officials can be trusted to recognize a fair election when they see one.

Monitoring elections in non-Western societies is so common that it does not even merit any serious discussion. Nobody asks how the British people would react if the verdict of Cambodian or Brazilian monitors was required to pronounce on the outcome of their election. No doubt it would be considered an impudent intrusion into a purely British affair. And yet when it comes to Western interference in 'their' elections, national sovereignty ceases to be an issue. It is not considered to be a case of foreign intervention in the domestic affairs of another nation.

The moral denigration of Third World societies helps contribute to the creation of a climate where *intervention is rarely experienced as such. We live in an age of 'peacekeeping' and 'humanitarian' missions.* Today's humanitarian colonialism explicitly avoids the language of *realpolitik* and presents itself as non-interventionism. Indeed, Western ministers continually argue that they do not want their troops to intervene in the affairs of another country. And when a military operation is sanctioned, it is invariably promoted as a sacrifice, carried out with reluctance by a selfless power. Few Americans would have disagreed with the *New York Times*, when it described the invasion of Somalia as 'a turning point in American foreign policy', since this was the first time that the charitable motive of feeding 'starving people' inspired a major military operation (5 December 1992).

This rhetoric of non-intervention has led many experts to speculate about the new isolationism in the West. The discourse of isolationism has led to the situation where often it is those associated with liberal causes who are most vociferous in demanding intervention. The mission to save them from their governments or themselves excites the imagination of the morally outraged. In Britain, it is publications like the *Guardian* and the *New Statesman* who have been the most vociferous proponents of military intervention in Iraq – on the side of the Kurds – and in Bosnia. In the United States, liberal and left-wing writers were in the forefront in demanding intervention in Haiti. Their support for an interventionist foreign policy was no doubt motivated by humanitarian and moral concerns. But an important effect is to legitimize the right of the West to dictate the rules of international affairs. The conversion of some of the most critical observers to the stance of interventionism indicates that today the right of the West to intrude and regulate the life of other societies is virtually unquestioned. It also suggests a new fault line between North and South on the moral plane.

THE NEW MORAL CONSENSUS

The establishment of a new moral equation between the North and South has helped legitimize a two-tiered international system. It is a system where few ask questions about who gave institutions like the 'Gulf War Coalition', NATO or the UN the authority to militarily intervene in different parts of the world. These institutions – which have become Western diplomatic conveniences – can *de facto* abrogate conventional notions of national sovereignty. It is now routinely argued that issues like the environment, ethnic violence, female genital mutilation, or fundamentalist intolerance are too important to be hidden behind the principle of national sovereignty. The right of the West to intervene has become a moral imperative.

The consensus behind Western intrusion is underwritten by the acceptance of the moral differentiation of the world into two kinds of people. This differentiation has become intellectually acceptable at all levels of Western society. The uncritical acceptance of the term fundamentalism by conservative, liberal and radical commentators is symptomatic of the way in which a 'them' and 'us' outlook on the world has become intellectually plausible. At its most banal, this outlook proposes that they are irrational while we are rational or that they are intolerant while we are permissive. The fundamentalist label provides a moral and cultural condemnation of millions of people.

At its simplest, the fundamentalist label helps to recycle the old Orientalist stereotypes about fanatical, frustrated people. 'Muslims are frustrated and frustrated people snarl', concluded the editor of *The Economist* (August 1994). The *Guardian* opted for the more liberal version of the schema. It drew the line between those who are tolerant and those who are not. Taking sides against the fundamentalists in the civil war in Sudan, it observed that 'the tolerance exhibited in the Nuba mountains is the mirror image of Khartoum's intolerance' (22 July 1995). For the reporter of this story, the discovery of an example of tolerance in Africa was itself nothing short of 'remarkable'.

Serious liberal and leftist theoreticians and social scientists are no less prey to the attractions of the two-tier moral system that underpins the fundamentalist concept. The concept plays a central role in the recent writings of Anthony Giddens. According to Giddens, fundamentalism represents a refusal to dialogue. In some cases it 'demonizes the alien'. At times Giddens's diagnosis sounds suspiciously like the bearded irrational fanatic of the Western media. It does not occur to Giddens that fundamentalists may not have a monopoly over demonizing aliens (Giddens, 1994,

p. 190). The mechanistic counterposition of the fundamentalist to the non-fundamentalist continues to perpetuate the sociological legacy of the rational/irrational couplet in a new form.

Even Fred Halliday, usually a critical observer of international affairs, has come to accept the new moral consensus. Perturbed by the 'intolerance' and 'antidemocratic character' of fundamentalism, Halliday argues for taking sides against them. 'Politically, it is not possible to ignore the threat that these movements pose the citizens of the countries in which they live and, by extension, to the world', he concluded (Halliday, 1995, pp. 46, 55). This diagnosis of the fundamentalist threat to the world necessarily invites the response of some form of intervention. The absence of any clear intellectual differentiation among the Western intelligentsia on this elementary aspect of North–South relations is one of the most disturbing developments of our times.

Our aim is not to celebrate political movements characterized as fundamentalist or any particular cultural practices prevalent in the South. The argument of this contribution is that the discovery of certain objectionable practices in the South by people from the North cannot be explained as the outcome of humanitarian and altruistic motives. Regardless of the motives, the effect has been the manipulation of such practices to strengthen the moral authority of the West and to morally condemn societies of the South. The acceptance of this moral division of the world in the West has helped encourage a culture of international intrusion into the affairs of the South. *Such intrusion, of course, has a long history. What is new is the silence of critical voices in the North. In Europe and America the right of the West to intervene is simply not in question.*

NOTES

1. For illustrations of this trend see Furedi (1992), pp. 114–19, 141–50.
2. See, for example, the report of this event in the *Guardian*, 24 July 1995.
3. This point is discussed at length in Furedi (1994).

REFERENCES

Ayubi, N. N. (1995) 'Radical Islamism and Civil Society in the Middle East', *Contention*, 4, 3.

Bell, D. (1980) *Sociological Journeys: Essays 1960–1980* (London: Heinemann).

Bissell, R. E. (1990) 'Who Killed the Third World?', *The Washington Quarterly*, 13, 3.

Bongaarts, J. and Bruce, J. (1995) 'The Causes of Unmet Need for Contraception and the Social Content of Services', *Studies in Family Planning*, 26, 2.

Casey, J. (1991) 'All Quiet on the Liberal Front', *Evening Standard*, 20 August.

Elton, G. R. (1991) *Return to Essentials: Some Reflections on the Present State of Historical Study*, in J. Gardiner (1990) *The History Debate* (London: Collins & Brown).

Fromkin, D. (1975) 'The Strategy of Terrorism', *Foreign Affairs*, 53, 3.

Furedi, F. (1992) *Mythical Past, Elusive Future: History and Society in an Anxious Age* (London: Pluto).

Furedi, F. (1994) *The New Ideology of Imperialism* (London: Pluto).

Fukuyama, F. (1992) *The End of History and the Last Man* (New York: Free Press).

Giddens, A. (1994) 'Living in a Post-traditional Society', in U. Beck, A. Giddens and S. Lash (1994) *Reflexive Modernization: Politics, Tradition and Aesthetics in the Modern Social Order* (Cambridge: Polity).

Gough, B. M. (1990) 'Pax Britannica: Peace, Force and World Order', *The Round Table*, 314.

Halliday, F. (1995) 'Fundamentalism and the Contemporary World', *Contention*, 4, 2.

Kaplan, R. D. (1994) 'The Coming Anarchy', *Atlantic Monthly*, February.

Kennedy, P. (1993) *Preparing for the Twenty-First Century* (London: Harper Collins).

Lukács, J. (1993) 'The End of the Twentieth Century', *Harper's Magazine*, January.

Macrare, N. (1990) *Sunday Times*, 11 March.

Mearsheimer, J. (1990) 'Why We Will Soon Miss the Cold War', *The Atlantic Monthly*, August.

Pfaff, W. (1995) 'A New Colonialism?', *Foreign Affairs*, January/February.

Rotberg, R. I. (1993) 'The Clinton Administration and Africa', *Current History*, May.

UNFPA (1995) *The State of World Population 1995* (New York: UNFPA).

Wichterich, C. (1988) 'From the Struggle against "Overpopulation" to the Industrialization of Human Production', *Reproductive and Genetic Engineering*, 1, 1.

6 Universal Human Rights: Imposing Values
Tony Evans

INTRODUCTION

A central theme of this volume is that the capitalist world economy and a dominant liberal ideology provide the context for processes of globalization. While international relations scholars and political theorists have come to recognize these processes only in the last ten years, in retrospect they can be traced back considerably further. *One example of the early signs of globalization is the attempt to legitimate a set of internationally recognised human rights norms, begun at the end of the Second World War.*

Although the rhetoric of human rights is often couched in the language of idealism, an understanding of the politics of rights reveals that economic and ideological considerations condition the moral claims made. Furthermore, the existence of an extensive body of international law on human rights contrasts with the international community's inability to take any systematic action on continued reports of genocide, disappearances, social deprivation, malnutrition and starvation. While 'human rights talk' (Vincent, 1986) is commonly presented as a philosophical or legal discourse, this is often a cloak for political and economic interests (Watson, 1979). Less developed states of the South have sought consistently to resist the promotion of these interests from the beginning of the attempt to create a human rights regime, often with some success. However, under conditions of further globalization the distinction between the formal regime, as represented at the United Nations, and the practice of states, will continue to diverge (see Furedi, Chapter 5, this volume).

The most commonly offered explanation for the centrality of human rights to the post-war international political agenda is the moral shock of Nazism, including the Holocaust, the concentration camps and medical experimentation. While moral shock undoubtedly played a role, the promotion of the human rights discourse by the United States and its western allies was also motivated by less noble concerns. Important among these was the promotion of human rights as a moral foundation on which to support global economic expansion at the expense of people in the South. Throughout the Cold War, less developed states of the South sought to include rights that challenged liberal values concerned with economic and social interests. The socialist countries of Eastern Europe supported this challenge and the alternative view of rights proposed by the South. With the end of the East–West ideological struggle, alternatives to Western views of rights are less likely to be heard. The South's strategy of presenting economic claims in the language of rights is likely therefore to be less effective than in the past.

Following a brief examination of power and rights, this chapter will examine the post-war human rights discourse and hegemony. This is necessary to gain an insight into political and ideological aspects of human rights as a central feature of the post-war international political agenda. A further section will consider human rights under conditions of globalization in the post-Cold War world order. Finally, some conclusions will be drawn on the liberal world order and human rights.

IMPOSING VALUES

Universal human rights are imposing in two senses. Firstly, they are imposing in the sense that they offer a coherent claim to authority over the sovereign state. Western states promoted this understanding of universal human rights at the founding of the United Nations in 1945, when the prospects for protecting human rights were first considered. It is a meaning that offers individuals and human rights activists the authority to challenge those who violate rights anywhere in the world. The realization that the atrocities of the war were inflicted on people by the state caused a moral outcry and the demand for the protection of human rights, defined as the rights of people by virtue of being human. Therefore, in constructing a new, post-war international order, the reformation of old ideas of domestic jurisdiction became a central issue. Sovereignty was no longer absolute, at least in the sense a that state could not expect to treat its citizens as it will and remain free of condemnation. The emergence of universal human rights placed conditions of legitimacy upon all states in the form of universally recognized duties to guarantee the rights of their citizens.

In a second sense, human rights are imposing because they represent part of a further attempt to forge new structures of colonial dominance. For many people living in the South, international human rights are understood increasingly as a set of values that support the expansion of global capital, exploitation and control. When Western statespeople and academics speak of rights today, they usually make the unspoken assumption that legitimate rights are civil and political claims.[1] In formal terms, civil and political rights are recognized as having equal status to economic, social and cultural rights. In practice, however, the forces of globalization ensure that economic rights have received considerably less attention than civil and political rights. For example, the rights to self-determination and development are recognized under international law, but economic dependency denies the realization of these rights. The dominant liberal–capitalist world order relies upon a set of values that prioritize civil and political rights. Throughout the history of the human rights regime, less developed states have resisted this limited conception of rights and attempted to promote rights that supported their demand for economic security and development. With the 'triumph of capitalism', the future success of this challenge seems in doubt.

Thinking of rights claims as imposition and resistance – as part of the political discourse on rights rather than the philosophical – helps to clarify post-war interest in human rights. Historically, rights claims have always been concerned with power relationships. While the rationale for the Magna Carta or the American Declaration of rights is often wrapped up in the language of reason and philosophy, rights claims have always represented a political challenge to the existing economic, political and social order (Stammer, 1993). This has usually been a challenge to the dominant order defined by the state, which is an order that offers moral legitimacy for the actions of particular groups or classes.

The post–1945 relationship between power and rights claims is distinguished from previous periods in two important respects. First, claims for universal human rights are not claims made against the state but against all people and societies. In future, the state could not invoke sovereignty and domestic jurisdiction as a defence against violation of rights. Second, while in the past rights claims were used to challenge the status quo, in the aftermath of the Second World War no such order existed. The United States sought to assume the role of architect of the new post-war order, including a liberal view of rights that placed the freedom of the individual at the centre of international politics. Against this, and within the context of growing anti-colonial fervour, the South sought to prioritize the rights of peoples, including a right to self-determination, the right to development and the right to control natural resources. Asserting these rights placed a duty on the wealthy to help the poor, and potentially challenged liberal values of enterprise, endeavour and the free market. The post-war human rights discourse was not therefore a challenge to an existing status quo, but a challenge to the potential emergence of that order. Recognizing the political, ideological and economic challenge this represented to its power, the United States sought to degrade the importance of the formal human rights discourse conducted within the United Nations and, instead, assert a view that supported its own interests and those of global capital. For universal human rights, the struggle over determining the legitimate limits of rights led the post-war hegemon to attempt a strategy of disabling the creation of a human rights regime (Evans, 1995a).

HEGEMONY AND HUMAN RIGHTS IN THE POST-WAR ORDER

Writers in international relations often fail to distinguish hegemony from empire. Empires are maintained with military force, which denies sovereignty to colonial peoples, imposes political leaders and sustains order by linking the interests of local élites to those of the imperial power. Hegemony, on the other hand, is characterized by legitimating political, economic and social institutions that gain the consent of the governed, who accept their weaker, subservient role as natural. *For the hegemon consensus is as important as coercion in maintaining order.* This requires that the hegemon exercise 'intellectual and moral' leadership (Gramsci, 1971, pp. 57–8). While analysis of economic and military capabilities remains a necessary task in understanding hegemony, reducing hegemony to economic and military power alone misses important insights concerned with moral, social and ideological control (Cox, 1983).

The hegemon must therefore ensure that secondary actors undergo some form of 'socialization' that promotes the 'common acceptance of a consensual order that binds the ruler and the ruled and legitimizes power' (Ikenberry and Kupchan, 1990, p. 287). In short, the actions taken by the hegemon in pursuit of its interest are understood as 'common sense' (Augelli and Murphy, 1988).

Those rights promoted by the United States and its allies from the end of the Second World War reflect a liberal ideology, including freedom of the individual, non-interference by the state in economic and social matters and the principle of *laissez-faire* (Addo, 1987). Transposing this into a list of internationally accepted human rights norms meant that human rights became defined as those rights that required government abstention from acts that impaired the freedom of the individual (Tetreault, 1988). As far as possible within the confines of maintaining a minimum order, liberal ideology offers the individual the widest possible freedom to innovate and to invest time, capital and resources in the processes of economic production and exchange. Applying liberal principles to human rights points to acts of omission rather than those of commission. Therefore, liberal–capitalist hegemony attempts to deny acts of commission by defining human rights as civil and political rights, which liberals claim require little or no government resources.[2]

Furthermore, 'hegemonic logic' (Falk, 1980) determines that human rights are utilized in the drive to further the interests of the hegemon, just like any other tool of foreign policy. Therefore, applying the principle of *laissez-faire* to human rights can be understood as part of a post-war programme to promote the interests of the hegemon. These interests were served by acknowledging civil and political rights and rejecting all claims that threatened to undermine the liberal ideology on which those interests were based. Furthermore, the rights proposed by the West can also be understood as reparations to be pressed upon the defeated by the victors, rather than as a display of global moral concern (Henkin, 1965). For example, many rights promoted by the victors during and immediately following the war were never intended as universally applicable principles, particularly where universal application challenged hegemonic superstructures. As Churchill made clear, the right to racial equality was a necessary feature for drawing all racial groups into the fight against fascism.

In addition the right to self-determination would not be extended to all peoples of the British Empire (Laurens, 1988). *The inclusion of universal human rights as a central feature of the new post-war order must therefore be seen against the background of hegemony.* Universal human rights were placed on the international political agenda during the Second World War by wartime leaders who were anxious to provide some idealistic purpose in their foreign policies. This was particularly necessary for the government of the USA for several reasons. First among these was a concern for the future economic prosperity of the US once victory had been won. The manufacturing output of the US nearly doubled during the war, while that of the UK, for example, marginally declined.[3] Aware that the US would emerge from the war as the dominant military and economic power, Roosevelt was anxious to ensure that the opportunities offered by this position were fully exploited. Unless new markets were secured, continued growth would mean post-war overproduction, high levels of unemployment and the potential for social unrest. These fears were heightened by continued calls from isolationists to bring troops home immediately victory was assured, potentially adding further millions of demobilized men and women to the ranks of the unemployed.

Appeal to human rights was therefore an appeal to promote liberal values and a counter to isolationist tendencies that threatened the US's chances of pursuing new, global markets (Loth, 1988, especially ch. 1). To achieve this policy, the Roosevelt Administration sought to link Americans' traditional love of freedom with global economic engagement: as a way of getting the US out of the 'vicious circle of isolation, depression, and war'.[4] To be an American was to assert a set of universal values associated with the liberal tradition, particularly individual freedom, liberty and self-determination. These were the values that inspired the early settlers to emigrate to America, which they later defended in their struggle for independence (Augelli and Murphy, 1988). Importantly, Americans claimed that these freedoms were achieved not by eliciting the intervention of the state, but by exercising the initiative and imagination of individuals free of government interference. This assertion was seen as the right of all people everywhere. Therefore, Americans could not ignore the appeals of others when their rights were threatened, because the defence of human rights was the rationale for America itself. As

Stanley Hoffmann has argued, '[i]f one believes in the values of liberalism, it is not enough merely to try to practice them at home' (Hoffmann, 1977, p. 5). Making a similar point, Tracy Strong has observed that 'being an American means that anyone has a potentially legitimate claim on you' (Strong, 1980, p. 51).

To reject appeals for assistance in securing rights would therefore deny the legitimacy of such universal claims and threaten the identity of all Americans. The US therefore took upon itself the role of architect of the post-war human rights regime, built upon American values expressed in quasi-constitutional terms. The Universal Declaration, it has been said, represents an attempt to secure 'American constitutional rights projected around the world' (Henkin, 1970, p. 115). However, the policy of using human rights as a symbol that justified America's expanding global influence did not remain uncontested for long. In the age of anti-colonialism, the South soon came to realize that the West's concern for human rights had more to do with finding outlets for surplus production and exploitation, rather than a genuine concern for human dignity (Lummis, 1991). For many in the South, the development of the human rights regime symbolized a 'manifestation of capitalist, individualist, liberal ideology, involving a capitalist view of the individual', which did not include a concern for human welfare, human dignity or economic security (Tamilmoran, 1992, p. 74).

The West soon discovered that the post-war human rights discourse promised to expose its preferred definition of rights as a façade for Western interests. Consequently, the West faced a threat to its moral status and authority. As discussion turned from establishing a set of generally accepted human rights norms without legal obligations (the Universal Declaration) to formulating legally binding international law, the South's resistance hardened. Amid growing US fear of 'socialism by treaty' (Eisenhower, 1963, p. 675), and suspicions of a communist plot to affect a 'withering away of our principles of human freedom [and] the decay of the free institutions we have established to secure them',[5] the West sought to withdraw from having to accept the full extent of rights proposed by the South, and thus avoid the correlative duties they would impose. In particular, the West made several proposals designed to limit their obligations on economic and social rights. Important among these were proposals to allow the constituent parts of federal states the option of not undertaking obligations in human rights treaties; a proposal that excluded colonial territories from human rights treaties; and objections to self-determination, particularly if the term included a right to 'sovereignty over natural wealth and resources'.[6] However, in every case the West saw its proposals overturned.

The US's intention of using human rights based on liberal principles as a means of legitimating global interests was therefore undermined. Increasingly, this aroused domestic interests which opposed any involvement that might impair the US's freedom to act either domestically or internationally. Isolationist and conservative groups began to question the necessity for any global role for the US, particularly if that role meant compromising cherished liberal values and restricting the activities of Americans. These same groups also began to realize that the racist, segregationist and property laws of many southern states would be rendered unconstitutional by the proposed human rights covenants.

The US responded to this by formally announcing that it had no intention of ever ratifying any international treaty on human rights.[7] Rather than suffer further defeats that promised to damage further the US claim to global moral leadership, withdrawal from the formal discourse on rights seemed preferable. The protection of rights in the US, it was argued, was already at a higher standard than that proposed by the United Nations (Evans, 1995b). This left the post-war project to protect universal human rights without hegemonic leadership, which according to many is a necessary if not sufficient requirement for moving any issue beyond rhetoric and towards decisive action to establish international institutions (Keohane, 1977, 1984). While the rhetoric of rights achieved a central place in international politics, mechanisms for the protection of rights have remained weak.

Between 1953 and the end of the Cold War human rights became a central focus for Cold War rhetoric. While the US sought to promote its superior record of civil and political rights, and to castigate the USSR and its allies for their poor records, the socialist and less developed countries pressed ahead with a programme of international law and General Assembly declarations on almost every aspect of rights. This included a covenant of economic, social and cultural rights, a declaration on the right to development and other commitments on the right to the use of natural resources. Although the amount of international law generated during the period suggests wide agreement on rights, the *West still maintained its emphasis on civil and political rights while the South*

continued to pursue economic claims. The expansion of global capital and
a liberal ideology had, however, favoured a view of rights supported
by the West. At a formal level economic rights are given parity with
political rights. However, the rhetoric and actions of Western states
and international organizations suggest that the West's view
predominates. *With the end of the Cold War, the barrier to prosecuting a
liberal view of rights has been lifted.*

GLOBALIZATION AND HUMAN RIGHTS

The rationale offered by Western states for dealing with regimes
known for persistent violations of human rights was usually that
they were avowedly anti-communist. This rationale has been
removed with the collapse of the Soviet Union and many other
communist states, suggesting that the West is now free to denounce
authoritarian states and take decisive action for the protection of
rights. However, the much vaunted 'New World Order' may not
prove as favourable to human rights conditions as leaders like
George Bush suggested.[8] Unless political and economic interests
are threatened, the economic imperative of globalization suggests
that victims of rights abuses will still be ignored. While profitable
and stable relations exist between states human rights do not
become an issue.

This has left those who deal with repressive regimes the problem
of finding a new rationale that justifies continuing economic
relations. The distinction between authoritarian and totalitarian
regimes, which assumes that the former are moving towards
democratization and the latter are not, offers a well-known
foundation for developing a new rationale. The success of this
move can be judged in the way the human rights discourse is
increasingly displaced by the democracy discourse (Carothers,
1994). Support for those governments who introduce the
institutions of democracy legitimates the continuation of economic
relationships, strengthens calls to extend aid programmes and opens
up the possibility of developing new trade and business relationships
unhindered by moral concerns.

While establishing the formal institutions of democracy may be a
necessary condition for claiming human rights, it is not a substitute
for them. Many states continue to be democratic in formal–
institutional terms only. These states do not provide for the

reform of social and legal systems that are essential for r
the conditions for protecting human rights, including a ɪ
inequality, a free press and access to public office.
relations with powerful economic interests, many newly
democratic states attempt to create favourable conditions for
foreign investment (Gills *et al.*, 1993). The recent emphasis on
democracy may therefore have more to do with pre-empting
social unrest, as previously authoritarian states prepare to
embrace an economic system that supports the interests of capital.
Introducing democratic institutions justifies the suppression of
opposition even if democratic processes are absent. Such 'low
intensity democracies' are indifferent to rights claims and may
actually encourage violations. For example, trade unions are
weakened, wages are depressed below the level possible to sustain
a dignified life, legislation on environmental, health and safety
questions never reaches the statute books and all movements
aimed at social reforms are quashed (Burbach, 1993). The claim
to be a democratic state often legitimates a particular order that
favours investment and supports the rationale for continuing
economic relationships (see Wilkin, Chapter 2, this volume).

For many people in the South the change of emphasis to the
institutions of national democracy, without regard for the
institutions of globalization, is of little significance when the
activities of transnational corporation, multinational banks and
global and regional trading organizations play a greater part in
shaping their future. These institutions are beyond the control of
national democratic institutions, although their activities are often
incompatible with the struggle for greater equality, justice and rights
(Donnelly, 1994). Indeed, sometimes these actors appear to
legitimate undemocratic practices that lead to further violations of
human rights (Kothari, 1994).

The World Bank offers the most obvious example of the potential
for international institutions to create the conditions for violating
human rights. The Bank has always viewed human rights issues as
political and therefore beyond its terms of reference. However, the
political neutrality defence of its operations cannot be sustained.
The Bank accepts a definition of the state that derives from liberal
ideas. These ideas concern the free individual acting in a civil
society under rules implemented by state institutions that regulate
the competition over differing concepts of the good. This challenges
the Bank's claim that it confines itself to economic calculations

when assessing requests for funding. The imposition of structural adjustment programmes as a condition of funding also belies the Bank's neutrality claim and is a fundamental challenge to national democracy (Kothari, 1994).

A further concern is that although human rights are presented as a claim by all on all other human beings, the human rights regime remains a state-centric mechanism. International law is concerned with relations between states, not individuals and peoples. Furthermore, international law relies upon reciprocity as its main tool of implementation. This contrasts with the coercive nature of domestic law with its legislature, judiciary, courts, police forces and prisons. Sanctions for non-compliance with international law on human rights are not administered by some disinterested third party with a capability of enforcing compliance, as is assumed in domestic law, but by those with political, economic or social interests in curbing further violations. Action against those who violate rights is therefore selective. In the case of human rights, the need for reciprocity is more difficult to establish than in any other area of law since, in most cases, how a state treats its citizens is of little interest to others. Perhaps this explains why states are more willing to tackle humanitarian issues concerning transnational refugee movements than those confined within the state (Watson, 1979).

The inconsistency that characterizes much human rights activity has given Southern leaders the opportunity to plead for special tolerance of their human rights records. Many Southern leaders argue that their attitude to human rights is conditioned by two important factors that do not pertain in developed countries. The first is the need to build a nation on the remains of colonial institutions. These leaders argue that governments must therefore apply a 'stability' test when thinking about human rights: does the application of the right help or hinder the process of nation-building and the move from a post-colonial to a mature state? Second, the South acknowledges that economic development is of paramount importance to the long-term stability and security of the nation. Governments must not allow traditional values and conservative thinking to deflect the nation from achieving the goal of development. Suppression and coercion of those who attempt to stand in the way of necessary social, cultural and political change is therefore legitimate in the interests of future generations (Tamilmoran, 1992).

This raises important questions to do with the purposes and subjects of development. Development can be understood in two ways; as the economic growth of the state or as fulfilling the aspiration of the people living in the state. Development as economic growth is the definition generally accepted by most countries. Following this definition, development becomes an end in itself, rather than a means to an end, which should include human rights, democracy and social justice. Since 'liberty and justice do not exist as technical terms in economic science' (Lummis, 1991, p. 52), development often means a negative outcome for the very people it should serve.

Attitudes to aid demonstrate this point clearly. Development aid is given for development defined narrowly as economic growth measured in terms of gross domestic product. The effectiveness of aid is usually measured in terms of output–input calculation; for example, increased energy supply or grain yield against capital and human resources. Missing from this type of calculation are people, including those who are advantaged by the economic growth and those whose rights are violated in the name of growth (Tomasevski, 1989). Governments remain the main recipients of aid. Donor states are content to assume a secure link between aid and the people whenever the institutions of democracy are evident. These assumptions fail to recognize that the democratic institutions of many countries fail to produce democratic outcomes, including economic justice, so that the interests of the people remain overlooked. Thus, if human rights, sustainability, equitability and environmentally sound development are considered at all they are confined for the most part to the level of rhetoric.

CONCLUSION: THE LIBERAL WORLD ORDER AND HUMAN RIGHTS

With the emergence of a dominant global liberal–capitalist order based on market principles, the future of economic claims is once again brought into doubt. The old distinction between political and economic rights is less likely to provide a focus for international human rights as the claim that 'the best hope for political freedom in some countries lies in opening them up through trade' gains even wider acceptance (*The Economist*, 1993). This approach to rights already has the status of 'common sense' in the West to the extent that many are incredulous that others do not share their definition of freedom in a free-market society (Augelli and Murphy, 1988). Therefore, the South will find it more difficult than ever to sustain claims for economic rights. Now that it is widely believed that the ideological battles of the Cold War are no longer relevant, many people in the South will encounter greater difficulty in asserting their rights to both political and economic security. Importantly, as the concern for democracy replaces a concern for rights in the day-to-day language of international relations, the human dignity of people will be increasingly overlooked.

After decades of procrastination, the US has ratified several human rights treaties.[9] This may suggest that the US has now lifted its long-held objections to the human rights regime and is at last prepared to support some rights claims. However, a close examination of the various reservations, declarations and understandings registered by the US when ratifying these treaties suggests that this is not the case. Instead, the US seems to have taken the opportunity to bolster its economic and political superiority by associating itself with human rights in a way that reflects its earlier, post-war ambitions.

This is clearly the concern of the UN Human Rights Committee. At its 1994 meeting, and without expressly naming the US, the Committee expressed concern for reservations that 'essentially render ineffective all Covenant rights which would require any changes in national law to ensure compliance' so that 'no real international rights or obligations have been accepted'.[10] The influential Lawyers Committee on Human Rights has also argued that ratifying the Covenant subject to important reservations suggests that 'one set of rules applies to the United States and another set to the rest of the world' and goes on to accuse the Administration of hypocrisy.[11] Similarly, Louis Henkin has accused the US of seeking the benefits of participation by pretending to assume international obligations while in reality doing no such thing. Furthermore, Henkin argues that such an attitude signals to many that 'the Conventions are for other states, not for the United States' (Henkin, 1995, p. 344).

Even during the Cold War years the prospects for securing the rights of people in the South were bleak. However, a view of rights that supported the aspirations of the South was kept alive as part of the ideological conflict. Now that the US 'seems content to gloat over 'winning the cold war', bombing Iraq into temporary submission, and praising the virtues of elections and markets' (Donnelly, 1994, p. 163), the prospects for even keeping the South's claims on the international political agenda seem poor.

NOTES

1. This was seen in the recent Ford Foundation-funded seminars on Humanitarian Intervention held at the London School of Economics during 1994–95.
2. For a well-known version of this argument see Cranston (1983).

| | *Manufacturing output* | |
	USA	*UK*
1938	79	94
1946	150	90

Index 100–1937, *Statistical Yearbook for 1948* (New York: United Nations, 1949).
4. Statement by Secretary of State Stettinius in *Department of State Bulletin*, 12, 301 (1945), pp. 1007–13.
5. George Finch (American Bar Association) testifying before the Senate Committee on human rights aspects of the Bricker Amendment (see Kaufman and Whiteman, 1988).
6. Proposal by Chile, revised later to become Article 1(2) of both the Covenant on Civil and Political Rights and the Covenant on Economic, Social and Cultural Rights. UN Doc.E/CN.4/L.24.
7. See speech by Mrs M. Lord (USA), the Commission on Human Rights, 9th Session, Geneva, 8 April 1953.
8. Speech by George Bush at Maxwell Air Force Base, 15 May 1991, *Vital Speeches of the Day*, 57:15 (1991), pp. 450–2.
9. These include the Convention Against Torture (1994), the International Convention on the Elimination of All Forms of Racial Discrimination (1994), the Genocide Convention (1989) and the International Covenant on Civil and Political Rights (1992).
10. Human Rights Committee, 52nd Session, November 1994, Doc.CCPR/C/ 21/Rev.1/Add.6.
11. Letter from the Lawyers Committee for Human Rights to Senator Claiborne Pell, 2 March 1992, published in *Human Rights Law Journal*, 14, 3–4 (1992), p. 129.

REFERENCES

Addo, M. K. (1987), 'The Implications for Some Aspects of Contemporary International Economic Law on International Human Rights Law' (University of Exeter: Ph.D. thesis).

Augelli, E. and Murphy C. (1988) *America's Quest and the Third World* (London: Pinter).

Burbach, R. (1993) 'The Tragedy of American Democracy', in B. Gills, J. Rocamora and R. Wilson (eds) *Low Intensity Democracy: Political Power in the New World Order* (London, Pluto), pp. 100–23.

Carothers, T. (1994) 'Democracy and Human Rights: Policy Allies or Rivals?', *Washington Quarterly*, 17, 3, pp. 109–21.

Cox, R. (1983) 'Gramsci, Hegemony and International Relations: An Essay in Method', *Millennium*, 12, 2, pp. 162–75.

Cranston, M. (1983) 'Are There Human Rights?', *Daedalus*, 112, 4, pp. 1–118.

Donnelly, J. (1994) 'Human Rights and the New World Order', *World Policy Review*, 9, 2, pp. 249–77.

The Economist (1993) 'The Red and the Blue', 8 May, p. 22.

Eisenhower, D. D. (1963) *The White House Years: Mandate for Change – 1953–56* (London: Heinemann).

Evans, T. (1995a) *UN Hegemony and the Project of Universal Human Rights* (New York: St. Martin's).

Evans, T. (1995b) 'US Hegemony, Domestic Politics and the Project of Universal Human Rights', *Statecraft and Diplomacy*, 6, 3, pp. 314–41.

Falk, R. (1980) 'Theoretical Foundations of Human Rights', in R. P. Newbury (ed.) (1980) *The Politics of Human Rights* (New York: New York University Press), pp. 65–109.

Gills, B., Rocamora, J. and Wilson, R. (eds) (1993) *Low Intensity Democracy: Political Power in the New World Order* (London: Pluto).

Gramsci, A. (1971) *Selections from the Prison Notebooks*, Q. Hoare and G. Howell (eds and trans.) (London: Lawrence & Wishart).

Henkin, L. (1965) 'The United Nations and Human Rights', *International Organization*, 19, 3, pp. 504–17.

Henkin, L. (1970) 'Rights: American and Human', *American Journal of International Law*, 64.

Henkin, L. (1995) 'U.S. Ratification of Human Rights Conventions: the Ghost of Senator Bricker', *American Journal of International Law*, 89, 2.

Hoffmann, S. (1977) 'The Hell of Good Intentions', *Foreign Policy*, 29, Winter, p. 5.

Ikenberry, G. J. and Kupchan, C. A. (1990) 'Socialisation and Hegemonic Power', *International Organization*, 44, 3.

Kaufman, N. H. and Whiteman, D. (1988) 'Opposition to Human Rights Treaties in the United States: The Legacy of the Bricker Amendment', *Human Rights Quarterly*, 10, 3, pp. 309–37.

Keohane, R. O. (1977) 'The Theory of Hegemonic Stability and Changes in International Economic Regimes', in Ole Holsti *et al.* (eds) (1977) *Change in the International System* (Boston, MA: Little, Brown).

Keohane, R. O. (1984) *After Hegemony: Cooperation and Discord in the World of Political Economy* (Princeton, NJ: Princeton University Press).

Kirkpatrick, J. 'Dictatorship and Double Standards', *Commentary*, 68.

Kothari, S. (1994) 'Global Economic Institutions and Democracy: A View From India', in J. Cavanagh, D. Wysham and M. Arrunda (eds) (1994) *Beyond Bretton Woods* (London: Pluto), pp. 39–54.

Laurens, P. G. (1988) *Power and Prejudice: The Politics and Diplomacy of Racial Discrimination* (Boulder, CO: Westview).

Loth, W. (1988) *The Division of the World – 1941–45* (London: Routledge).

Lummis, C. D. (1991) 'Development Against Democracy', *Alternatives*, 16, pp. 31–66.

Stammer, N. (1993) 'Human Rights and Power', *Political Studies*, XLI, pp. 70–82.

Strong, T. B. (1980) 'Taking the Rank with What is Ours: American Political Thought, Foreign Policy, and the Question of Rights', in P. R. Newberg (ed.) (1980) *The Politics of Human Rights* (New York: New York University Press).

Tamilmoran, V. T. (1992) *Human Rights in Third World Perspective* (New Delhi, Har-Anand Publications).

Tetreault, M. A. (1988) 'Regimes and the Liberal World Order', *Alternatives*, 13, pp. 5–26.

Tomasevski, K. (1989) *Development Aid and Human Rights* (London: Pinter).

Vincent, J. (1986) *Human Rights and International Relations* (Cambridge: Cambridge University Press).

Watson, J. S. (1979) 'Legal Theory, Efficacy and Validity in the Development of Human Rights Norms in International Law', *University of Illinois Law Forum*, 3, pp. 609–41.

7 Organizing Hunger: the Global Organization of Famines and Feasts
Julian Saurin

INTRODUCTION

There appears to be a perplexing paradox when *global food production reaches record levels and yet tens of millions of people either starve or suffer from chronic malnutrition or malnourishment.*[1] Numerous commentators, and certainly popular understandings, hold that the paradox obtains either because population growth in fact outstrips food production; or, that hunger – a catch-all term encompassing acute starvation to malnourishment – is the consequence of so- called natural disasters, or at least extraordinary and exceptional happenings.[2] In both cases, there is a barely-spoken *assumption that pre-social or 'inescapably natural' forces continue to retain a hold over the ordering of human society.*

Such accounts sit permanently, if uncomfortably, alongside the promises of modernity: *a modernity which asserted the ultimately triumphant ability of human society to subject nature to human will and design.* Hitherto the principal instrument of such design has been the modern state, operating through public policy, regulating the accumulative processes of capitalism. Thus, at the same time as famines appeared to increase in frequency and as malnutrition increased in absolute terms, one of the central claims and indeed promises of the modern state was to protect its population from the ravages of starvation and, albeit to a lesser extent, to insure against the persistence of malnutrition. Curiously, the perennial assurance that the state indeed had the capacity to avoid the shadow of hunger seems to have reinforced the plausibility of the 'act of nature' explanations when 'disasters' continued to strike.

Now – at the 'end of history' – as if embarrassed by the apparent inability of the state and public policy to safeguard us from hunger, the revelations of postmodernism demand apostasy to the rationality of the 'market' with its assurances of 'optimal' production and

price responsiveness to 'effective demand'. Whilst *state-led public
action has been unable to insure against hunger* – though not as unsuccessfully as most critics allege – simultaneously, *the 'free' operation
of markets has organised hunger across the world* to still greater effect. The
real pain of the famines that kill – usually silently and usually
orderly – has begun to melt into air. The self-evident claim on
nutrition and demand for equity has, it would appear, been
displaced and forgotten for the sterile demand for 'efficiency' and
'competitiveness'. Yet as Dreze and Sen insist,

> *The enormous expansion of productive power that has taken place over the
> last few centuries has made it, perhaps for the first time, possible to
> guarantee adequate food for all, and it is in this context that the persistence
> of chronic hunger and the recurrence of virulent famines must be seen as
> being morally outrageous and politically unacceptable'* (Dreze and Sen,
> 1989, p. 3).

To the extent that the contradictions between hunger and plenty
can be explained, then the paradox disappears. The argument
developed here is one in which *provision and access to food along with
its correlate – hunger – is understood to be organized globally.* The use of the
term 'organize' is deliberate, and is intended to convey the notion
that order is not accidental, haphazard nor unforeseeable (though
not necessarily intentional) and nor, therefore, beyond our
explanatory powers.

After identifying the broad dynamics of globalization, attention is
turned to the standard explanations of hunger and famines as
developed in a nationally – or, more accurately, a state-constituted
world. Noting the limitations of such explanations, *the significance of
the social relations developed through agribusiness, including new insecurities, is
highlighted.* Some final remarks identifying resistance to globalization
point to the actuality and possibilities of alternative forms of social
organization.

GLOBALIZATION AS CAPITALIST RENEWAL

*The current global organization of hunger is to a large extent simply an
expression of a broader reorganization of capitalist accumulation.*
Globalization is first and foremost a term which describes the
latest accumulation strategy of capitalism, in which globally rooted
accumulation has come to displace national, i.e state-based,

accumulation.[3] In so far as the global has displaced the national–territorial as the primary (dynamic) site of accumulation, so the regulatory capacity of the state has become increasingly subverted. As such, both the responsibility of the state and the capacity of public policy to address questions of hunger has been brought into question.

Globalization should be understood as something more than neo-liberalism. Whilst it is true that the collapse of the Eastern Bloc and the fragmentation of the Soviet Empire presaged the apparent triumph of liberalism,[4] the neo- liberal turn is just one – albeit an extremely important one – amongst several dynamics responsible for the reorganization of world order. *Globalization refers, more generally, to the global organization of social order* just as internationalization referred to the previously predominant national organization of social order.

Whereas the territorially-constituted state (national or otherwise) provided the structure and host to capitalist accumulation and from which key regulative functions of the state were located, globalization entails the subversion of the territorial regulation of social and economic structures of accumulation. The crucial distinctiveness of the global organization of social order is to be found in (1) the use and disposal of material and ideational resources and authority which are not territorially delimited or restricted; and (2), following Giddens, there is a pronounced organization of distanciated locales through the sophisticated global co-ordination of time and space (see Giddens, 1992). Those that can co-ordinate globally have a tendency to prosper: those that cannot have a tendency to redundancy and marginalization.

'Globalization' clearly refers, then, not to a static condition nor a completed project, but to a process which is characterized by relatively novel articulations of social power (which, crucially, were not available during earlier historical periods). In this sense, 'globalization' has been contingent and immanent in capital- ist modernity, only now emerging and becoming realised: globalization as an unfolding social process could have been forestalled, and it continues to remain subject to resistance and alternatives. Neo-liberalism, the most evident manifestation of globalization, can be seen not as the resolution of capitalist crisis but as 'the politics of the unresolved crisis' (Peck and Tickell, 1994, p. 318). Centrally, then, globalization does not constitute a historical rupture but rather a modernization of capitalism and imperialism.

Lest one becomes enthralled by the term 'globalization' there is a permanent caution: reference to 'globalization' does not tell us what specific form of social order actually obtains: Rather, it tells how, in what context and upon what social and technical resources, a given social order derives strength. Thus, the contemporary revival of fundamentalism – whether Christian, Hindu, Muslim, or neo-liberal – is an attempt to organize social order in a particular fashion, but which arises from the globalization of power, i.e. that power is rooted and expressed through global social formations and articulated through global networks or communities, and not primarily through national-territorial entities. Equally, to invoke 'globalization' in an explanation does not mean that the particular events or changes are happening all over the world, still less in the same way. It does mean, however, that these events, changes or social organizing are only made possible as consequences of globalized power relations. Thus, to follow in the footsteps of critical realism, the globalized relations and the particular social formations in question are dialectically dependent on each other, whether this be in the realization of particular social formations, their collapse, or indeed their non-appearance.

In this respect, it is important to revitalize the concept of combined and uneven development; that is to say, global social organization is characterized by intrinsically related, contingent, but unequal transformation. Of immediate concern in this chapter is the uneven and differentiated manner in which agribusiness develops and organizes to both act upon and structure the local and global organization of hunger. There is, for example, stronger and stronger linkage between different locales as a consequence of downward levelling, in which the global economic integration arising from concentrated competition for global markets ensures that the success of one economy is contingent on the losses of another. George Monbiot writes, in an article entitled 'True Costs of Aubergines All Year Round', that

> As one of our best apple harvests ever known rots on the ground, the autumn air shudders with lorries delivering out-of-season Granny Smiths from South Africa and lifeless Coxes from New Zealand. Potatoes are being flown in from Australia just as ours are being lifted from the ground; Kenyan beans are filling the shelves while British farmers are ploughing theirs back in. Heathrow airport was built on the market gardens that

once fed London; now its traffic renders British horticulture void (Monbiot, 1995, p. 15).

Downward levelling, which is a consequence of desperately competing locales, constitutes one type of 'localization' response. But as Peck and Tickell argue, 'local strategies – aimed particularly at securing mobile (public and private) investment – have become more prominent and more pervasive not because they provide the "answer", but because they represent a common tactical response to globalization' (Peck and Tickell, 1994, p. 318). This said, localization should not be seen as inconsistent with globalization. Instead it is one of the consequences of globalization: an attempted organization of social activity which seeks to resist the alienation and abstraction of power from the local to the global. Thus, ethnic particularism or the promotion of local economies are two examples of attempted self-determination in the face of apparently anonymous and abstract forces: in the first case coalescing around some essentialized and mythical chauvinism, and in the second case focused on the practice of a self-sustaining economy.

Accepting the argument that social order is increasingly organized globally, and not nationally, it follows that inequality – the permanent consequence of capitalist social relations – is similarly organized globally. As such, globalization represents the further modernization of inequality or the promotion of new and innovative organizations of poverty and wealth.

As hinted at earlier, *globalization refers to a renewed and reorganized phase of capitalism and indicates the trajectory or tendency of capitalist modernization. It is within this context that agri-industrial development and the organization of hunger needs to be understood.*

However, before analysing this reorganization, the history of organized hunger hitherto needs to be reviewed.

UNDERSTANDING HUNGER

The path-breaking work of Friedmann and McMichael argues that two basic processes have developed over the twentieth century: first, the *development of a state system within which specific agricultures were increasingly protected*; and second, the *continuous industrialization of agriculture and food*. Central to this analysis is the contention that each was the condition for the other in the period 1870 to 1914, but that accumulation by agri-food capitals has in the late twentieth century so subdivided and restructured agriculture everywhere...that the capacities of states and the state system for further regulation are in question (Friedmann and McMichael, 1989, p. 94).

How did the development of agri-industry, accelerated and accentuated through globalization, subvert the national organization of agriculture and food provision? And what relationship do these changes have to the organization of hunger?

Whilst we may recognize the tremendous growth in productivity over the century, in large part attributable to these very agri-industrial innovations, how is it that 'in the majority of countries [there has been] a widespread *deterioration* in the human condition [with p]overty and malnutrition worsening, not merely persisting as for so long before'? (Jolly, 1986, p. 81).

The central shibboleth to be overturned is that contained in the dominant assumption that adequate food production is equivalent to adequate nutrition for all. Such assumptions in turn rest upon simplistic national–territorially-based speculation about 'carrying capacity'.[5] That the central challenge is still set by a 'productivist' logic whereby more food production is taken to mean better nutrition is an indictment of populist understandings of poverty.[6] Criticism of 'productivist' or 'food availability decline' arguments seem to be plainly counter-intuitive: how couldn't producing more food lead to better and more nutrition? A brief specific answer would be because 'What we eat depends on what food we are able to acquire. The mere presence of food in the economy, or in the market, does not entitle a person to consume it' (Dreze and Sen, 1989, p. 9). More generally, 'food availability decline' theories simply ignore every relevant social distributional question.

Fifteen years after the publication of Amartya Sen's seminal work, *Poverty and Famines* (1982), the orthodox discourse of international relations remains attached to an anti-social, abstract 'paradox' which licenses a set of crude, ill-reasoned and simply wrong accounts of hunger. Possibly the most significant contribution of Sen's work was to have dealt a fatal blow to those 'explanations' , labelled as 'food availability decline' (FAD) theories by Devereux (1993, pp. 23–8); i.e. those Malthusian-inspired claims which assert that famine and malnutrition occur because of a relative lack of food, that is to say there are more mouths to feed than there is food available.

Explaining how it has come to pass that productivism appears to be popularly intuitive is an important part of the enquiry. For example, the apparent simplicity and hence attractiveness of the Malthusian argument reflects the abiding appeal of 'act of nature' explanations, that is to say it deflects accountability for mass human deprivation from existing social structures or named social agents to a supernatural explanation: there are just too many of us. Or, the 'invisible hand' of the economy – upon whom no blame can be attached – contrived a disequilibrium between supply and demand resulting in hunger.

So effective are Sen's criticisms of FAD claims that they are worth rehearsing briefly. In what must be one of the clearest statements of a thesis ever published, Sen begins his book with the lines: '*Starvation is the characteristic of some people not having enough food to eat. It is not the characteristic of there not being enough food to eat.* While the latter can be the cause of the former, it is but one of many possible causes' (emphasis added). Later he identifies the heart of his analysis as follows:

> *A person's ability to command food . . . depends on the entitlement relations that govern possession and use in that society.* It depends on what he owns, what exchange possibilities are offered to him, what is given free, and what is taken away from him (pp. 54–5: emphasis added).

Whilst Sen's analysis has been rightly characterized as arising out of individualist claims, it nevertheless seems readily applicable to collectivities which share broadly similar entitlement profiles. Notwithstanding some limitations (see Devereux, 1993 and de Waal, 1989) in Sen's thesis on entitlements – particularly with regard to entitlement breakdown in war; the alleged excessive legalism of the notion of entitlements; and the individualistic account of deprivation – the essential argument is worth developing in order to deal with larger collectivities.

Two matters for reminder are required here. First, specifying the conditions of hunger will serve to reinforce why it has been at the forefront of public concern. Second, and allied to this, Sen's account of entitlements and hunger provides a ready framework from which public action to limit hunger has been undertaken, and how food security has so readily been conceived as a national public problem.

When speaking of hunger a quite extensive and complex set of concerns are invoked. These concerns coalesce primarily around three social questions. First,

> the subject of nutrition is concerned with how people stay alive and well by means of food. This includes how people obtain their food and everything that influences this, and how this is used by the body and contributes to health (Young, 1992, p. 4).

Second,

> In relation to food scarcity and famine, nutrition is concerned with the *process leading to hunger and malnutrition* as well as the *state of malnutrition* itself. This process includes the immediate causes of inadequate nutrition, which are associated with diet and health, as well as the less direct causes associated with 'livelihood' (p. 5, original emphasis).

Third,

> Malnutrition usually starts either with the failure of an individual to acquire enough to eat, or ill-health. Nutritional inadequacy can lead to malnutrition, which is the state in which an individual's physical functions are impaired (p. 5).

And finally,

> In addition to the effect of nutrition on disease, the presence of disease leads to further malnutrition, through malabsorption of nutrients, altered metabolism, loss of appetite and by affecting feeding practices. Thus, the relationship between malnutrition and infection is cyclical (p. 5).

The debilitating effects of chronic malnutrition are evident not only upon direct victims, but also have severe implications for future generations in all social respects. As implied at the outset, the scale and depth of contemporary hunger is alarming and historically unprecedented (see Newman *et al.*, 1995; and also Dreze, Sen and Hussain, 1995). Historically, where the modern state has sought to limit the scourge of hunger, it has done so by directing public action at the support or creation of new entitlements, principally through more or less complex social security systems. It is difficult, if not impossible, to see how in capitalist society there could be a private guarantee of entitlements that did not fall at the first hint of hunger and poverty. In this sense, public action in support of entitlements and through the state is a *sine qua non*.

However, intervening through entitlements has at least two faces. Once again Dreze and Sen note that 'The distinction between the problem of chronic hunger (involving sustained nutritional deprivation on a persistent basis) and that of famines (involving acute starvation and a sharp increase of mortality) is particularly important' (Dreze and Sen, 1989, p. 7). For example, famine prevention may rely on the speedy use of existing distributional mechanisms (for example, see Clay and Stokke, 1991), whereas chronic hunger may require slower development of mechanisms and institutions. In both cases, though, the centrality of public action is not in question, nor the interventionary role and responsibility of the state.

Unfortunately the limitations of this analysis and prescription are that – without wishing to overstate the degree of change – *the assumption that the prevention of hunger and the assurance of adequate nutrition as being a public problem and a basic question of public policy is no longer secure.* First, in most states there is a fundamental crisis of capacity which the neo-liberal assault has actively provoked (e.g. Mexico), fostered (e.g. India), compounded (e.g. Romania) or guaranteed (e.g. Mozambique); and second, in those states where capacity seems to be more robust (mainly the OECD states), a crisis of legitimacy has been openly solicited by trashing the precepts of the welfare state, collective responsibility and social security. In the specific case of the limitation of hunger it is now highly questionable whether the guarantee of entitlements retains any significant hold in the neo-liberal agenda. Moreover, where public action continues to be directed at the enhancement of entitlements (or the more effective exercise of entitlements), there is substantial evidence to suggest that the process of globalization has subverted the mechanisms and institutions which would have made this form of public action viable.

A renewed capitalism – which is not just about economic reorganization but is equally, amongst other things, a story about the manufacture of collective identities, the reassertion of patriarchal relations and the appropriation of nature – represented by globalization entails the reorganization of hunger. Whereas with the rise of the modern state the regulation of hunger had been increasingly carried out by state or public authorities on a national–territorial basis, it is increasingly evident that this responsibility has either been dramatically questioned (a matter of legitimacy) or undermined (a matter of capacity).

By next addressing the development of a globalized agri-industrial complex one can see how the discourse of entitlements and public action has been marginalized such that *state capacity and legitimacy have ceded considerable ground to globally privatized interests*. The core argument to be developed is that the *de-facto* organization and regulation of hunger have been privatized.

The analytical, and hence political, limitations characteristic of much food study work are in keeping with the inherited intellectual division of labour, as well as the bureaucratic division of labour. The concern with food and nutrition has tended to display a number of common characteristics. First, food studies have typically been nationally based, presupposing a relatively discrete socio-economic and political entity within which food security can be organized. The correlative of this is that the international study of food is generally limited to inter-state trade relations or the operation of dedicated international organizations such as the UN's Food and Agriculture Organization (FAO). Second, food studies which relate to poverty or famines have been prompted, unsurprisingly, by aid-based analysis, focusing on emergencies and relief. Third, food studies have been marked by a notable problem-solving approach which is policy-based and attentive almost exclusively to public action.

In this regard, food studies have tended to neglect structural analyses of the global food order; have a 'thin' notion of international/global organization; have a rather limited interest in the structural power of agribusiness; and tend to ignore, or at least treat as discrete changes, the myriad of technological innovations which have shaped global food complexes.

RESTRUCTURING OF GLOBAL AGRIBUSINESS

Having sketched out the broad dynamics of globalization and the traditional modes of analysis associated with the study of hunger, the central research question to be addressed is: *how does globalization transform − intensify, diminish, redistribute − the experience of hunger?*

The broad changes of capitalist agriculture which Bernstein identified, but which have now been informed further by globalized relations, continue to be the main concerns. So, class and gender differentiation; division of access to land, of labour and the fruits of labour are refined through globalization; property and livelihood, affluence and poverty are reorganized through globalization; colonial legacies and state activity are redefined; agricultural development into the agri-industrial complex and the complication of global markets accelerates in globalization; and relations of power and inequality are rearticulated (Bernstein, 1995, p. 41). In these key ways the primary concerns have not changed: globalization as capitalist modernization has simply accentuated and further concentrated powers and inequalities.

The manner in which changes have come about through globalization is, however, distinctive. By focusing on the development of global agribusiness the manner in which a global food complex and organization of hunger has come about will become clearer. The examination of food supply, food entitlement and broader food security, as well as the analysis of poverty and famines, has continued with relatively little attention paid to the structuring of global food markets, nor to the activities of the agents which predominate in global food markets, namely, transnational corporations.

Globalized agribusiness acts in a combination of three principal ways: (1) by commoditizing production it concentrates capitalist agricultural production upon a relatively narrow range of food crops, especially grains and durable foods, i.e. fats and sweeteners; (2) the operation of markets across the global space and time ensures that global prices have direct and often immediate bearing on local prices. By operating in, as well as creating, these markets across the world, agribusiness is able to capitalize on time-space compression in ways which are severely restricted for local agricultures; (3) historically the relatively low market price for staples – characteristic of EC/US supported agriculture – has encouraged 'third world' imports and the disruption of local markets.

The reorganization of agriculture and food provision transforms not only total availability of food but every other aspect of food production and provision. It disrupts and reshapes local diets; it upsets and redefines local farming practices; it reconstitutes the division of labour with all attendant social relations; and it erodes the foundations of food security – and ultimately challenges the basis of local entitlements.[7] Ultimately relative autonomy or relative self-determination is wrested from the local to the global.

Global reorganization entails a series of intimately interconnected transformations. Goodman, Sorj and Wilkinson have identified two prominent transformative processes in agriculture: *appropriationism and substitutionism*. First, appropriationism refers to the transformation of specific aspects of agricultural activity into industrial activity followed by 'their re-incorporation into agriculture as inputs', e.g. manure fertilizer, a by-product of farming, is replaced by industrially produced synthetic fertilizers to be sold to the farm. Thus, an activity previously carried out exclusively on the land is appropriated and increasingly controlled from industry.

Second, substitutionism refers to the process wherein 'industrial activity account[s] for a steadily rising proportion of value added but the agricultural product, after first being reduced to an industrial input, increasingly suffers replacement by non-agricultural components' (Goodman, Sorj and Wilkinson, 1987, p. 2).

Appropriation and substitution alter both food availability as well as food quality, thereby structuring taste, food status, price, diversity and nutritional quality. Thus, not only are key parts of diet mediated through global markets, but the key controllers of such markets are a relatively small number of agribusinesses. Intimations of the significance that globally-organized agribusiness possesses can be derived from the monopolistic or oligopolistic sectoral control which vertical integration holds for them. The processes of appropriationism and substitutionism,[8] though characteristic of capitalist agriculture, have entailed yet stronger consequences through globalized agribusiness. The industrial manipulation of nature is contingent upon the concentration of research and technical capital.

A brief profile of Cargill, with global revenues of $47.37 billion in 1992–93, serves to illustrate the point. Cargill, which is the largest private company in the US, is also the world's largest grain trader, largest malting barley producer, second largest phosphate fertilizer producer, and largest oilseed processor. In the US it is also the third largest beef packer, fourth largest pork slaughterer, third largest flour miller, and fourth largest cattle feeder. Cargill also has major interests in salt, cotton, coffee, transport, shipping, steel, biotechnology, citrus fruits, fruit and vegetables (see the meticulous history by Kneen, 1995). Furthermore, Cargill is one of the largest agents in agri-industrial finance, ranging from farm credit to agricultural futures markets.

As already observed above, food–availability–decline (FAD) explanations are inadequate accounts of famine and hunger, and yet the argument made so far is that the modernization of agribusiness has reorganized on a global scale – not entitlement to food – but the availability of food.

However, the argument to be emphasized here is that the power of agribusiness, typified by Cargill, is such that the social basis through which entitlements evolve and are articulated are continuously but erratically disrupted. For example, the global integration of agri-industry has had a profound impact on the concentration in landholdings and the concentration of landownership; in the increased casualization of labour; increasing specialization of production, particularly for export; the corresponding reduction in land area and labour dedicated to local staples; the mechanization of agriculture; the 'technologizing' of farming and the gendering of labour. For example, taking the case of grain, which constitutes 83 per cent of food crop production in the Third World and 87 per cent of the growth in food production between 1960 and 1980, Barkin *et al.* show how 'cereal food crops historically produced and consumed locally [have] give[n] way to commercial production of grain destined for other uses' (Barkin, Batt and DeWalt, 1992, pp. 6–7, 10).

The overall conclusion is that food crops for local consumption have been substituted on a very large scale by feed crops for export consumption. The rapidity and scale of such change – with the attendant transformation of the social organization of production and reorganization of the social structures of accumulation – has been effected through the global integration and co-ordination of agribusiness. All these social transformations qualify both the security and diversity of entitlements.

The detailed work of Barkin, Batt and DeWalt has clearly demonstrated that the success of 'agricultural modernisation – leading to huge increase in the output of feed for animals, as well as of higher valued crops for urban markets and export – was accompanied by a growing inability to produce basic food stuffs' (1992, p. 1). Here the requirements of global agri-industrial capital transformed the character of local diets, the cultural status of different foods, the division of household labour, the security of employment, and so on, whilst at the same time removing or at least severely limiting the food resources available for local reproduction. As labour becomes commoditized and as the number of wage labourers therefore increases, the lack of money amongst poorly paid or unemployed labour ensures that there is little local effective demand. Simultaneously effective demand is being exercised globally.

It is in the light of these patterns of development that *'Third World' countries have become more and more dependent on imports in the attempt to provide basic food supplies.* The world's richest countries have become the world's granaries, and the growing discrepancy between what is produced, in what locations and by whom, and what is consumed, in what locations and by whom, is accounted for by the far faster growth in trade in agricultural products than by growth in production.

In general terms, as McMichael and Raynolds argue, globalization and 'de-peasantization' entail 'the elimination of centuries-old agricultural practices that only now are we beginning to recognise as a serious ecological, cultural and demog raphic consequence of the fetishism of industrialism and its associated consumerism' (McMichael and Raynolds, 1995, p. 317). The globalization of agriculture in essence constitutes the permanent destabilization of food security.

RESISTANCE, THE LOCALITY AND FOOD SECURITY

We can continue with the examination of world order as if states were determining of order and remain frustrated by the persistence of famine and malnutrition, since state action is ineffective. Or we can acknowledge now that *world order is framed not by states but by a host of social agents and structures over which most states have little determining control.*[9] On the contrary, these other social agents and structural forces set the terms within which and through which states may operate. The argument put forward here is that the world food order – crucial elements of which were instituted by explicit state action – has developed primarily through the operation of global markets, the concentration of capital, and the organization of the agri-industrial complex over which most states have virtually no control. In brief, *the world food order can neither be portrayed as a state order, nor can it be analysed primarily in terms of state action.*

The central change which the process of globalization has achieved is the fracturing of national capital accumulation as the accumulation strategy of modern capitalism, for capitalism to be gradually reconstituted as globalized accumulation. To an increasing extent this globally-based accumulation has made redundant – or at least relatively ineffective – the regulative and insurance capacity of most states. This is not to say that states do not continue to act in concert with one another in international fora, such as GATT, the EC, etc., but it does mean that the 'sovereign veto' previously enjoyed by at least some of the most powerful states is no longer open even to these.

A powerful example of globalization is that of changes to the constitution of Mexico in 1992. Article 27 of the 1917 revolutionary constitution had provided for national landownership and the guarantee of community access to land and water sufficient for the citizens' survival, principally through the institution of the *ejido*. As Klein-Robbenhaar notes, the February 1992 constitutional changes allowed for (1) *ejido*s or *ejidatario*s to engage in independent commercial agreements to finance production on their land; (2) *ejidatario*s on communal lands to enter long-term land leasing arrangements and (3) for land to be alienated through sale or mortgage (Klein-Robbenhaar, 1995, p. 395). Through these constitutional changes, in association with the already dominant position of globalized agribusiness, *state and agribusiness 'conspire' to reorientate agriculture towards the demands of privileged consumers.*

However, globalization should be regarded as the *resistible* renewal of capitalism. Critics of capitalist modernization should be able to identify precisely the coincident changes in capitalist regulation (e.g. the Mexican constitutional changes just noted) and the particular innovations in agri- industrial development (e.g. feed-for-food substitution), and demonstrate how basic human need is not satisfied by such developments. Clunies-Ross and Hildyard point to the heart of the matter: *'At issue is the question of power – of who controls the land, inputs, production, marketing, research, decision-making and policy'* (Clunies-Ross and Hildyard, 1992, p. 8).

However, the next step is as crucial: *how are alternative practices which satisfy human need to be effected?* Fortunately, globalization is always partial and incomplete, although the aspiration is one of universality and generalization. Any theory of historical change must address the question of how alternative projects arise, how resistance is articulated and how dominant effects of enterprises are subverted. *Any theory of capitalist hegemony is incomplete without a corresponding theory of counter-hegemony.* It is to that action that we should now turn.

NOTES

1. Aggregate and average figures should be used with great caution, not least because they form part of the problem of the reification of hunger analysis outlined below. As such the UNDP/FAO estimates which focus on three indicators – the food production per capita index, the food imports dependency ratio index, and the percentage of daily calorific requirement supplied – suggest that almost forty countries do not meet basic calorific requirements. Furthermore, 15 African countries alone, plus 13 other countries required exceptional and/or emergency food assistance in 1995. Thus, 64 of the 104 countries for which the food production index data is available (1995) are worse off than in 1979–81. These and other standard aggregate figures do not show the 'hidden hunger' caused by chronic dietary deficiencies in micronutrients (see Food and Agriculture Organization, 1995; and UNDP, 1995).

2. 'Exceptionalist' or 'natural disaster' explanations frequently include war as an exceptional cause of hunger, though I see little reason to regard war as anything other than usual and often banal (in the Arendtian sense). See the explanations, noted below, which Devereux calls 'food-availability decline' theories.

3. However, globalization should not be understood to mean homogenization. Since accumulation is not just an economic process (but is inherently cultural, social, political, etc.) developing in a myriad of different social circumstances, subject to a host of differing social forces, then we should neither expect uniformity nor homogeneity. Globalization, then, does not mean, for example, that the process of neo-liberalization will entail the same results all over the world. This is most important, not least in respect to the shape and character of counter-hegemonic forces and strategies. We cannot 'read off' from neo-liberalism either what any local results will be nor, especially, what local resistance will be.

4. This orthodox tale of history's march in which liberalism triumphs is only possible through a perverse myopia. Liberalism has not triumphed in Indonesia, Korea, Taiwan, the Middle East, including Israel, most of Africa and Latin America: that is unless one interprets liberalism as permitting – even sponsoring – the denial of basic freedoms and fundamental rights such as labour organization, rights of women, religious tolerance, civil liberties, free speech, etc.

5. The many works in ecological economics effectively demolish the notion of national carrying capacity. See also Scoones and Zaba, 1992.

6. The emphasis in this chapter is upon food complexes and the generation of poverty. Clearly the food complex also creates wealth and the rich, but whereas it is undoubtedly the case that those vulnerable to starvation are the poor – this vulnerability is part of what is meant by 'being poor' – and those most vulnerable to malnutrition are also the poor, the rich – essentially those with much wider or stronger entitlements – will never suffer malnutrition, still less starvation, though they may suffer inadequate nutrition due to mistaken dietary habits, and so on.
7. This is not to romanticize the local and vilify the global, but it is to recognize that the alienation inherent in logics of global accumulation are inconsistent with basic human need and autonomy.
8. Ben Fine uses a slightly different definition of these terms: appropriationism refers to 'the encroachment by capitalist products and processes within agriculture itself' and substitutionism refers to 'the displacement of products and the production process from agriculture to industry, most marked in food processing and the substitution of inorganic for organic products' (Fine, 1994, p. 534).
9. The thesis put forward here is not arguing that the state is irrelevant or redundant. It is though one in which the regulative capacity of the state has been dramatically transformed, and, furthermore, that historically in the majority of states the regulative capacity has been much more tenuous than typically assumed.

REFERENCES

Barkin, D., Batt, R. and DeWalt, B. (1992) *Food Crops vs. Feed Crops: Global Substitution of Grains in Production* (London: Lynne Rienner).
Bell, D. and Reich, M. (eds) (1986) *Health, Nutrition and Economic Crises: Approaches to Policy in the Third World* (Dover, MA: Auburn House).
Bernstein, H. (1995) 'Agrarian Classes and Capitalist Development', in L. Sklair (ed.) (1995) *Capitalism and Development* (London: Routledge).
Bernstein, H., Crow, B., Mackintosh, M. and Martin, C. (eds) (1990) *The Food Question: Profits versus Peoples* (London: Earthscan).
Clay, E. and Stokke, O. (eds) (1991) *Food Aid Reconsidered: Assessing the Impact on Third World Countries* (London: Cass).
Clunies-Ross, T. and Hildyard, N. (1992) *The Politics of Industrial Agriculture* (London: Earthscan).
Devereux, S. (1993) *Theories of Famine* (Hemel Hempstead: Harvester Wheatsheaf).
de Waal, A. (1989) *Famines that Kill: Darfur, Sudan, 1984-85* (Oxford: Clarendon).
Dreze, J. and Sen, A. (1989) *Hunger and Public Action* (Oxford: Clarendon).
Dreze, J., Sen, A. and Hussain, A. (1995) *The Political Economy of Hunger: Selected Essays* (Oxford: Oxford University Press).
Fine, B. (1994) 'Towards a Political Economy of Food', *Review of International Political Economy*, 1, 3.
Food and Agriculture Organization (1995) *The State of Food and Agriculture* (Rome: FAO).

Friedmann, H. and McMichael, P. (1989) 'Agriculture and the State-System: The Rise and Decline of National Agriculture, 1870 to the Present', *Sociologia Ruralis*, 29, 2.

Giddens, A. (1992) *The Consequences of Modernity* (Cambridge: Polity).

Goodman, D. and Redclift, M. (1991) *Refashioning Nature: Food, Ecology and Culture* (London: Routledge).

Goodman, D., Sorj, B. and Wilkinson, J. (1987) *From Farming to Biotechnology: A Theory of Agro-Industrial Development* (Oxford: Blackwell).

Jolly, R. (1986) 'A UNICEF Perspective on the Effects of Economic Crises and What can be Done', in D. Bell and M. Reich (eds) (1986) *Health, Nutrition and Economic Crises: Approaches to Policy in the Third World* (Dover, MA: Auburn House).

Klein-Robbenhaar, J. (1995) 'Agro-Industry and the Environment: the Case of Mexico in the 1990s', *Agricultural History*, 69, 3.

Kneen, B. (1995) *Invisible Giant: Cargill and its Transnational Strategies* (London: Pluto).

LeHeron, R. (1993) *Globalised Agriculture: Political Choice* (London: Pergamon).

McMichael, P. and Raynolds, L. (1995) 'Capitalism, Agriculture and World Economy', in L. Sklair (ed.) (1995) *Capitalism and Development* (London: Routledge).

Monbiot, G. (1995) 'True Costs of Aubergines All Year Round', The *Guardian* (London), 31 October.

Newman, L. *et al* (eds) (1995) *Hunger in History: Food Shortage, Poverty and Deprivation* (Oxford: Blackwell).

Peck, J. and Tickell, A. (1994) 'Jungle Law Breaks Out: Neo- Liberalism and Global-Local Disorder', *Area*, 26, 4.

Raikes, P. (1988) *Modernising Hunger: Famine, Food Surplus and Farm Policy in the EEC and Africa* (London: Catholic Institute for International Relations).

Redclift M. and Benton, T. (eds) (1994) *Social Theory and the Global Environment* (London: Routledge).

Scoones, I. and Zaba, B. (1992) 'Is Carrying Capacity a Useful Concept to Apply to Human Populations ?', in *Population and Environment Annual Conference* (Oxford: British Society for Population Studies).

Sklair, L. (1991) *The Sociology of the Global System* (London: Harvester Wheatsheaf).

Sklair, L. (ed) (1995) *Capitalism and Development* (London: Routledge).

Twose, N. (1984) *Cultivating Hunger: An Oxfam Study of Food, Power and Poverty* (Oxford: Oxfam).

UNDP (1995) *Human Development Report, 1995* (New York: UNDP/Oxford University Press).

Young, H. (1992) *Food Scarcity and Famine: Assessment and Response* (Oxford: Oxfam, Oxfam Practical Health Guide No. 7).

8 Global Ecologism and its Critics

Mohamed A. Mohamed Salih

INTRODUCTION

The universal consensus that the environment holds the key to human (and non-human) survival lends itself to no agreement as to how to create a globally sustainable society. Varying perceptions and interpretations of the promises and predicaments posed by the pursuance or lack of pursuance of 'sustainable development' have engulfed the South and the North in competing claims over who is responsible for the environmental damage and who should pay for it. Although the North is aware that its economic prosperity is responsible for most of the environmental damage done thus far, its search for viable solutions has been centred around a covert desire to maintain the status quo. In the event, it is not surprising that *global ecologism has been largely perceived by the South as an exclusionist ideology used to feign and hence mystify the deeds of the Old World Order under pretext claims about the emergence of a New World Order.*

This chapter argues that the development imperative in the South has been shaped by historical and structural determinants dictated by the international political economy of resource management. Because of an impending need to utilize its resources in order to improve the quality of life of its impoverished populations, the South is increasingly suspicious of the political designs of global ecologism, and views them as subversive ideologies delineated to deprive its populations of the opportunity to utilize their natural resources for the benefit of themselves and future generations. It is between these two perspectives that the South has to choose in determining its future destiny: development or maintaining the status quo under the pretence of the preservation of nature. Hence it is argued that the discrepancies between the core values of global ecologism, the life-styles of the industrial societies and the politics of global environmental management do not prescribe to the former perspective nor the requirements of a sustainable 'global' future.

124

In this chapter, global ecologism is defined as a host of contemporary trends in eco-political thought and practices which assume a global crusade in the struggle for halting what is increasingly perceived as a global ecological crisis. However, it is important to make clear that nowhere in this chapter will global ecologism be used to refer to a coherent body of literature, ideology or theory. Global ecologism combines diverse ideological and theoretical positions whose focus of analysis is the globe. Furthermore, there is no denying that different schools of thought within global ecologism advocate different interpretations of the ecological crisis in order to support their claims or to negate the claims and discourses put forward by others.

Although there is nothing novel or basically wrong with addressing ecological or other questions from a global perspective, what is important is how the globe is defined and whose interest a given global discourse serves. This chapter suggests that *the debate over the meaning of the global ecological crisis reflects prevailing inequalities of power between North and South*. The key sites of conflict are: (1) who defines the causes of the global ecological crisis; (2) what interests are at stake and what prevail; and (3) to what extent has the South been able to influence this agenda? We can begin by looking at the way in which global environmental governance has emerged on to the agenda of world politics.

THE RETURN OF THE STRONG: GLOBAL ENVIRON-MENTAL GOVERNANCE

The Return of the Strong is unwittingly quoted from Robert Harvey's (1995) widely acclaimed book in which he warns against symptoms showing that the world is drifting towards global disorder. The attempt to develop the linkage between global environmental governance and the return of the strong is an attempt to pave the way for my argument that the New World Order is based on a neo-colonial ideology code-named globalization. Basically, I argue that following the end of the Cold War, many thought that the environment would be a sufficient reason to rally the South and the North for the common goal of protecting the environment (Mohamed Salih, 1994). The global environmental forums and negotiations have so far shown that South–North differences and confrontations are far from over. The evolution of the concept of global environmental governance has been characterized by the South as continuous contestation of the manner in which the global and the ecological are hideously linked to serve the interests of the North. A short synopsis of how the concept has evolved during the last two decades or so will be a useful introduction to the South's positions.

Recent debate on environment and sustainable development often begins by acknowledging the Stockholm Conference on Human Environment (1972) as a key event in the emergence of global environmental concern (WCED, 1987; Adams, 1990; Thomas, 1992; Tolba *et al.*, 1992). According to Adams (1990, p. 36), the Stockholm Conference was only partly and belatedly concerned with the environmental and developmental problems of the South. The primary pressure behind the UN's decision to hold the conference came from the developed world, with the initial focus on the environmental problems of industrialization in the North. However, the evolution of the global environmental movement from Stockholm to Rio has developed into the concept of global environmental governance, which is part of the wider notion of global governance. The background to the emergence of a global project to facilitate the dominance over natural resources goes back centuries, but its contemporary relevance is related to the global environmental forums, negotiations and conventions which followed the Stockholm Conference.

Global governance is explicit about the need to establish a global resource management system to save the global commons from abuse by what is often referred to as some irresponsible nation–states. Biswas and Biswas (quoted in Adams, 1990) pointed out that the developing countries felt that the concept of global resources management (later to became global environmental governance) was an attempt by the North to take away from them (the developing countries) the national control of their resources. Furthermore, as the industrialized countries used the lion's share of the world resources and contributed to most of the resulting pollution, the South did not see much reason to be fined and pay for the solutions.

Thomas (1992, p. 25) observes that

the global notions already advanced by the North had raised questions about sovereign states dealing with environmental issues which often traverse national boundaries. Developing countries voiced their belief that environmental matters could not be tackled in isolation from the divide between rich and poor countries.

In other words, the link between environment and development in a South–North context was being formally elaborated in an intergovernmental forum probably for the first time, and by implication the perceived inadequacies of the prevailing international economic and financial systems to deal with these issues.

The South's concerns with sovereignty and poverty issues continued to dominate the working of all UN commissions on environment and development. Brandt's Report (1980), *North–South: A Programme for Survival*, the South Commission's *The Challenge to the South* (1990), and the reply to it in South Commission Report (1993), *Facing the Challenge*, were particularly designed to allay the South's fears about the emergence of neo-colonial environmentalism in the name of the common good. However, the North has successfully managed to impose a linkage between development aid and an implicit (and sometimes explicit) environmental conditionality. The South Commission (1990, p. 218) argues that

> the countries of the South are today victims of the deleterious environmental effects of policies and patterns of development in the North. These include, such global phenomena as the thinning of the ozone layer, nuclear radiation, and the green house effect, as well as such direct acts as the dumping of hazardous wastes and the location of polluting industries in the South. Attempts by the developing countries to bring the global commons – in particular the oceans and outerspace – under effective international jurisdiction have been defeated in practice by the lack of cooperation of the developed countries.

In *Facing the Challenge* (1993), the South Commission was able to elaborate on several issues related to environment and development. Of particular relevance to this chapter is the fact that the South Commission began to foresee the importance of South–South co-operation in environmental issues as a priority to South–North. The overview of *Facing the Challenge* (1993, pp. 32–3) emphasizes that in their effort to protect the environment, developing countries could co-operate with each other in several directions: in managing shared natural resources, especially river basins, coastal areas, forests and wildlife; in such activities as offshore oil exploration, the management of exclusive economic zones and the prevention of desertification; and in such areas of research as renewable energy, especially biomass and solar power, and the efficient use of energy in industry, agriculture, transport and homes.

Facing the Challenge has also emphasized (p. 33) that 'the South should adopt a common approach in negotiating with the North to ensure an equitable management of the global environment and should sponsor arrangements for sharing technologies that help to conserve energy and reduce environmental pollution'.

According to MacArthy (1993, p. 60),

> cognizant of continued global ecological decline and serious economic and social deterioration of the South, the UN General Assembly called in September 1983 for the creation of special independent commission to provide 'a global agenda for change' by seriously addressing the relationship between environment and development, and by proposing environmental strategies for achieving long-term sustainable development.

The discussions of the United Nations Commission on the Environment and Development which gave birth to the Brundtland Report were also marred with South–North confrontations. Sandbrook (quoted in *Our Common Future*, 1987, 64) argues that

> it has not been too difficult to push the environmental lobby of the North and the developmental lobby of the South together. And there is now in fact a blurring of distinction between the two, so they are coming to have a common consensus around the theme of sustainable development. The building blocks are there. Environmental concern is common to both sides. Humanitarian concern is common to both sides. The difference lies in the methods of each and the degree to which each side tries to achieve its economic interest through development assistance.

In the build-up to the Earth Summit and increased national and international efforts to promote *sustainable development*, the South was keen to unite in the face of increasing pressure from the North which was not eager to make concessions. Fears of neo-colonial environmentalism were voiced again by the G77, particularly by the newly industrialized countries (NICs). The South argued (Weizsacker, 1994) that the countries of the North, which have polluted and damaged the environment should: (1) reduce the emission of pollutants; (2) provide new technology so that the South can develop without harming the environment; and (3) provide finance to reduce emissions worldwide. The current pattern of development in all three areas reveals that little to no progress has been achieved (Bartelmus, 1994; Brown *et al.*, 1993). The South could be waiting for decades and even longer before its demands are met.

Despite the importance of the Earth Summit, it was marred by South–North confrontations. This, according to MacArthy (1993), was exemplified in at least two obvious developments: firstly the Global Forum, which represented sectors of the global civil society known for their detachment or autonomy from state and business interests; and secondly the strong G77 lobby representing the poorest countries in the world *vis-à-vis* the most industrially advanced countries, the G7. The most difficult areas for negotiation included how to compensate the South for the genetic resources extracted freely from its semi- preserved eco-systems. The forestry convention and the financing of environmental protection worldwide were also amongst the contested areas between the South and the North.

In response to the North's failure to make any genuine concessions, the South's frustration became obvious. An Indian delegate (quoted in *Down to Earth*, 1992) commented that the North–South conflict during the Rio Summit was secondary to the US's conflict with Europe. Unfortunately, the failure of the industrialized world to harmonize its position was often glibly transformed into a North–South conflict, as an explanation of their own – i.e. the North's – failure. Indigenous peoples (Brascoupe, 1992; LaDuke, 1992) whose natural resources have been looted by transnational corporations (TNCs) for centuries, charged that to globalize natural resources is to take them even further away from the people who depend on them for their survival. For the South, the Rio summit was seen as an attempt to take the control of natural resources from local communities and nation–states and give it to global-level managing institutions.

The Earth Summit and Agenda 21 have laid the foundations for the advocacy of global environmental governance within the wider concept of global governance. According to *Our Global Neighbourhood* (Commission on Global Governance, 1995, pp. 3–7), as a concept, global governance:

(1) is viewed primarily as intergovernmental relationships, but it must be understood as also involving non-governmental organizations (NGOs), citizens' movements, multinational corporations, and the global capital market. Interacting with these are global mass media of dramatically enlarged influence;

(2) there is no single model or form of global governance, nor is there a single structure or set of structures. However, recognizing the systemic nature of the issues with which it deals, it promotes systemic approaches in dealing with major global concerns;

(3) the aims of global governance include reforming and strengthening the existing system of intergovernmental institutions, and improving its means of collaboration with private and independent groups. Among other things, global governance will strive to subject the rule of arbitrary power – economic, political, or military – to the rule of law within global society.

Global environmental governance operates within the confines of, and consistent with, the principles laid down in global governance: legal instruments, conventions and international environmental policy proclamations. *Our Global Neighbourhood* (p. 216) also indicates that global environmental governance emphasizes the need:

(1) to put to action a global legal, intellectual and institutional groundwork for a concerted effort to achieve sustainable development;

(2) to establish a Trusteeship of the Global Commons (TGC) and to be made responsible for acting on behalf of all nations, including the administration of environmental treaties;

(3) to enact an Earth Charter for world endorsement pending the outcome of the global efforts exerted by the Earth Council and Green Cross to achieve this endeavour.

It has become obvious that *one of the most conspicuous outcomes of the Earth Summit is that the stage has been set for global governance, aided by diverse trends of eco-globalism, to become the dominant paradigm and the most influential actor on the global scale.* According to Rich (1994, p. 273),

the premise of the Earth Summit was that global environmental management can work. The project as it emerged out of Rio has two principal approaches – a growing body of international environmental treaties among nation–states and increased foreign aid for environmental protection and management as well as poverty alleviation, channelled and managed mainly through the Global Environmental Facility (GEF) and other financing arms of the World Bank.

Such notions imply not only that the natural economy has already been rendered subject to capital, but also that sustainable development has been defined according to the logic of capital and the dominant structures that supports it.

It is now over four years since the Rio Conference proclaimed Agenda 21 as the guiding principle for global sustainable development; the question remains as to why contradictory Northern political discourses have converged to agree on the assumption that what is ecological is by necessity global and hence concerns the whole of humanity and not an economically and politically differentiated globe. The second question is whether the South fairs better in the eco-centric than the anthropocentric eco-global designs.

CONTRADICTORY DISCOURSES; IDENTICAL AGENDAS

The *ideological foundations of global ecologism draw on two broad, but apparently divergent and contradictory discourses – eco-centricism and anthropocentricism* – with their diverse political strands. Anthropocentricism argues that the root of the ecological crisis is neither anthropocentric attitudes about humanity's place in nature, nor the political–economic structures that embody those attitudes. Ecological destruction stems from ignorance, greed, and shortsigh tedness. Hence such human failures may be addressed by enacting legislation, changing public policy, increasing education, altering tax laws, returning public lands to private ownership, emphasizing moral obligations to future generations of humans, promoting wise stewardship of nature and encouraging more prudent use and more equitable allocation of natural resources (Dobson 1990). As shown earlier, these are the issues with which the global environmental forums and negotiations have been grappling.

By and large, *anthropocentricism informs the utilitarian socio-economic and political values in global ecologism*. This has, to a large extent, reinforced the core values which justify the North's dominance over the globe. At a higher level of abstraction, eco-centricism provides an ideological base which justifies the need for keeping the South underdeveloped for the sake of global ecological sustainability. However, this argument does not suggest that there is a coherent conspiracy theory which divides the functions of dominance between anthropocentricism and eco-centricism.

On the other hand, eco-centricism criticizes the utilitarian approaches advocated by anthropocentricism and argues that non-human living species also have the right to live and that they should not be subject to human domination. For instance, Dobson (1990, p. 15), argues that

> ecologism makes Earth the physical object of the very foundation-stone of its intellectual edifice, arguing that its finitude is the basic reason why infinite population growth and economic growth are impossible and why, consequently, fundamental changes in our social and physical behaviour need to take place.

In its most radical forms, ecologism calls for the abandonment of affluence (Trainer, 1995), glorification of the life-styles of preliterate societies, and a quest for the return to the ethos of the 'noble savage' in social ecology (Bookchin, 1980; Bookchin and Foreman 1991).

Global ecologism goes beyond sustaining ecology for human self-interest to the care for nature whether it is useful for human beings or not. Deep ecology elaborations of the Gaia (Earth) hypothesis (Goldsmith 1988, Bunyard and Morgan-Grenville 1987) represent the philosophical foundation of 'radical' ecologism and its aim to dissolve humans into the natural world and thus displace humans from their tendency to exert dominance on all forms of the living world. However, the problem here is that modern ecologism has failed miserably in changing the life- styles of Western societies and therefore it has no right to call upon preliterate societies 'to enjoy their wonderful way of life', because they are closer to nature. It sounds like calling upon preliterate societies to go on 'enjoying' ill health, famine, poverty, lack of public amenities and relative isolation in a world eco-centricists describe as 'globally interdependent'. While anthropocentricism uses political, economic and technological dominance to subdue the South, eco-centricists use what they perceive as their moral superiority to tell poor peasants and forest dwellers what is good for them because the societies of the North have experienced that 'better standards of living' are not good for ecology. Let us recall Lohmann's argument (1993, p. 204) that 'it is better for Euro-ecologism not to perceive Southern farmers or forest dwellers as nothing more than characters in Northern environmentalists stories, but to acknowledge that Northern societies themselves are in part characters in criticizable tales told by others'.

Second, it is ethically and morally irresponsible of deep ecologists who live under the cradle of the welfare state to debate more about the protection of seals, elephants, whales and lion-tailed monkeys, than about the dispossessed dwellers of the rainforests or the famine victims of the African Sahel. The same goes for some eco-theologians who argue that the shift in social paradigms requires shifts in the types of moral reasoning made available by secularism. Therefore, sustainable development is conceived by some eco-theologians (Engel and Engel, 1990; Regenstein, 1991; Gore 1992) as a moral ideal which challenges the traditional separation of theory from practice. The failures of secular society, therefore, urge religions to play, with vigour, their historical role and provide the moral grounds for global environmental ethics. Either way, both eco-centricism and anthropocentricism play an important role in justifying the need for global environmental governance and in informing the South and the North of the debate on how to halt and eventually reverse the so-called global ecological crisis. Furthermore, because of their global nature, both contain utilitarian and non-utilitarian ideological manifestations, with discernible consequences on the South.

It is implicit that there is an analogy between how colonialism and religion assumed a common mission of extending civilization to the primitive South and its savage societies. The former is guided by anthropocentricism and the latter by religious zeal. Evidently, religion had perceived certain common interests with the colonial powers, even though they might have disagreed with some of their policies. As far as the South is concerned, what eco-centricism shares with anthropocentricism is more than what religion shared with colonialism.

In short, *eco-centricism provides the ideological and moral reasoning for global ecologism,* and from a South point of view, it shares with anthropocentricism the grand aim of dominating the global ecology. The underlying theme in both is a *covert interest to control the 'globe',* albeit with different tools and under different ideologies. The only real difference between them is how and under what pretext: anthropocentricism or eco-centricism. In both cases, the discussion remains a Northern discussion targeted at a Northern audience, but one which will eventually have serious consequences for the South. The tenets of the position which I have presented so far will be delineated when the manner in which the South has been conceptualized by ecologism is examined.

It is important to emphasize here that anthropocentricism and eco-centricism agree on at least two broad assumptions: (1) the world is synonymous with the North and a global mission controlled and directed by the North is justified under claims of the global nature of ecology; and (2) the South is an extension to nature and therefore a natural extension to the North's eco- global designs. These two points have far-reaching ramifications on the North's attitude towards the South and the South's response to the North's eco-global designs.

NEO-COLONIAL RECIPES FOR A NEW WORLD ORDER!

There is an extensive literature on how global environmental negotiations have been debated (Agarwal and Narian, 1991; Thomas, 1992; Tolba *et al.*, 1992; Sjostedt *et al.*, 1993; Finger 1993; Barbier *et al.*, 1994; Read, 1994; Weizsacker, 1994; Bhaskar and Glyn, 1995; Brenton, 1995; and several others) and there is no need to repeat it here. One of the main objectives of colonialism was the exploitation of the South's natural resources under the guise of expanding civilization to its 'primitive' people. The objectives of neo-colonialism are not different, even though they have been conceived during an era of relative political independence. Merchant (1992, p. 23) reminds us that 'the patterns of uneven development and their differential economic and ecological effects are the products of a global market economy that has been emerging since the sixteenth century'. She (pp. 24–5) also remarks that

> accumulation of economic surplus occurred as natural resources (or free raw materials) were extracted at minimum cost (minimum wages) and manufactured goods were sold at market value.... Today's global system is based on this same fundamental division of labour between industrialized or centre economies of the First World and the underdeveloped or peripheral economies of the Third World.... Instead of enslavement by force or theft of resources, neocolonialism uses economic investments and foreign aid programs to maintain economic hegemony.

These 'development' programmes are in themselves many of the factors contributing to the environmental crisis and poverty in the South. De La Court (1992) laments that

> The North has been able to develop because it has exploited the South. Slaves, gold and silver, spices, tropical wood and all the other products from the colonies form the foundation on which Western development has been built. As a result, we now have a situation in which 20 percent of the world's population has 80 percent of the world raw materials at its disposal; a situation distinguished by flagging economic development for millions of people, political instability and far-reaching ecological disruption. (p. 21)

In this respect, the global ecological crisis is a result of centuries of cumulative Northern industrialization which dates back to the colonial legacy, increasingly reinforced by the international division of labour and the prevailing international economic order. In *Mortgaging The Earth*, Rich (1994) argues that

> the market driven rationalization and administration of the earth's surface and natural resources for economic production has had a brutal corollary: the uprooting and dispossession of huge rural populations from *what is misconceived by 'development agents'* as their less efficient modes of production (emphasis added). (p. 155)

In other cases, the poor are pushed on to marginal lands and are thereby forced to ruin their environments.

In the same context, the example presented by Rich (1994) about the linkage between poverty and state-sponsored policies in Latin America is also relevant to many other parts of the South where the prevalence of

> highly unequal land tenure systems in many tropical countries, have been major factor in deforestation, both by forcing populations with smaller holdings to overwork the land, and by pushing millions of others into marginal tropical forest ecosystems, often with government and World Bank support. (p. 156)

One of the most conspicuous outcomes of these development programmes, according to Brecher and Costello (1994, p. 24), is that 'almost one-third of the population of the developing countries live in absolute poverty – too poor to provide for the minimum diet required for full human functioning'. In this particular situation, the processes of environmental damage in the South are inseparable from the development policies advocated by global economic institutions such as the World Bank and the International Monetary Fund (IMF).

The management of global natural resources is ultimately linked to socio-economic processes and relations (production, distribution and consumption of goods and services) which result in what is abstracted as a global ecological crisis. The South Commission (1990, p. 218) argues that

> the pressure is made worse by the developing countries resulting from the debt burden. . . . Equally fall in commodity prices leads to pressure to increase production and step up exports. The result is, on the one hand, that developing countries are forced to over-exploit their resources, harming the environment, and, on the other, to accept environmentally damaging deals with the North, e.g. deals for the disposal of toxic wastes.

On the same theme, Sachs (1993, p. 20) makes the point that

> the purpose of global environmental management is nothing less than control of a second order; a higher level of observation and intervention has to be installed in order to control the consequences over the control over nature. Such a step becomes the more imperative as the drive towards turning the control into a closely interrelated and expanding economic society.

In a similar situation, Shiva criticizes the well- celebrated concept of sustainability and the way it has been conceived as part of the instruments for the advancement of the rule of capital over nature. She (1992, p. 189) argues that 'the false notion of the concept of sustainability as has been advocated so far is based on three flaws: assigning primacy to capital, dependence on capital and substitutability of nature and capital'. The global crisis, therefore, is a direct result of global capitalism and its expansion throughout the world, and if that process was initiated by colonialism, it has been maintained by neo-colonialism under the banner of globalization and the emergence of the concept of global governance.

Mainstream globalists are in the habit of praising the current process of globalization as a historical opportunity for global interdependence as a result of the integration of markets for money, finance and technology, the prominence of transnational enterprises with transport and communication and information networks which expand the globe. Put together, these processes are linked to a biosphere which reacts globally to human interventions regardless of their geographical locations. Politically, the concept of global governance is a response to what is also perceived as an expanding global civil society. As mentioned earlier, global environmental governance is part of the globalization process and has therefore been integrated into the economic, social and political processes which will prepare the globe under Agenda 21 and other environmental conventions and treaties.

Contrary to the claims put forward by the advocates of global environmental governance, McRae (1995, p. 139) reminds us that in the era of the New World Order, 'the West will bully and bribe the developing countries not to exploit their resources, or at least exploit them only in the most environmentally-friendly way possible'. Smil (1993, p. 2) is of the view that

> four centuries of the European expansion had finally encompassed the whole planet. But this end of a centuries-old quest was not an occasion for a reflection on limits and vulnerabilities of the Earth: such feelings were still far in the future, in the time of Apollo spacecraft providing the first views of the blue-white Earth against the blackness of cosmic void.

The symbolism cannot be more revealing for those who have experienced a steady decline in their standards of living and to 1.5 billion people who live under absolute poverty worldwide.

Global environmental governance is not merely about how to save the global environment, but about how to maintain the status quo which originated during the colonial legacy. Despite attempts by the dominant power-structures to depoliticize the global and the ecological, the New World Order and hence global governance have not transcended the core values of the Old World Order and its handling of policies of global influence which have for centuries reinforced the South–North divide. This demonstrates that the globalization of ecology is an extension to the colonization of nature, and both processes are implicitly expressed in an attempt to ensure mechanisms for global environmental management. Global environmental management is, therefore, encompassed in the diverse ecological, spiritual, economic and political interests served by global ecologism. In essence, the critique of global ecologism is a critique of the control over nature which has historically gone hand in hand with the control and domination of the 'other'.

CONCLUSIONS

Evidently, the current process of globalization has offered greater opportunities for capital and business élites, supported by an advanced communication and transport system, which have enabled a privileged few to operate at a global scale. However, the disproportionate glorification of this process has concealed its negative consequences on the excluded: the poor and the disadvantaged worldwide. Despite diverse and at times contradictory positions as how to save the environment, global ecologism has been adopted by and converged into a globalistic vision whose objectives are, to a large extent, consistent with those of global governance. The positive aspects of global environmental governance have been highlighted by many authors, while the negative ones are whispered or else faded away.

This chapter has presented a counter-argument to those glorifying the concept of global environmental governance. The main premise, therefore, is that *global ecologism has developed out of the North's interest in eliminating or minimizing the adverse consequences of industrialization on a global level.* However, because such a project may entail the acceptance of certain levels of pollution reduction (de- industrialization or the introduction of new technologies, both of which will have negative implications for employment in the North), the South has often been presented as the major future threat to the global environment.

The political designs of global ecologism are irrelevant to the South's interest in achieving a different pattern of development from the one prescribed by the North. The global ecological vision which may satisfy the requirements of a truly 'common future' will be attained when the North abandons the 'old ways of doing things' and changes its life-styles, including its wasteful consumption patterns. Democratic global institutions and actions could emerge only if these are based on equity and justice where global partnership is not a matter of sustainable charity, piecemeal injection of development aid, or bribery of obedient governments and signatories of global environmental treaties and conventions. By implication this means that an equitable and just globalization process cannot be attained within the confines of the New World Order and global governance, including global environmental governance. *This observation should not be understood to suggest that the critics of global ecologism and the South are ambivalent about the future and the need for a concerted effort to protect the global ecology. However, they are genuinely ambivalent about the manner in which the global and the ecological have been defined to serve the interests of an 'exclusive' Northern sustainable future.*

REFERENCES

Adams, W. M. (1990) *Green Development: Environment and Sustainability in the Third World* (London and New York: Routledge).

Agarwal, A. and Narian, S. (1991) *Global Warming in an Unequal World: A Case Study of Environmental Colonialism* (Delhi: Centre for Science and Environment).

Barbier, B., Burgess, J. C. and Folke, C. (1994) *Paradise Lost?: The Ecological Economics of Biodiversity* (London: Earthscan).

Bartelmus, P. (1994) *Environment, Growth and Development: Concepts and Strategies of Sustainability* (London and New York: Routledge).

Beck, U. (1995) *Ecological Politics in an Age of Risk* (Cambridge: Polity Press).

Beney, G. (1993) 'Gaia: "The Globalization Temptation"', in W. Sachs (ed.) (1993) *Global Ecology: A New Arena of Political Conflict* (London and Atlantic Highlands, NJ: Zed).

Bhaskar, V. and Glyn, A. (eds) (1995) *The South, The North and the Environment: Ecological Constraints and the Global Economy* (London: United Nations University Press and Earthscan).

Bookchin, M. (1980) *Towards and Ecological Society* (Montréal: Black Rose).

Bookchin, M. and Foreman, D. (1992) *Defending the Earth: A Debate between Murry Bookchin and Dave Foreman* (Montréal: Black Rose).

Brandt, W. (1980) *North–South: A Programme for Survival* (London and Sydney: Pan Books).

Brascoupe, S. (1992) 'Indigenous Perspectives on International Environment', *ALL OF US Akwe:kon*, 9, 2, Summer.

Brecher, J. and Costello, T. (1994) *Global Village or Global Pillage* (Boston, MA: South End).

Brenton, T. (1995) *The Greening of Machiavelli: The Evolution of International Environmental Politics* (London: Royal Institute of International Affairs and Earthscan).

Brown, L. R., Kane, H. and Ayres, E. (1993) *Vital Signs: The Trends that Are Shaping Our Future* (London: Earthscan).

Bunyard, P. and Morgan-Grenville, F. (eds) (1987) *The Green Alternative* (London: Methuen).

Capra, F. (1985) *The Turning Point* (London: Flamingo).

Commission on Global Governance (1995) *Our Global Neighbourhood, Report of the Commission on Global Governance* (Oxford: Oxford University Press).

De La Court, T. (1992) *Different Worlds: Environment and Development Beyond the Nineties* (Utrecht: International Books, Jan van Arkel).

Devall, B. (1980) 'The Deep Ecology Movement', *Natural Resources Journal*, 20.

Dobson, A. (1990) *Green Political Thought* (London: Harper Collins).

Down to Earth (1992) 'Rio: The Green Farce', special issue, 31 May.

Engel, J. Roland and Engel, J. Gibb (eds) (1990) *Ethics of Environment and Development: Global Challenge and International Response* (Tucson, AZ: University of Arizona Press).

Escobar, A. (1995) *Encountering Development: The Making and Unmaking of the Third World* (Princeton, NJ: Princeton University Press).

Finger, M. (1993) 'Politics of UNCED Process', in W. Sachs (ed.) (1993) *Global Ecology: A New Arena of Political Conflict* (London and Atlantic Highlands, NJ: Zed).

Fox, W. (1984) 'Deep Ecology: A New Philosophy of Our Time', *The Ecologist*, 14, 5/6.

Goldsmith, E. (1988) 'The Way: The Need for an Ecological World View', *The Ecologist*, 18, 4/5.

Gore, Al (1992) *Earth in the Balance: Ecology and the Human Spirit* (Boston and New York: Houghton Mifflin).

Harvey, R. (1995) *The Return of the Strong: The Drift to Global Disorder* (London: Macmillan).

LaDuke, W. (1992) 'Indigenous Environmental Perspectives: A North American Primer', *ALL OF US Akwe:kon*, 9, 2, Summer.

Lipietz, A. (1995) 'Enclosing the Global Commons: Global Environmental Negotiations in a North-South Conflictual Approach', in V. Bhaskar and A. Glyn (eds) (1995) *The South, The North and the Environment* (London: United Nations University Press and Earthscan).

Lohmann, L. (1993) 'Green Orientalism', *The Ecologist*, 23, 6.

MacArthy, J. (1993) 'The Rio Summit: Rhetoric and Wisdom', *Social Action*, 23, January–March.

McKibben, B. (1990) *The End of Nature* (London: Viking).

McRae, H. (1995) *The World in 2020: Power, Culture and Prosperity: A Vision of the Future* (London: Harper Collins).

Meadows, D.H., Meadows, D.L. and Randers, J. (1992) *Beyond the Limits: Global Collapse or a Sustainable Future* (London: Earthscan).

Merchant, C. (1992) *Radical Ecology* (London and New York: Routledge).

Mohamed Salih, M. A. (1993) 'The Role of Social Science in Conflict Analysis', *Nordic Journal of African Studies*, 2, 2.

Mohamed Salih, M. A. (1994) 'NGOs' Response to the Ecological Crisis in the South', in W. Mlay and A. M. Ahmed (eds) (1994) *Global Environmental Crisis and African Development* (Addis Ababa: OSSREA).

O'Riordan, T. (1981) *Environmentalism* (London: Pion).

Paterson, M. (1992) 'Global Warming', in C. Thomas (ed.) (1992) *The Environment in International Relations* (London: Royal Institute of International Affairs).

Pepper, D. (1993) *Eco-socialism: From Deep Ecology to Social Justice* (London and New York: Routledge).

Read, P. (1994) *Responding to Global Warming: The Technology, Economics and Politics of Sustainable Energy* (London and Atlantic Highlands, NJ: Zed).

Redclift, M. (1984) *Development and the Environmental Crisis: Red or Green Alternatives* (London and New York: Methuen).

Redclift, M. and Benton, T. (1995) *Social Theory and the Global Environment* (London and New York: Routledge).

Regenstein, L. G. (1991) *Replenish the Earth: A History of Organized Religion's Treatment of Animals and Nature, Including the Bible's Message of Conservation and Kindness towards Animals* (New York: Crossroad).

Rich, Bruce, (1994) *Mortgaging the Earth: The World Bank, Environmental Impoverishment and the Crisis of Development* (London: Earthscan).

Sachs, W. (ed.) (1993) *Global Ecology: A New Arena of Political Conflict* (London and Atlantic Highlands, NJ: Zed).

Sale, K. (1984) 'Mother of All: An Introduction to Bioregionalism', in S. Kumar (ed.) (1984) *The Schumacher Lectures Vol. II* (London: Blond and Briggs).

Sandbrook, R. (1987) in *Our Common Future*, The Brundtland Report (Oxford and New York: Oxford University Press).

Shiva, V. (1992) 'Recovering the Real Meaning of Sustainability', in D. E. Cooper and J. A. Palmer (eds) (1992) *The Environment in Question: Ethics and Global Issues* (London and New York: Routledge).

Shiva, V. (1993) 'The Greening of the Global Reach; Global Environment or Green Imperialism ?', in W. Sachs (ed.) (1993) *Global Ecology: A New Arena of Political Conflict* (London and Atlantic Highlands, NJ: Zed).

Sjostedt, G., Svedin, U. and B.H. Aniansson (eds) (1993) *International Environmental Negotiations: Processes, Issues and Contexts* (Stockholm: Swedish Institute of International Affairs).

Smil, V. (1993) *Global Ecology: Environmental Change and Social Flexibility* (London and New York: Routledge).

South Commission (1990) *Challenge to the South: The Report of the South Commission* (Oxford: Oxford University Press).

South Commission (1993) *Facing the Challenge* (London and Atlantic Highlands, NJ: Zed).

Taylor, R. G. (1970) *The Doomsday Book: Can the World Survive?* (London: Book Club Associates).

Thomas, C. (1992) *The Environment in International Relations* (London: Royal Institute of International Affairs).

Tolba, M. K. *et al.* (1992) *The World Environment 1972–1992: Two Decades for Challenge* (London, Glasgow, New York, Tokyo, Melbourne and Madras: Chapman and Hall for United Nations Environmental Programme).

Trainer, F. E. (1995) *Abandon Affluence* (London: Zed).

UNEP (United Nations Environment Program) (1991) *State of The Environment* (Nairobi: UNEP).

United Nations (1990) *Global Outlook 2000: Economic, Social and Environmental* (New York: United Nations Publications).

WCED (World Commission on Environment and Development) (1987) *Our Common Future* (Oxford and New York: WCED/Oxford University Press).

Weizsacker, E. U. von (1994) *Earth Politics* (London and Atlantic Highlands, NJ: Zed).

9 Fast-track Capitalism, Geoeconomic Competition, and the Sustainable Development Challenge in East Asia
Walden Bello

The explosive economic growth in the Asia-Pacific region continues to fixate the attention of economic policy-makers, corporate leaders, and academic thinkers throughout the world. For the *US economic and political establishment, East Asia has moved from being a partner in the Cold War to being a competitor for global economic hegemony.* In Europe, there is much worry in government and corporate circles about the contrast between what is fashionably termed *'Eurosclerosis'* and East *Asian dynamism. And in much of the South, 'Asian capitalism' has replaced socialism as the new paradigm of development.*

Within the region itself, *'fast-track capitalism'* has been accompanied by a region-wide consensus celebrating East Asian economic growth. This consensus is a powerful, persuasive, and ideologically hegemonic alliance of government technocrats, private interests, and established intellectuals. Today, this consensus stresses three points: that much of East and Southeast Asia has left or is leaving the Third World; that high-speed growth will mark the region far into the twenty-first century; and that East Asia will increasingly be the 'driver' of the world economy as the US and European economies continue to be marked by weak or low growth. In short, it is the Asia-Pacific's turn to be at the centre of the world stage.

But while there is a consensus on the celebration of high-speed growth and its desirability, there is intense debate on the causes of this growth and, related to this, on the policies to be followed to sustain it. Moreover, while the consensus is hegemonic, it is not total, for other voices are now questioning both the impact and the direction of high-speed growth.

143

THE FREE-MARKET EXPLANATION

Within establishment circles, *two competing schools have emerged to explain the so-called 'East Asian Miracle'*. One sees Asian growth as the flowing of *free-market policies*. (For an analysis of the way in which the human rights regime supports such policies, see Evans, Chapter 6, this volume). The other attributes it to a combination of neo-mercantilism, protectionism, and government activism that one can appropriately term *'state-assisted capitalism'*.

The *free-market model of East Asian development* is espoused by orthodox economists such as those connected with the World Bank, the International Monetary Fund (IMF), and the 'Eminent Persons' Group' identified with the Asia-Pacific Economic Cooperation (APEC) initiative. In their view, the market was the central mechanism of rapid growth in Japan and the newly industrializing countries (NICs) in the past, and freeing market forces even more fully from government controls is the key to even more dynamic growth in the future.

Currently, the free-market/free-trade approach has been institutionalized in World Bank and IMF-imposed structural adjustment programmes (SAPs) which promote radical deregulation, sweeping privatization, trade and investment liberalization, export-oriented trade and investment strategies, containment of wages, and cutting back of government expenditure. Purportedly inspired by the East Asian experience, SAPs have been generalized over the last decade to sub-Saharan Africa, North Africa, Latin America, and South Asia.

The problem with this model, say its critics, is that hardly any of the fast-growing countries of the region achieved 'NIC-hood' by following the free-market formula, except possibly Hong Kong and Singapore, which are really dependent urban economies masquerading as national economies. The Southeast Asian 'stars' of the last 10 years – Malaysia, Thailand, and Indonesia – are often portrayed in the business press as examples of growth through the implementation of liberal economic policies. But this interpretation is problematic. Certainly, these three countries did engage in some liberalization in the mid-1980s, but these programmes did not substantially reduce the state's leading economic role:

* *Malaysia*, which has been experiencing a growth rate of 10 per cent per annum in the last few years, is one of the few Third

World countries that escaped stabilization or structural adjustment by the World Bank and the IMF in the 1980s, though its leadership on its own did undertake some liberalization. For the most part, however, the Malaysian state intervened heavily in economic life to give Malaysia more control of the national economy, maintained a protectionist trade regime, and engaged in what is called 'picking winners', or targeting certain industries to develop through various incentives, including direct government participation in production. It was not unfettered market forces that produced what is now Malaysian industry's crown jewel, the Proton Saga, also known as the national car. It was a partnership between a state enterprise and the Japanese corporation Mitsubishi that produced the car as part of a state-managed rationalization of the car industry.[1] With close to 80 per cent of its components now sourced locally, the Proton Saga is trumpeted by official circles as an example of how foreign investment can be manipulated not to marginalize but to strengthen an activist government role in the economy.

* *Indonesia*'s growth rate of 5–6 per cent in recent years is often attributed by World Bank officials to free-market policies. But the reality is that economic liberalization has been quite limited, with the economy continuing to be marked by a high degree of protectionism, control by monopolies linked to key individuals or groups in government, and significant state influence on foreign investors. And while the Malaysian state has targeted the car industry, the Indonesian government has heavily subsidized the creation of an increasingly sophisticated aircraft industry, which was roundly criticized by World Bank and other neo-classical economists.[2] Recently, however, the successful test-flight of the N-250, the first Indonesian-designed and manufactured passenger plane, has impressed even the critics.

* Of all the large economies of Southeast Asia, *Thailand* is perhaps the closest to a market-dominated economy. Yet one finds the seeming anomaly that the Thai economy actually became more protectionist as it moved to a second stage of import substitution in the mid- and late 1980s, precisely the period when it began to register the 8–12 per cent growth rates that dazzled the world (Sakasakul, 1992, p. 19).

STATE-ASSISTED CAPITALISM

Dissatisfaction with both the explanatory power and prescriptive thrust of the free-market school has spawned a perspective on East Asian growth that goes in the opposite direction, to claim that state intervention in the bigger NICs or 'Near NICs' has been the central factor in the take-off of these economies. Specifically, development was produced by a strategy consisting of:

(1) strategic economic planning managed by government, exemplified in some countries by 5–10 year plans;

(2) government targeting of specific industries for development, and generous subsidy of private enterprises to support the targeted industries;

(3) building strategic economic depth by moving in a planned fashion from the development of consumer goods industries to intermediate goods and capital goods enterprises;

(4) reserving the domestic market for local entrepreneurs by maintaining tight restrictions on imports and foreign investments;

(5) adopting a mercantilist trade strategy consisting of limiting the entry of foreign imports into the domestic market while aggressively winning and dominating export markets, results in a growing trade surplus; and

(6) bold, Keynesian-style manipulation of macroeconomic mechanisms such as deficit spending, loose credit policies, massive borrowing, and strict undervaluation of the currency relative to hard currencies in order to keep exports competitive in world markets.

The mix of these policies, of course, differed from economy to economy, and in some economies some elements of these formulas were not even implemented. Taiwan, for instance, did not engage in massive foreign borrowing but resorted to the massive dollar reserves it had built up from exports. However, *the main thrust of economic policy in all the key NICs was government leadership of the economic process via activist, interventionist policies that disciplined the private sector and controlled the market.* To borrow economist Alice Amsden's phrase in her classic study of Korean industrialization, 'not only has Korea not gotten relative prices right, it has deliberately gotten them wrong' (Amsden, 1989, p. 139).

True, market mechanisms operated, but they were deliberately distorted and much inefficiency was tolerated in the short term to build up strategic economic depth. For instance, Korean technocrats deliberately violated the classical free-market principle of consumer sovereignty – 'Give the consumer the best product at the lowest price' – for the larger strategic goal of strengthening national economic sovereignty. Thus, if the price of Korean-made computers in the domestic market was three to four times that in export markets, this was in order to allow local conglomerates and monopolies to recoup the losses they incurred in battling against the formidable Japanese in highly competitive export markets.

To take another example, in contrast to the neo-classical dictum that macroeconomic stability is a key condition of growth, proponents of state-assisted capitalism see imbalance as a necessary feature of development. And they point to the fact that the heavy and chemical industry drive in Korea in the 1970s may have provoked many short-term dislocations and triggered inflation, but it also laid the basis for Korea's successful push to export capital-intensive, high-tech products like microchips and cars in the 1980s (see Bello and Rosenfield, 1991, pp. 44–57).

THEORETICAL MODELS AND ECONOMIC *REALPOLITIK*

Exasperated by what it saw as the World Bank–IMF's doctrinal commitment to the free-market/free-trade paradigm, Japan's famous Ministry of Industry (MITI) has been known to become cautiously critical of World Bank–IMF structural adjustment programmes. Japan has argued that it might be the dismantling of an activist economic role for the state through indiscriminate liberalization, deregulation, and privatization that is prolonging economic stagnation in countries being subjected to adjustment.

More important, the Japanese prodded the World Bank to review the Asian region's development experience and came forward with the bulk of funding for the study. Released in late 1993, the World Bank study, entitled *The East Asian Miracle*, grudgingly agreed that Japan, Korea, and some other NICs had not unsuccessfully employed state-activist policies such as 'picking winners', compensating market failure through subsidized loans to the private sector, and strategic protectionism. But much to the consternation of the Japanese, the World Bank asserted that these policies, while possibly successful in the earlier NICs, were not applicable to other developing countries in East Asia and elsewhere, and that they were constructive for certain countries only during a specific historical period, which had passed (World Bank, 1993).

The study's guiding lessons for countries still seeking to break out of underdevelopment was: 'It is still better not to intervene than to intervene.' Interestingly, this advice against replicating the NICs' experience with industrial policy drew the following response from a prominent critic of the free-market school:

> There is reason to worry whether the World Bank's refusal to countenance selective industrial policies for industries with high entry barriers reflects an underlying unwillingness to help developing countries enter industries that are already well-established in the West, especially when Western plants have excess capacity.... Given the governing structure of the Bank, it is not difficult to imagine why (Wade, 1994, pp. 74–5).

Some may dismiss this as crude conspiracy theory, but the Bank study's readiness to attribute success to market policies, while raising the standard of proof when it comes to assessing interventionist industrial policies, does reflect the fact that more than just academic and technocratic issues are at stake in the NIC debate.

Indeed, *the debate over models has become caught up with the ongoing trade conflict between the US and Asian economies.* The 1980s and early 1990s saw the aggressive pursuit of unilateralist trade policy in the name of free trade. Japan was, of course, a key target for the US. But practically all the other East Asian countries have been assaulted by American unilateralist trade policy. Korea, in particular, is often cited as a prima facie case of the opportunistic use of free trade to aggressively push US economic interests. In bilateral trade negotiations with Korea, free trade has been the slogan deployed by US trade negotiators in what Koreans have seen as an effort that goes beyond rectifying the trade balance to transforming the very foundations of their economy. Free trade and free markets have been invoked to legitimize an assault on a broad front that includes completely opening up an agricultural market that is already one of the US's biggest markets, doing away with restrictions on foreign investment aimed at the domestic market, limiting Korean access to high technology, and even seeking to change Korean consumer behaviour to favour imports over domestic products and consumption over saving. Appeals to free trade were, of course, coupled with the threat to invoke Super 301 and Special 301 provisions of the US Trade Act, which mandated the president to take retaliatory action against 'unfair traders' and 'intellectual pirates'.

Though they were not subjected to a full-court press in the same way Korea was, the other Asian countries were also subjected to the US trade offensive. Taiwan, Singapore, and Hong Kong were 'graduated' from the General System of Preferences (GSP), which accorded developing countries preferential tariff rates. The US also forced Taiwan to revalue its currency to make its products more expensive to US consumers, subjected a number of its electronics exporters to additional duties on anti-dumping grounds, imposed tight limits on its farm and textile exports, and placed it on the Special 301 watch list.

Indonesia was also placed on the Special 301 watch list for prohibiting foreign film distributors from directly importing or distributing their films in the country.

As for Thailand, it lost up to $644 million in GSP benefits following the US Department of Commerce's determination that it 'did not fully provide adequate and effective intellectual property protection' (US Dept of Commerce, 1992, p. 241). The country was also designated a 'Priority Foreign Country' under Special 301. Some US moves indeed bordered on the outrageous and absurd, as when the US Trade Representative's Office made Thailand the target of investigation for allegedly 'exploiting its [monsoon] climate to hold on to the number one slot in world rice export markets'. The investigation was triggered by the American Paddy and Rice Industry League's claim that '[t]he last straw was the 1988 logging ban in Thailand', a move which 'would further reduce the opportunity for the US to gain its rightful place as the world's top rice exporter' (*Bangkok Post*, 1992, p. 25). The logging ban, it must be noted, was enacted to reverse the rapid rate of deforestation that is producing an ecological calamity in that country.

APEC AS A BATTLEGROUND

The Asian political and economic élites' suspicion of the free-market/free-trade model and their increasing identification with state-assisted capitalism was recently heightened by US initiatives connected with the Asia Pacific Economic Cooperation (APEC), a loose consultative grouping founded in 1989. At the first APEC summit in Seattle in November 1993, Washington, backed by Australia, pushed hard to have the association transformed from a consultative forum to a formal trading bloc with a timetable for the disappearance of trade and investment barriers. This effort, which was also promoted heavily at the second summit in Bogor, Indonesia, a year later, has been seen almost universally by Asian governments as an 'end run', to borrow a term from American football – as a US effort to outmanoeuvre them by institutionalizing, via a multilateral organization, the free-trade agenda that it had been trying to force the Asians to swallow in bilateral trade negotiations.

A key element in the American game plan was the creation of an APEC 'Eminent Persons' Group' (EPG), to provide the intellectual muscle for the creation of an APEC free-trade area. Made up largely of pro-free trade economists, technocrats and policy-makers from the APEC member countries, this quasi-official body was largely set up, with the blessings of the US trade bureaucracy, by Dr Fred Bergsten, head of the Washington-based Institute of International Economics, to push the US free-trade agenda. A stalwart of Washington's economics establishment, Bergsten is widely known as an unabashed promoter of US economic interests via free trade, and he has served as a lobbyist not only for APEC but for the General Agreement on Tariffs and Trade (GATT) and the North American Free Trade Area (NAFTA). In Bergsten's view, according to one report on his comments to a forum in Washington, DC, 'Given the fact that all of the countries in the region, outside North America in particular, have lots of trade barriers... very little would actually be required from the United States'. Thus, 'trade liberalization or moving to totally free trade in the region means enormous competitive gain to the United States'(Kyodo News Agency, 1994).

With aggressive self-promotion, Bergsten and the EPG managed to project themselves as a quasi-official body pushing a multilateral consensus rather than a body whose ideological agenda coincides with the US trade agenda. The blueprint they have come out with, the so-called '2020 Plan', was, in fact, adopted at the Bogor Summit in November 1994. The '2020 Plan' would commit APEC member countries to the formation of a free-trade area, eliminating all trade and investment barriers among them by the year 2020. But the surface unanimity of the document, in fact, masked deep rifts among the participants. The US, Australia, New Zealand, Canada, Mexico, and Chile are earnest believers in the 2020 Plan. But these countries are seen by Asian technocrats as the outsiders seeking to gatecrash the party known as the 'East Asian Miracle'. For most of the so-called 'core' Asian members of APEC, agreeing to a statement that was long on vision but vague on implementation was less a declaration of belief than a relatively costless manoeuvre to accommodate American economic power. Indeed, shortly after the Bogor declaration, Thai and Malaysian officials declared that the 2020 Declaration was 'non-binding'.

In response to the APEC free-trade area initiative, the Southeast Asian governments moved to speed up the timetable for their own sub-regional trading bloc, the ASEAN Free Trade Area (AFTA). But more dramatic was the Malaysian Prime Minister's proposal to create the East Asia Economic Group (EAEG), a regional trade bloc that would include the ASEAN countries, China, Korea and Japan but exclude Australia, Canada, the United States, and the Latin American countries. EAEG resonated with the East Asian and Southeast Asian élites, and the reason it did so was that it addressed a central problem: the Asia-Pacific economies were becoming an integrated production base but many of the economies of the region continued to be dependent on the US as their principal market. With Washington becoming more and more unilateralist in trade policy towards them, government and business élites realized more and more their deep vulnerability to US trade retaliation. EAEG promised to make the region itself the main market for its production, accelerating what was already a trend: the trade among the Western Pacific economies was growing faster than their trade with other regions. In 1994, for instance, Southeast Asia had overtaken the US to become Korea's biggest export market, while, despite an official ban on direct transportation links, Taiwan's exports to China were expected to match in value those to the US. Earlier, Japan's trade with Asia had overtaken its trade with the US.

The US response was, of course, predictable. 'We can never approve this regionalism which is designed to split the Asian-Pacific region and divide Japan and the United States', then Secretary of State James Baker asserted when Malaysian Prime

Minister Mahathir first floated the proposal in 1991. The Japanese response has been a mixture of positive statements about the goals of EAEG coupled with a studied hesitation to explicitly endorse the formation – to the chagrin of Mahathir. Japan's reticence is understandable. Endorsing EAEG would earn it the wrath of the US, something it cannot at the moment afford. Indeed, for the Japanese the ideal situation is neither EAEG nor the APEC free-trade area but the status quo, which one might characterize as a *de-facto* trade and investment bloc dominated by Japan.

THE REGIONALIZATION OF THE JAPANESE ECONOMY

This *de-facto* integration of the region around the Japanese economy can be traced to the Plaza Accord of the mid-1980s, when Japan was forced by the US and Europe to get the yen to appreciate *vis-à-vis* the dollar and other hard currencies in a draconian effort to reduce their trade surpluses with the former. With the rise in production costs in Japan that this move automatically produced, Japanese manufacturers, in an effort to remain competitive in the US and other export markets, transferred a substantial part of their manufacturing operations to cheap labour sites in East and Southeast Asia. Between 1985 and 1990, for instance, some $40 billion worth of Japanese investment swirled through the region, in the process creating an impressive integrated regional platform composed of the Japanese conglomerates' complementary manufacturing operations located in different countries.

With the continuing rise in the value of the yen relative to the dollar, the transfer of Japan's industrial operations to that region has accelerated, so that many analysts now talk about the 'hollowing out' of Japan (*Far Eastern Economic Review*, 1995, pp. 28–45). A survey of over 140 firms carried out by the Japan Machinery Exporters' Association in mid-1994 'revealed that their companies expected their Japan-based production to decrease by eight per cent during the period FY 1992–1994, while their Asian-based production rose by 41 per cent (Cronin, 1994, p. 23). By the end of that period, production in Asia was expected to reach the equivalent of a quarter of the surveyed firms' domestic production (Cronin, 1994, p. 23). For some companies, in fact, overseas production had already outstripped production in their domestic factories; for example, the

Japanese electronics producer Aiwa now manufactures 90 per cent of its output at Asian sites (*Republika* (Jakarta), 1995).

One dimension of the Japanese sponsored regional integration taking place is horizontal; that is, splitting up the production of different goods or the components of one product among different countries. In Matsushita's strategy, for instance, each country is assigned specific items to produce for export: colour TVs and electric irons in Malaysia, semiconductors in Singapore, and dry-cell batteries, floppy disk drives, and electronic capacitors in the Philippines (Steven, 1990, p. 116). A more functional level of integration has been undertaken by car companies like Nissan, Toyota, and Mitsubishi. In Toyota's scheme, Indonesia specializes in petrol engines and stamped parts, Malaysia turns out steering links and electrical equipment, the Philippines produces transmissions, and Thailand manufactures diesel engines, stamped parts, and electrical equipment.[3]

In addition to integration along lines of product specialization, a process of backward integration is tightening the links of the region to the core economy. In the first phase of this process, which began in the mid-1980s, Japanese automobile and consumer electronics firms relocated their plants to the region. This was followed by the outmigration of smaller Japanese companies that supply parts and components for the automobile and electronics manufacturers. A third phase of backward integration may be about to begin, with the relocation of heavy and chemical industries that provide basic inputs to both the big assemblers and their suppliers (*This Is* (Tokyo), 1992).

Describing the process, one prominent Japanese diplomat, Hisahiko Okazaki, noted: 'Japan is creating an exclusive Japanese market in which Asia-Pacific nations are incorporated in the so-called *keiretsu* [financial/industrial bloc] system' (*This Is* (Tokyo), 1992). The essential relationship between Japan and Southeast Asia, he contended, is one of trading 'captive imports, such as products from plants in which the Japanese have invested', in return for 'captive exports, such as necessary equipment and materials' (*This Is* (Tokyo), 1992).

But *unlike the American design of integration via free trade, the Japanese design of integration via investment has not demanded that the Asian governments change their investment laws.* It has not required that they reduce their tariffs. It has not stipulated that they end their subsidies for local firms. It is all very informal, 'very Asian', say envious US trade officials. As one Washington-based government analyst put it, 'the Japanese don't need free trade' to create a trading and investment bloc (Nanto, 1989, p. 10).

As a result, although Asian governments and business groups occasionally bemoan the lack of technology transfer from the Japanese, most feel that they have a more strategic partnership with Japan than with the US, though the US continues to be the main export market for many of them. And while some may be upset at Japan's refusal to endorse the EAEG, they are likely to work with the Japanese behind the scenes to slow down, if not sabotage, the 2020 Plan.

Increasingly, *what Asian technocrats feel is at stake are not just trade relationships but their way of organizing economic life.* The 2020 Plan is ultimately threatening not only because the US may regain a strong foothold in Asian markets but because the ideology and strategy of free trade that underpins it aims to dismantle the system of state-assisted capitalism that, in their view, has been responsible for their success. Indeed, in view of Jeffrey Garaten, the US Under-Secretary of Commerce, the Clinton Administration must draw the line in the sand and counter 'the demonstration effect Japan is having on the rest of Asia... [I]t's already been made into a model for China and other up-and-coming countries' (quoted in Hirsh, 1995, p. 45).

Underneath the diplomatic manoeuvrings in Seattle, Jakarta and the Osaka Summit in November 1995 has been a struggle between contrasting ways of capitalist organization and the ideologies legitimizing these 'capitalisms'. Perhaps one of the best analyses of the implications of this conflict is provided by an Australian commentator, Kenneth Davidson, who writes that:

> The unstated Anglo-Saxon assumption behind APEC is that if the Anglo-Saxon countries can persuade Asian countries to play the economic development game according to Anglo-Saxon rules, the game will be translated into a neoclassical, laissez-faire, positive-sum game in which the players will be transmuted from countries or tribes into firms and individuals (Davidson, 1994, p. 19).

However, managed capitalism of the Asian variety, Davidson continues, is proving more successful than the Anglo-Saxon variety and 'more resistant to cultural and political convergence imposed by globalizing forces and the growth in Asian living standards that many in the West had hoped'. In this context the Australian–American goal at APEC is 'to try to get the Asian winners of the economic game to deny the cultural basis of their success in order to create the conditions whereby the losers can become winners' (Davidson, 1994, p. 19).

On the other hand, the Japanese and East Asian game plan is to emasculate any attempt to make APEC a free-trade area, deflecting its energies instead to becoming an Organization for Economic Development (OCED) of the Pacific, a largely consultative group that would co-ordinate on eliminating not tariff and investment restrictions but 'technical barriers' to trade.

THE SUSTAINABLE DEVELOPMENT CRITIQUE

While regional élites have battled to define the direction of Asia-Pacific development along free-market lines or along the lines of state-assisted capitalism, many NGOs, people's movements, and progressive academics have, over the last few years, evolved a powerful critique of both approaches. *The essence of this critique is that despite some very real differences, the free-market model and the Asian capitalist or NIC model have more to unite them than to divide them*:

(1) Both the free-market and NIC models fetishize economic growth as the be-all and end-all of development.
(2) Both intrinsically generate and perpetuate social inequality even as, in the case of the Asian capitalist model, rapid growth takes place. Indeed, high growth rates are necessary to allow a rise in absolute incomes without having to undertake redistribution of wealth. This conjunction of a rise in absolute income and worsening income distribution has characterized Korea, Taiwan, Singapore and Thailand in the last 20 years.[4]
(3) Both models – again intrinsically – are ecologically destructive and unsustainable. In the case of the market approach, there is a rundown of natural capital since ecological costs are typically not factored into the real costs of production. And in the case of NIC capitalism, there has been a deliberate sacrifice of the environment to attract local and foreign capital in order to deliver high-speed growth. Indeed, the prospect of zero investment in pollution control is one of the two cornerstones of the NIC model, the other being cheap labour. In the NICs,

market and state, in fact, act in a complementary fashion to create an accelerated plunder of the environment. In Taiwan, the policy of decentralized industrialization decreed by the KMT government pushed small and medium industries to settle helter-skelter throughout the country, in residential areas and close to waterways, in the process decentralizing pollution and converting the island into an ecological wasteland. In Thailand, the market, private interests, and state policy have created the convergence of two ecological catastrophes: massive deforestation and massive water pollution.

(4)   Both strategies have detrimental effects on agricultural communities, with both market signals and state policy channelling capital and personnel from agriculture to industry and promoting terms of trade adverse to agriculture. In Korea and Taiwan, agriculture is on its last legs, while in Thailand and the Philippines it is entering severe crisis.

(5)   Both approaches have very destructive effects on communities: in the case of the market approach, because of the dissolving effect of unchecked market forces on communal and community bonds; in the case of the NIC model of state-assisted capitalism, through the deliberate breaking up and resettling of organic communities that stand in the way of state-managed development projects. In Thailand, the Philippines, Indonesia, and Malaysia, the story is depressingly similar: big dam schemes imposed from the centre, uprooting and resettlement of communities, particularly indigenous communities, and the gradual erosion and silent destruction of resettled communities.

THAILAND AS NEGATIVE PARADIGM

Thailand, which only a few years ago was proclaimed as an example to the Third World during the 1991 World Bank–IMF conference in Bangkok, has become instead an example of the unsustainable character of the high-speed growth model among many NGOs concerned with development.

*   Bangkok booms, but the gap in average income between rural people and urban people widens each year. Thailand's growth

indeed benefits largely the 15 per cent of the population concentrated in the Bangkok metropolitan region.

* Bangkok prospers but the north-east of the country stagnates, with a significant part of the latter's population converted into cheap labour for the industrial sector of the capital region. Many north-eastern villages are said to now be made up largely of grandchildren and grandparents who are sustained by remittances from the middle generation that is for all intents and purposes resident in Bangkok.

* Bangkok grows rapidly, but this growth is fuelled by the rundown of natural capital, with the area of the country covered by forests down to less than 20 per cent, from 60 per cent in the 1950s. Rapid growth has also led to what many call Thai 'resource imperialism', with Thai entrepreneurs now leading the plunder of the timber resources of Burma, Laos, and Cambodia.

* Bangkok's industrial growth is impressive, but air and water pollution are out of control, with the lower reaches of the mighty Chao Phraya River now considered 'biologically dead' and the Gulf of Thailand believed to be in a state of irreversible crisis. So serious is the pollution problem that government planners are seeking to decentralize it in the guise of de-centralizing industry!

* Bangkok is indeed a great, vibrant city, but unplanned growth has brought it to a standstill, so that planners are now thinking of setting up a new politico-administrative capital at some distance from the Bangkok metropolitan area.

TOWARDS AN ALTERNATIVE DEVELOPMENT STRATEGY

Dissatisfaction with both the free-market and NIC models is increasingly becoming vocal, especially among NGOs and peoples' organizations. East Asian NGOs have often been criticized as being long on critique and short on prescription. This has, however, changed in the last few years. Though their ways of expressing them may vary, NGOs throughout the region are beginning to articulate a similar set of core ideas that, for want of a better term, come under the rubric of 'sustainable development'. (See also Lohmann, Chapter 12, this volume and

Gyawali, Chapter 11, this volume for similar South Asian examples.)

(1) In opposition to the blind play of market forces in the free-market approach and to state fiat in the NIC model, the sustainable development perspective would make transparent, rational, and democratic decision-making the fundamental mechanism of production, distribution, and exchange.

(2) In contrast to the impersonal control by the 'invisible hand' of the market and the hierarchical and centralizing thrust of decision-making in the NIC model, the sustainable development model would decentralize economic decision-making and management to communities, regions, or ecological zones, and make national planning a bottom-up process.

(3) In opposition to the premium put on economic growth by the free market and NIC models, the sustainable development model de-emphasizes growth in favour of equity, the quality of life, and ecological harmony.

(4) Whereas both the free-market and NIC models are heavily biased towards urban-based industry, sustainable development would make agriculture and the reinvigoration of rural society the centrepiece of the development process.

(5) Whereas in both the free-market and NIC models, the pursuit of profitability dictates the adoption of capital-intensive high technology in industry and chemical-intensive technology in agriculture, the sustainable development approach would try to reverse what it considers uncontrolled technological change at the expense of the people, favouring the development of labour- intensive appropriate technology for industry and organic, chemical-free agro-technology.

(6) Whereas in the free-market model, the private sector calls the shots and in the NIC model, the state-big business partnership has a 'duopoly' over political and economic decision- making, the sustainable development approach would organize the popular sector, represented by NGOs, as the third pillar of the political and economic system – as a balance to state and business in the short term, but with the perspective of making it the dominant force in the triad in the long term.

(7) Finally, in contrast to a property system based on the division between private and public ownership in both the free-market and NIC models, the sustainable development approach

growth. Articulating this alternative future is, more than ever, a necessity. While the rampant consumerism that comes with high-speed growth continues to dazzle many in Asia, there is a growing feeling that a process which is accompanied by the decline of agriculture, increasing inequality, and uncontrolled ecological degradation is a recipe for an unliveable future.

NOTES

1. See the excellent analysis of Robert Doner (1987), pp. 511–96.
2. For an interesting account of the development of the aircraft industry, see *The Australian* (1994). See also McBeth (1995).
3. Diagram provided by Toyota Motor Company.
4. For these figures see Bello and Rosenfeld (1991).

REFERENCES

Amsden, A. (1989) *Asia's Next Giant: South Korea and Late Industrialization* (New York: Oxford University Press).

The Australian (1994), 'Hero Flying High on Indonesia's First Passenger Plane', 10 November, p. 15.

Bangkok Post (1992) 'Environment, Industry Groups Resist US Trade Accusations', 1 April, p. 26, reproduced in *FBIS Environment Report*, May 1992, p. 25.

Bello, W. and Rosenfield, S. (1991) *Dragons in Distress: Asia's Miracle Economies in Crisis* (London: Penguin).

Cronin, R. (1994) *Japan and US Economic Involvement in Asia and the Pacific: Comparative Data and Analysis* (Washington, DC: Congressional Research Service), 27 September.

Davidson, K. (1994), 'Hard Lessons Ahead as We Learn to Deal with Asia', *The Age*, 15 November, p. 19.

Doner, R. (1987) 'Domestic Coalitions and Japanese Auto Firms in Southeast Asia' (University of Michigan, Ann Arbor: Ph.D. dissertation).

Far Eastern Economic Review (1995), 'Nippon's Choice', 8 June, pp. 38–45.

Hirsh, M. (1995) 'The Great Debate', *Newsweek*, 1 May, p. 45.

Kyodo News Agency (1994), 'APEC to Fulfill U.S. Goals', 2 November, reproduced in *FBIS Environment Report*, 3 November 1994, p. 1.

McBeth, J. (1995) 'In the Clouds', *Far Eastern Economic Review*, 24 August, p. 47.

Nanto, D. (1989) *Pacific Rim Economic Cooperation* (Washington, DC: Congressional Research Service), 3 April.

Republika (Jakarta) (1995), 'Region Expects Greater Japanese Investment', 10 March, reproduced in *FBIS Environment Report*, 14 March, p. 57.

Sakasakul, C. (1992) *Lessons from the World Bank's Experience of Structural Adjustment Loans: A Case Study of Thailand* (Bangkok: Thailand Development Research Institute).

Steven, R. (1990) *Japan's New Imperialism* (Armonk, NY: M.E. Sharpe).

This Is (Tokyo) (1992) 'New Strategies Toward Super-Asian Bloc', August, reproduced in *FBIS Environment Report*, October, p. 18.

US Dept of Commerce (1992) 'Thailand', Washington, DC.

Wade, R (1994) 'Selective Industrial Policies in East Asia: Is the East Asian Miracle Right?', in A. Fishlow (ed.) (1994) *Miracle or Design: Lessons from the East Asian Experience* (Washington, DC: Overseas Development Council).

World Bank (1993) *The East Asian Miracle* (New York: Oxford University Press).

10 The World Bank's Finances: an International Debt Crisis

Patricia Adams

INTRODUCTION

Western governments that jointly own the World Bank with Third World governments have turned a blind eye to the perverse set of financial incentives and responsibilities on which the institution rests. *The World Bank, the single largest source of development finance for Third World leaders and, according to Standard and Poor, itself 'one of the world's largest borrowers', has played financial charades to hide irresponsible lending and to appear fiscally sound* (quote from Standard and Poor's Credit Analysis Service, 1993).

Because of the industrialized countries' uncritical support, and because of its own iron-clad constitution, the *Bank faces little or no incentive to behave responsibly.* That spells tragedy for people in the developing world affected by the Bank's uneconomic 'development' projects and hardship for Western taxpayers who unwittingly hold the world's riskiest loan portfolio and over $100 billion in liabilities.[1]

CRACKS IN THE WORLD BANK'S FINANCIAL EDIFICE

In 1985 two World Bank agencies – the International Bank for Reconstruction and Development (IBRD), which operates on a near-commercial basis, and the International Development Association (IDA), the World Bank's concessionary loan wing – approved a $450 million loan to help India finance a massive irrigation–hydroelectric scheme on the Narmada River. With over 3,000 dams and a labyrinth of canals that would forcibly displace over one million people, the project offended almost everyone.

Public outrage within India over the World Bank's stubborn support for the megaproject led to a *'Quit India' campaign* – a revival of Gandhi's campaign against British colonial rule – to expel the World Bank. International outrage over the project, meanwhile, was threatening the World Bank's bid for an $18 billion capital fix for the IDA from the Western countries that periodically refill the association's coffers. Both Finland and Canada cut their contributions, and the US Congress – the World Bank's biggest benefactor – was threatening to withhold its hefty 20 per cent share of the IDA's budget.[2] *An independent project review, financed by the World Bank itself to quell critics, backfired*: it confirmed that the project would perform poorly and impoverish some 240,000 people whose land would be swallowed up by the dam complex (Morse and Berger, 1992). *The project, and especially Sardar Sarovar, the largest of the Narmada dams, had become an albatross around the World Bank's neck.*

But the World Bank could not walk away from the project without offending the Indian Government. Faced with a balance-of-payments crisis and public opposition to its economic reform package, the Indian Government was also furious with foreign environmentalists' meddling in its sovereign affairs and with the World Bank over Sardar Sarovar. In a daring game of financial brinkmanship, *India threatened to default on its World Bank debts* if the Bank stopped supporting the dam (Rich, 1994, p. 254). As *the World Bank's biggest borrower, the Indian Government had it over a barrel: an Indian default would put 15 per cent of the World Bank's entire portfolio in the limbo of nonaccrual status, threatening the IBRD with its first annual loss* (World Bank, 1993b, pp. 194–5, 214–15).[3]

The World Bank clumsily capitulated in March 1993. After nearly a decade of controversy, and after India had failed to satisfy the loan's requirement for a comprehensive resettlement plan, the Bank cancelled the remaining $170 million in disbursements for Sardar Sarovar to appease its critics. Almost simultaneously, to please its client state, the World Bank offered India over ten times as much as the cancelled loan, half of it not pegged to specific projects with their potential for embarrassmen but for the general purposes of the Indian Government (IBRD Deputy Secretary, 1993, pp. 128–9). The Indians won that showdown with the Bank, which could not risk the unknown world that lay beyond a major borrower's going into arrears. (For more on the World Bank and hydro projects, see Gyawali, Chapter 11, this volume.)

THE BANK FROM BRETTON WOODS

Buckling to pressure over a dam project seemed uncharacteristic of the World Bank, an institution considered the world's most unflappable financier. With a *reputation for imposing discipline on its borrowers*, for cool-headed, unsentimental economic analysis, and with an unshakeable AAA credit rating, *the World Bank, particularly the IBRD, had always seemed the most prudent of financial institutions.*

Established 51 years ago at Bretton Woods, New Hampshire, by John Maynard Keynes and the world's leaders, *the IBRD finances its roughly $16-billion annual lending operations primarily from borrowings that are 100 per cent backed by its member governments.* Such bond-rating institutions as Standard and Poor's, which rates IBRD bonds AAA, credit 'strong membership support' with 'virtually eliminating the possibility of insolvency'.[4] The IBRD then lends money – $103 billion is now outstanding – to developing countries at just below commercial interest rates (World Bank, 1995a, p. 2).

In contrast to the IBRD's near-commercial loans, the IDA provides 'soft loans' – long-term loans (35 to 40 years) at no interest (but with a 0.75 per cent annual 'service charge') – to the Bank's poorer members. Unlike those of the IBRD, IDA's lending operations – about $6 billion annually, $62 billion in total – are funded by triennial grants from its rich-country members (World Bank, 1994, pp. 198–200).

Although the IBRD and the IDA are two legally and financially distinct entities, they are known colloquially as the 'World Bank': they publish one joint annual report, and the staff who prepare loans and the executive directors who approve them are identical. Over the years, 63 countries have borrowed from both the IDA and the IBRD, and some projects, such as Sardar Sarovar, received financing from both.

Because capital infusions to the IDA are regular and more frequent than those to the IBRD, they more often attract public ire. But the IBRD created taxpayer liabilities, which are hidden from public view, that exceed IDA replenishments. The US Treasury's backing of the IBRD – approximately $28 billion (compared to $20 billion in IDA contributions since 1960) – has not been supported with appropriations since 1981, despite the sizable liability should the IBRD's borrowers, who defaulted on their commercial bank loans in the 1980s, do so with IBRD loans.[5]

The IBRD spares no effort to dispel worry over defaults. In its Information Statement (a prospectus for potential bond purchasers), the IBRD reassures investors that it 'does not make loans which, in its opinion, cannot be justified on economic grounds'. It boasts of having 'never written off any of its outstanding loans', nor will it reschedule loans as have other, by implication less adroit, financiers (World Bank, 1995a, pp. 10, 17). And, the IBRD is quick to point out, its *'preferred-creditor' status* ensures it gets paid back first, ahead of all other creditors.

All these factors contribute to the IBRD's blue-chip reputation. As Standard and Poor's quarterly credit report explains,

> both borrowing and nonborrowing member countries have powerful incentives to support the bank. Borrowing countries treat the bank as a preferred creditor to safeguard access to financing from the World Bank Group .... Nonborrowing countries enhance their relationships with developing countries by supporting the bank, and they may help develop new markets for their own exports in the process.[6]

All World Bank loans carry sovereign guarantees.

No factor contributes more to the IBRD's blue-chip status than do *pledges, by the IBRD's rich-country members, to repay bondholders should the IBRD's Third World borrowers default.* IBRD loans can therefore be money losers without affecting the IBRD's credit rating. *Money-losing loans, as it turns out, have been the order of the day.*

'STEADY AND PERVASIVE' DECLINE IN BANK'S LOAN PORTFOLIO

Evidence gathered by internal reviews, independent critiques, and an army of concerned citizens from around the world gives the lie to IBRD claims of supporting only economically viable projects.

The first outside, independent assessment of a World Bank project ever made – of India's Sardar Sarovar dam and irrigation complex – documented year after year of bureaucratic deception, incompetence, and negligence (Morse and Berger, 1992). Engineering studies to determine the dam's viability were never completed, and when it came to environmental matters, the review team accused the World Bank of 'gross delinquency'. The review team also rejected the argument that Sardar Sarovar was atypical, stating that 'the problems besetting the Sardar Sarovar Projects are more the rule than the exception [for] resettlement operations supported by the Bank in India'. In general, the review team concluded, 'assertions have been substituted for analysis' (Morse and Berger, 1992, pp. xxiv, 53, 234).

A flood of more damning evidence soon followed the review team's findings. In 1992 a leaked internal report, commissioned by then World Bank President Lewis Preston to investigate project quality, confirmed that the problems plaguing the Sardar Sarovar project were bank-wide.

That *report, prepared by high-ranking World Bank official Willi Wapenhans, found over one-third of the World Bank's $140 billion in projects to be failing and that deterioration of the Bank's loan portfolio was 'steady and pervasive'* (Portfolio Management Task Force, 1992b, p. 4).[7] *'The portfolio is under pressure', and 'this pressure is not temporary; it is attributable to deep-rooted problems',* the report explained (Portfolio Management Task Force, 1992a, p. 4). In a June 1992 presentation to members of the World Bank's Board of Executive Directors, Wapenhans declared, *'There is reason to be concerned!'* (Wapenhans, 1992).

Among Wapenhans's 'deep-rooted problems' were the World Bank's 'systematic and growing bias towards excessively optimistic rate of return expectations at appraisal' and an 'approval culture' in which 'staff perceive appraisals as marketing devices for securing loan approval (and achieving personal recognition)'. 'Appraisal,' observed Wapenhans with dismay, 'becomes advocacy' (Portfolio Management Task Force, 1992a, pp. iii, 4, 12).

What critics had long suspected was now confirmed at the World Bank's most senior level − *the Bank's investment analysis was shoddy, biased, and in some cases cooked to make unsustainable projects appear viable.* Instead of detached economics' calling the shots, everything was seen through rose-coloured spectacles by bureaucrats and borrowers out to build empires.

Wapenhans also found that the World Bank fails to carry out projects properly; he described borrowers' non-compliance with legal loan covenants, especially financial covenants (such as a failure to undertake proper financial audits), as 'gross' and 'overwhelming' (Portfolio Management Task Force, 1992a, p. 8). Between 1967 and 1989, for example, borrowers had complied with only 25 per cent of the financial covenants for the Bank's water-supply projects.

The World Bank's failure to live by its own creed of economic efficiency became front-page news. Bank projects might be reputed to ravage the earth's environment, but the public believed their economics justified them. *For the first time, a comprehensive study of World Bank projects had been conducted, and by the Bank's own analysis, here was evidence that its loans contributed, not to the wealth of nations, but to their impoverishment.*[8]

Impoverished nations, Wapenhans would have understood, make poor credit risks, which renders the World Bank's portfolio suspect. The state of the World Bank's own affairs, however, could not be attributed to the impoverishment of its clientele; its financial disarray was entirely of its own making.

STRUCTURAL ADJUSTMENT LOANS: ROUND-TRIPPING LOANS

The technique of paying off old debts with new borrowings, or otherwise obfuscating puffed-up asset values, generally enjoys a limited life. But its attraction may be irresistible: as long as new money satisfies old obligations, a lender's operations will appear financially solid. The World Bank is well-schooled in the technique; its tools are 'adjustment loans'.

When Third World countries began to default on their loans in the early 1980s, the World Bank shifted its lending to keep creditors — including itself — at bay. Instead of funding only specific projects, the World Bank began providing what are known as 'adjustment loans'. Third World countries receive those loans to pay for imports, even routine imports such as oil, in order to free other monies to repay debts. The adjustment money thus makes a round trip — from the World Bank in Washington to a Third World country and then back to the West, where much of it repays various creditors.

Those loans now represent approximately one-fifth of the World Bank's portfolio. In principle, they are supposed to help Third World countries make market-oriented adjustments to their economies; in practice, even the World Bank is at a loss to explain how those loans help Third World economies 'adjust'.

CONVERTING PRIVATE TO PUBLIC DEBT: THE BAKER AND BRADY PLANS

To stem the Third World's debt crisis, the US enlisted the World Bank and the International Monetary Fund (IMF) to administer its debt-workout plans, relieving commercial banks of the need to privately resolve their delinquent debts with Third World borrowers.[9]

From 1985 to 1988, under Secretary of the US Treasury James A. Baker's plan to replace private with public debt, commercial banks were repaid $17 billion more per year from the Third World than they lent, while government sources (including the World Bank, the IMF, and rich governments) paid out $700 million per year more than they received.[10] That 'slow transfer of relative LDC [less developed country] debt exposure from the commercial banks to Western taxpayers' was accomplished 'by using international institutions', says the Cato Institute's Melanie Tammen (Tammen, 1990, p. 248). 'As LDCs' private bankers increasingly pull the plug, the IMF and the World Bank are opening the spigot' (p. 250).

> While all money is fungible, this nonproject-related assistance is highly fungible. Indeed, the amount of a policy-based loan (or package of them) is determined solely by the size of a debtor nation's financing gap in a given period – a clear signal that the funds are largely used for private debt service (p. 249, note 10).

To pay for the private-sector bail-out, in 1988 IBRD shareholders contributed $75 billion – the IBRD's largest ever general capital increase. Debt expert Jeffrey Sachs, an adviser to Third World governments and international financial agencies, called the increase an 'explicit taxpayer contribution' to commercial bank interest payments. Although the World Bank had not written off outstanding loans, Sachs stated that 'so far, the official creditors [i.e. the taxpayers] have not suffered explicit losses, but rather losses that are implicit in new loans to uncreditworthy borrowers' (Sachs, 1989, p. 14).

Through those round-trip loans, Third World countries got deeper into debt; the World Bank held more of that debt, since it lent more new money than it received; and the private banks – the Chase Manhattans, Lloyds, and Deutsche Banks – were owed less, since old loans were being repaid while new loans were not extended. *Round-trip loans thus transferred the Third World's debt from the private sector to the public sector.*

Treasury Secretary Baker's successor, Nicholas Brady, continued the strategy of strengthening private banks at the expense of the portfolios of international institutions. Since March 1989 the IBRD has lent $3.3 billion under the 'Brady plan' to help restructure over half the developing 31 countries' total commercial bank debt (World Bank, 1993–94, vol. 1, p. 36). Under the Brady plan, commercial banks reduce either the outstanding principal or the amount of interest payable on their sovereign loans. The discounted principal and interest payments (converted into 'Brady bonds') are then secured by US Treasury bonds purchased with money borrowed from the IBRD, the IMF, and some bilateral contributors, such as Japan. The Brady plan has also provided IBRD loans to enable Third World countries to buy back their now-discounted commercial debt on secondary markets.[11]

The conversion of private bank debts to debts owed to multilateral institutions is only building up to a new debt crisis, which could force World Bank asset write-downs. One senior bank official, concerned about its risky portfolio, privately conceded to the *International Economy* in 1989 that, given increased overall lending to the highly indebted countries and the emphasis on adjustment loans, 'there's little doubt that the overall risk to the Bank and Fund has gone up. Anyone who says otherwise is a liar or a fool or maybe both' (Hager, 1989, p. 55).

Despite the rash of bad news about the World Bank's mismanaged projects and its increasing vulnerability to high-risk debtors, the IBRD's AAA credit rating remains unscathed. (The IDA, which does not raise funds in capital markets, has no credit rating.) Any other bank with such a disastrous portfolio would soon see its credit rating slashed and its investors flee. But the World Bank is unlike any other bank.

A QUIET WORLD BANK BAIL-OUT

Rather than a financial powerhouse governed by market discipline and exercising investment prowess, the World Bank is a financial cripple propped up by state guarantees and disguised government bail-outs.

Because all World Bank loans have sovereign guarantees from borrowing governments, the World Bank does not depend on the viability of the projects being financed. 'With such a setup', says long-time Bank critic Bruce Rich in his recent book *Mortgaging the Earth*, 'it makes no difference whether the projects the Bank lends for are well managed or mismanaged, or whether some or all of the money disappears' (Rich, 1994, p. 256).

The sovereign guarantees, in turn, are bolstered by routine transfers from the rich countries, disguising the fact that the World Bank, with the riskiest loan portfolio in the world, is a financial house of cards that could crumble at the slightest tremor.

Having seen to the bail-out of the private banks, and to maintain the disguise, the World Bank's members now need to bail out the World Bank itself – a situation that sends all concerned into denial.

TAXPAYERS PAY FOR THE BANK'S PREFERRED-CREDITOR STATUS

A 1992 investigation by the Canadian auditor general (a parliamentary watchdog over government expenditures) of the World Bank and four smaller regional development banks concluded that taxpayers have indeed been paying for the World Bank's ineptitude. Maintaining the preferred-creditor status of the development banks – the linchpin of their AAA credit ratings – said the auditor general, 'is not cost free to countries like Canada' (Auditor General of Canada, 1992, p. 286).

Not only has the IBRD maintained its status by round-tripping loans, but as the Canadian auditor general observed, the donor countries have been offering debt relief indirectly through the Paris Club.

THE PARIS CLUB, IDA, AND OTHER FRIENDS OF THE BANK

The Paris Club is a regular rendezvous of lending and borrowing nations, hosted by the French finance ministry, to renegotiate Third World debts to government lenders. While the World Bank does not participate in those negotiations, its rich-country members protect it by directing their own lending institutions (aid agencies such as the US Agency for International Development and export credit agencies such as the US Export–Import Bank) to reschedule or forgive the debts of Third World countries in danger of defaulting on World Bank debts. The hundreds of billions in rescheduled debts and the $12.5 billion in bilateral debts actually forgiven by the rich countries since 1982 have thus become important safety valves protecting the IBRD from loan defaults (Cobourn, 1994, p. 25; see also World Bank, 1993–94, vol. 1, p. 173).

Another IBRD rescuer – one even more inbred than the Paris Club – is the IDA, its sister organization at the World Bank. That rich-country-financed foreign aid agency helps to keep the IBRD solvent by keeping borrowers flush in foreign exchange, enabling them to service their IBRD debts. In 1989 that practice was formalized under the whimsically named 'Fifth Dimension' programme, through which the IDA has lent approximately $900 million interest-free to 'ease the debt service burden' of its borrowers' outstanding IBRD debts. According to the World Bank's World Debt Tables, 'This has amounted to over 90 percent of the interest due on loans contracted by these countries from the IBRD' (World Bank, 1993–94, vol. 1, p. 40; 1994).

Since the World Bank – to protect its blue-chip reputation – forbids round-trip loans to pull chronic debtors out of arrears, its rich members do the job instead. In 1990 a 'support group' of creditor countries, worried that the mounting arrears of various small borrowers would weaken the credibility of the World Bank and the IMF, pooled millions of dollars to pay off Guyana's World Bank and IMF arrears, thus restoring Guyana's good standing with both institutions (Melly, 1989, p. B8). Similar packages have been marshalled since: France recently paid Cameroon's debt service arrears to the World Bank, and in 1993, for the same purpose, the United States and Japan gave Peru a bridging loan (Reuters, 1993; Inter Press Service, 1993, p. 10; Lasagabaster, 1994).

Then, in September 1995, a leaked document revealed the Bank's latest off-balance-sheet mechanism to bail itself out. The *Multilateral Debt Facility*, as it has been named, would raise some $11 billion from grants, donors, and the multilateral organizations themselves and assume the debt servicing and principal repayment for heavily indebted poor countries' multilateral debts for the next 15 years (World Bank, 1995b).

Third World debtors have 'often been supported through bilateral and multilateral programs to enable them to service their debts with the World Bank', said Canada's auditor general, suggesting that a taxpayer bail-out has been quietly operating to keep a financial crisis from the World Bank's doorstep. But, he added, 'one must ask whether these flows can be maintained indefinitely' (Auditor General of Canada, 1992, p. 286).

THE BANK'S NET TRANSFER TRAP

In the real world of international finance, banks lend money to borrowers, who are then expected to repay the principal, with interest; if borrowers fail to repay more than they borrow, or if lenders suspect such intentions, there is great cause for concern.

The World Bank understands that banking truism and tirelessly explains it to the foreign aid lobby, development groups, and the press, who often do not understand. The following exchange at a press conference, which took place during the World Bank's 1988 annual meeting in Berlin, between a reporter and Ernest Stern, the man who many believe ran the IBRD, summarizes the debate.

> REPORTER: For the last couple of years or so, the Bank has been getting back more from past and present borrowers in interest and repayments than it has actually been relending. I know there are lots of complicated reasons for this, but can you say when, on present lending schedules, and repayment schedules, net transfers back to the Bank will come to an end?
> STERN: The people who argue that there should always be positive net transfers not just net positive disbursements are, in my view, saying something very peculiar. To maintain positive net transfers means that you have to refinance the repayments of principal plus the interest payments. Since interest runs around 8 percent a year, it means that a country's debt will grow by 8 percent a year.
> The reason I think this is peculiar is because if you do that, a country is destined for quick bankruptcy (World Bank, 1988).

But the World Bank does not belong to the real world of international finance, and neither do its Third World clients. Despite the Bank's official recognition of the way banking should work, and its claim to conform to those norms, the Bank itself panics when its transfers turn negative (that is, when borrowers are repaying more than they are borrowing).

BORROWERS BALK

After 43 years of transferring more to its borrowers than its borrowers were paying back in principal and interest, the IBRD moved into uncharted territory in 1987 when net transfers turned negative. Because of the borrowing binge of the early 1980s, when positive net transfers reached all-time highs, very high debt repayments became due by the late 1980s. Debt forgiveness and reschedulings of various kinds, through various institutions, were then required to facilitate the IBRD's debt repayments, which by 1992 had increased sixfold over 1980 levels (See World Bank, 1993–94, vol. 1, p. 172).[12]

Although those negative net transfers fit Stern's stated view of how the World Bank's operations should unfold, they nevertheless provoked fear. According to one senior financial officer, the 'disturbing' day will come when *borrowers may have a 'diminished incentive to pay'*.[13] Indeed, many in charge at the IBRD share that fear. Confidential notes from a 1992 presentation to its Board of Executive Directors warned that *'since 1980, there has been a significant deterioration in the quality of the portfolio'*, and *'almost half of the projected increase in bank exposure is to countries that are currently considered to be high risk'* (World Bank, 1992b, pp. 1, 2, 4, 6).

> It is possible that a few of today's high risk countries could slide into nonaccrual over the next few years ...
>
> The implications are clear .... The Bank should thus be prepared to support adjustment strongly and quickly, but also be ready to curtail support if the conditions for effective use of our resources are not met. There are clear risks to the Bank in implementing such a strategy. Where countries encounter difficulties in implementing reform, external financing pressures can quickly reach crisis proportions, and the Bank's preferred creditor status could come under stress. For the foreseeable future, the Bank's financial position will therefore continue to require an adequate capacity to withstand situations of temporary nonaccrual ....
>
> It is not possible to predict whether or where such a situation might trigger an arrears problem for the Bank .... But there is always a likelihood of new countries falling into nonaccrual. This likelihood, while difficult to measure, must be taken into account in our loan loss provisions (World Bank, 1992b, pp. 4–6).[14]

The IBRD's loan-loss provisions would not go far in protecting the institution. At 3 per cent of disbursed and outstanding loans (plus the present value of guarantees), they are meagre compared to the 100 per cent provisions set aside in 1989 by J. P. Morgan & Company when Preston was chairman. The IRBD's loan-loss provisions exceed by roughly $1 billion the arrears portion of its portfolio (World Bank, 1992b, pp. 2, 16–17). But that portion is artificially low – a fiction of round trip loans and other state bail-outs that keep more debtors from going into arrears.

Indeed, it would take only one large debtor, such as India (which continues to receive positive net transfers from the IBRD and the IDA combined), and a handful of smaller debtors defaulting on their loan repayments, and the unthinkable could happen: the IBRD would have to start calling on the capital of its member countries to meet its obligation to its bondholders.[15] Should taxpayers in member countries resist bailing out boondoggles, the Bank's credit rating would be lowered, the cost to it of borrowing money would increase, and its Third World borrowers would begin to question the wisdom of more World Bank borrowing – and the wisdom of repaying their IBRD loans. The IBRD's financial stability would be put at risk.

That doomsday scenario is not remote but a constant worry. As Canada's auditor general explained, the World Bank's authority – as embodied in its preferred-creditor status – is fragile and not 'based on a formal or legal subordination of the debts owed other creditors to the debts owed to the banks'. Rather, the auditor general explained, its preferred-creditor status stems from 'informal factors, like the willingness of the development banks to maintain a positive cash flow to their borrowing countries' (Auditor General of Canada, 1992, p. 286[16]). In the absence of that incentive, the World Bank worries that its most vulnerable – or most belligerent – borrowers will fall into arrears. In 1991, when the Bank projected continuing negative flows (by roughly $3 billion a year) for the first half of the 1990s, borrowers demanded a 'comprehensive review' to find new ideas for viable investment projects (Westlake, 1991). A decade earlier, at the peak of the Third World's debt crisis, the planning director for the Haitian ministry of finance, Claude Grand-Pierre, said, 'If we're not receiving fresh money, we can't pay', adding that his government felt no obligation to pay lending agencies that had cut Haiti off (Hampton, 1988).

Similarly, in explaining his government's September 1989 decision to miss a $1.6 billion interest instalment to private banks, Brazilian finance minister Mailson da Nobrega said, 'Normal relations with creditors are our desire'. Referring to some $3 to $4 billion in loans that had failed to materialize that year, he added, '*This is a two-way street, in which debt payments should open the way for new resources*' (Werret, 1989).

Over the World Bank's history, positive net cash flows have bolstered borrowing governments' willingness and ability to meet their debt service obligations; without a 'positive cash flow' − to allow delinquent Third World debtors to receive more in new loans than they must pay back − many Third World countries simply would be unable to repay the World Bank. Without the promise of new and often larger loans, strapped debtor nations might renege on their promise to repay the World Bank first.

To steer as far from that cliff as possible, the World Bank provides adjustment loans and donor countries provide other refinancing vehicles, and uncreditworthy Third World countries get deeper into debt. Ironically, deepening Third World debt can alleviate the IBRD's woes: countries that slip into the basket-case category ('reverse graduates', in World Bank lingo) now become eligible for IDA support. In his 1988 press conference, Stern confirmed that although the IBRD may collect more than it lends when IBRD borrowers become reverse graduates, 'this does not mean that these countries are net payers to the Bank Group'. No. While the reverse graduates repaid the World Bank a little over $300 million in principal and interest, they received over $900 million in disbursements from the IDA (World Bank, 1988).

In addition to the risk that debtor nations might go into arrears, negative net transfers also impose a heavy public relations penalty: *when the world's largest aid agency draws in more capital than it doles out, press coverage sours*. In a recent story marking the World Bank's golden anniversary, *Time* ran the caption 'Bank "Profiteering" ?' over a chart that showed Third World repayments to the Bank exceeding its disbursements to the Third World (Zagorin, 1994, pp. 32–4).

THE LENDER OF LAST RESORT: THE BANK KEEPS THE LEMONS

Negative net transfers also signify the Bank's growing irrelevance. 'Once the chief doctors to the world's ailing economies', a recent column in the *Wall Street Journal* began, the World Bank and IMF are being surpassed by a surge in private financial activity that offers emerging Third World nations 'a different – and often more efficient – funding option' (Carrington, 1994, p. 1). *In 1994, foreign direct investment in all developing countries climbed to more than $56 billion – greater than the $51 billion in official development assistance, and far greater than disbursements by the World Bank and the IMF – threatening to reduce the World Bank and the IMF to 'high-priced extras'.* Even more significant, *most of the private investment involves private Third World borrowers, signalling a shift away from lending to sovereigns* (World Bank, 1993–94, vol. 1, p. 3.).

Preston conceded that the IBRD should not be lending money to the twenty-odd countries in Latin America and East Asia to which the ballooning private capital flows have gone. But as the relatively 'safe-bet economies' go elsewhere for their funds, the Bank gets drawn deeper into the 'financially precarious territory of African countries inching their way back from collapse and former Soviet states stranded somewhere between Communism and free enterprise' (Carrington, 1994). That shift, the *Journal* columnist warns, would produce a riskier loan portfolio, 'which the Bank's member countries and bondholders should gird for'.

AN INTERNATIONAL DEBT DEBACLE

The OECD's taxpayers may be stuck with a bail-out of World Bank bonds. National guarantees from the OECD countries have given a cabal of government and IBRD officials the power to influence-peddle and gamble away taxpayers' money without fear of financial or legal reproach. If their loans to the Marcoses and Mobutus of the world end up in default, the governments of the IBRD's most creditworthy shareholders will pay the bondholders back.

The IBRD's loose lending was disguised by good motives: cheap loans to poor countries for presumably worthwhile development projects. But in the case of the World Bank, says Paul Craig Roberts, former assistant secretary of the US Treasury for economic policy, 'the guarantees meant that no one had to behave responsibly because, in the end, it was only taxpayers' money'.

The IBRD's liabilities for its members' taxpayers now total over $100 billion. If the IBRD went belly-up, the US Treasury would be on the hook for $30 billion, the G–7 countries for $78 billion, and the industrialized countries *for $103 billion, which, not coincidentally, just about matches the bonds issued by the IBRD* (World Bank, 1995a, p. 2, 6).

While the World Bank's PR department is working overtime to convince the public that the Bank is reforming, the fundamental facts remain unchanged. *The World Bank is above the law: the legal immunity of staff; the inviolable nature of its documents; the unenforceability of its guidelines; the bizarre voting structure of its Board of Executive Directors* (in which borrowers and lenders alike vote on loans, with some executive directors representing both yet being allowed to cast only one vote); the multilateral structure of the World Bank and the resultant demands of diplomacy; and the coinciding pork-barrel interests of member governments make *democratization of the World Bank impossible.*

Real reform is possible only in theory. For example, amending the World Bank's articles of agreement – its constitution – requires three-fifths of the members, which represents 85 per cent of the total voting power. But roughly four-fifths of the members are borrowers, so the articles give them an iron grip on the Bank's affairs and leave the lending countries emasculated.

In the final analysis, *the process by which development decisions are made matters most, and in that regard, the World Bank has failed spectacularly.* Because the Bank's decision-making process is constitutionally unaccountable to, and unamendable by, those it is supposed to serve, *the Bank continues to approve large projects that rearrange nations' resources for the benefit of élites and to set economic policy without accountability to the citizens of the nations affected.*

The World Bank's single most destructive accomplishment has perhaps been to free Third World governments from the need to deal with their own people, thereby undermining the growth of democratic institutions and legitimate tax regimes throughout the Third World. As Chinese dissident Fang Lizhi said in arguing for the withdrawal of World Bank loans and credits from China, 'We must make our government realize that it is economically dependent on its citizens'(Cuomo, 1989).[17] Two months after making that statement, Fang was forced to seek asylum in the US Embassy for his part in the democracy movement. China has since become the World Bank's biggest annual borrower.

ENDING THE WORLD BANK LEGACY

The World Bank, which has just celebrated its fiftieth anniversary, has long enjoyed a sound financial reputation. But *its AAA credit rating is not justified*. Because of the perverse incentives under which the World Bank operates, the *quality of its loan portfolio has diminished significantly*, and because the Bank is backed by rich-country governments, *its irresponsible lending exposes Western taxpayers to a possible $100 billion bail-out*.

For 50 years World Bank investments have destroyed environments, distorted economies, broken lives, and amassed over $100 billion in contingent liabilities for the world's taxpayers. For almost as long citizens have attempted and failed to reform the Bank, confirming that it is constitutionally unaccountable and incapable, however good its intentions, of contributing to the development of nations. *After half a century of laying waste to the Third World's physical and social fabric, shareholders should take stock, assume responsibility, and end the World Bank's operations.*

NOTES

1. As of March 1995 the International Bank for Reconstruction and Development's borrowings were $98.3 billion (World Bank, 1995a, p. 2).
2. The contribution was for the International Development Association, the soft-loan window of the World Bank, which makes interest-free loans to countries with per capita incomes below $1,305 (1992 figure). The World Bank managed to secure the $18 billion it sought, $3.75 billion of which would come from the United States. But the US Congress took the unusual step of making its third-year appropriation conditional on the World Bank's becoming more accountable and making information more accessible to the public (see Environmental Defense Fund, 1993).
3. India has almost $10 billion in outstanding loans from the IBRD, or about 9 per cent of the bank's total outstanding loans. It also has $15.4 billion in outstanding development credits from IDA, or about 27.5 per cent of all IDA credits. According to *Information Statement*, 'It is the policy of the Bank to place in nonaccrual status all loans made to or guaranteed by a member of the Bank, if principal, interest or other charges with respect to any such loan is overdue by more than six months, unless the Bank's management determines that the overdue amount will be collected in the immediate future' (World Bank, 1995a, p. 16). According to *The World Bank Annual Report 1993*, 'It is the policy of IDA to place in nonaccrual status all development credits made to a member government or to the government of a territory of a member if principal or charges with respect to any such development credit are overdue by more than six months, unless IDA management determines that the overdue amount will be collected in the immediate future. In addition, if loans by IBRD to a member government are placed in nonaccrual status, all development credits to that member government will also be placed in nonaccrual status by IDA' (World Bank, 1993b, p. 221).

4. Standard and Poor's Credit Analysis Service, 1993.
5. US backing for the IBRD from *Information Statement* (World Bank, 1995a, p. 6). When countries purchase shares in the IBRD, they pay in approximately 7 per cent of the cost of those shares, with the remaining 93 per cent of the capital being 'callable' as a guarantee. Those guarantees – especially those from the IBRD's AAA-rated members – enable it to raise money by borrowing in international capital markets.

   IDA contribution figure from Congressional Research Service 'World Bank: Answers to 26 Frequent Questions' (1991, p. 58). This report lists US subscriptions to the IBRD since 1944 and US subscriptions and contributions to IDA since 1960 (the year IDA was created). The United States also made a $3.75-billion subscription to the tenth replenishment of IDA in 1993.

   On lack of US appropriations since 1981 see Rich (1994), p. 78. According to the Congressional Research Service, 'Since 1981, the United States no longer appropriates money to back its callable capital subscriptions to the MDBs [multilateral development banks]' (1994, p. 2).

   The extent of the liability for Canadian taxpayers is also obfuscated. According to the *Report of the Auditor General of Canada to the House of Commons 1992*, 'We are concerned that the vote wording in the Appropriation Act, with respect to the 1988 World Bank general capital increase, does not clearly disclose that payments to the World Bank are for purchase of shares and represent only the paid-in capital portion, or about 3 per cent of the capital subscriptions for those shares. There is no mention of the callable capital portion, which represents about 97 per cent of the total subscriptions. As a subscriber to the shares, Canada is committed to the callable portion. Therefore, we are concerned that Parliament is not made fully aware that it is approving a potential financial commitment when it approves the payments to the World Bank. Since 1988, the callable capital portion of shares purchased by Canada has been almost $1.5 billion' (Auditor General of Canada, 1992, p. 314).
6. Standard and Poor's Credit Analysis Service. The World Bank Group includes the IBRD, IDA, and the IBRD's two affiliates, the International Finance Corporation (which promotes private-sector growth in developing countries by mobilizing foreign and domestic capital to invest alongside its own funds in commercial enterprises) and the Multilateral Investment Guarantee Agency (which encourages foreign direct investment in developing countries by protecting investors from non-commercial risk). (World Bank, 1993b, p. 4).
7. Wapenhans's review included both the IBRD's and IDA's portfolios.
8. Earlier internal project reviews had signalled a deterioration in project quality (see, for example, World Bank, 1983, 1987, 1990, 1992a, 1993a).
9. For an excellent review of that phenomenon, see Tammen (1990).
10. According to the World Bank (1993–94), net transfers on debt equal new loan disbursements minus old loan amortizations minus interest on old loans (vol. 1, p. x).
11. 'Loan Agreement (Debt and Debt Service Reduction Project) between República Oriental del Uruguay and International Bank for Reconstruction and Development', loan no. 3323UR, World Bank, Washington, 25 June 1992; and 'Loan Agreement (Debt Management Program) between Republic of the Philippines and International Bank for Reconstruction and

Development', loan no. 3149-PH, World Bank, Washington, 22 December 1989.

12. Debt repayments include loan amortizations and loan interest.
13. Interview with Kenichi Ohashi.
14. The IBRD raised its loan-loss provisions in 1993 from 2.5 per cent to 3 per cent of total loans disbursed and outstanding plus the present value of guarantees. According to the *Information Statement*, 'Until June 1991, the Bank maintained loan loss provisions only for Bank loans which were in nonaccrual status. The provisioning policy was broadened by the Bank's Executive Directors at that time to cover general collectability risks in the loan portfolio as a whole in addition to the specific risks for loans in nonaccrual status. On May 20, 1993, the bank's executive directors approved an increase in the provisioning rate from 2.5 per cent to 3.0 per cent of the overall portfolio' (World Bank, 1995a, p. 16).
15. For transfers to India, see World Bank (1993–94), vol. 2, p. 208.
16. Also, according to Hugh N. Scott, associate general counsel at the World Bank, 'The Bank's preferred creditor status is reflected in the arrangements between the borrower and its rescheduling creditors. There is no specific commitment to preferred creditor treatment in our Articles of Agreement or loan agreements' (correspondence with author, 27 June 1991).
17. Fang made one exception to his appeal for foreign divestment from China: he thought World Bank and other loans should continue for education projects.

REFERENCES

Auditor General of Canada (1992) *Report of the Auditor General of Canada to the House Commons 1992* (Ottawa, Ontario: Minister of Supply and Services).

Carrington, T. (1994) 'It's Time to Redefine World Bank and IMF', *Wall Street Journal*, 25 July.

Cobourn, C. (1994) 'Multilateral Debt: A Growing Crisis', *Bankcheck Quarterly*, 8, June.

Congressional Research Service (1991) 'World Bank: Answers to 26 Frequent Questions', CRS Report 91–847F (Washington, DC: Congressional Research Service), 25 November.

Congressional Research Service (1994) 'Multilateral Development Banks: US Contributions FY 1984–95', CRS Report for Congress 94–571F (Washington, DC: Congressional Research Service), 18 July.

Cuomo, J. (1989) 'Chinese Dissident Advocates Divestment', *Wall Street Journal*, 26 April.

Environmental Defense Fund (1993), press release, 'US Congress Puts World Bank on Short Leash' (Washington, DC: Environmental Defense Fund), October.

Hager, B. M. (1989) 'The World Bank Underwater', *International Economy*, September–October.

Hampton, E. (1988) 'Haiti Retrenches as International Aid Cut Off', *Globe and Mail* (Toronto), 12 January.

IBRD Deputy Secretary (1993) 'Monthly Operational Summary of Bank and IDA Proposed Projects (as of 15 May 1993)', SecM93–527 (Washington, DC:

International Bank for Reconstruction and Development, International Development Association), 1 June.

Inter Press Service (1993) 'Multilateral Lenders Claim Larger Share of Debt', *Third World Economics*, 16–30 November.

Lasagabaster, M. E. (1994) 'Peru: Back from the Brink', *The IDB*, August.

Melly, P. (1989) 'Canada Stage-manages Rescue Package for Guyana', *Globe and Mail* (Toronto), 18 May.

Morse, B. and Berger, T. (1992) *Sardar Sarovar: The Report of the Independent Review* (Ottawa, Ontario: Resource Futures International).

Portfolio Management Task Force (1992a) *Effective Implementation: Key to Development Impact*, confidential discussion draft (Washington, DC: World Bank), 24 July.

Portfolio Management Task Force (1992b), *Effective Implementation: Key to Development Impact*, report of the World Bank's Portfolio Management Task Force (Washington, DC: World Bank), 2 October.

Reuters (1993) 'Cameroon: France Bails Cameroon Out of World Bank Debt', 7 July.

Rich, B. (1994) *Mortgaging the Earth: The World Bank, Environment, Impoverishment, and the Crisis of Development* (Boston, MA: Beacon).

Sachs, J. D. (1989) *New Approaches to the Latin American Debt Crisis, Essays in International Finance*, 174 (Princeton, NJ: International Finance Section, Department of Economics, Princeton University), July.

Standard and Poor's Credit Analysis Service (1993) 'Supranational: International Bank for Reconstruction and Development' (New York), November.

Tammen, M. S. (1990) 'The Precarious Nature of Sovereign Lending: Implications for the Brady Plan', *Cato Journal*, 10, 1, Spring–Summer, pp. 239–63.

Wapenhans, W. A. (1992) 'Oral Briefing of the JAC [Joint Audit Committee] at Its Meeting on June 22, 1992 on the Portfolio Management Task Force, Notes', speaking notes (Washington, DC), 6 June.

Werret, R. (1989) 'Nobrega Explains Arrears and Seeks IMF Accord', *Annual Meeting News*, 25 September.

Westlake, M. (1991) 'Negative Transfers to Zoom in 90s', *Annual Meeting News*, 15 October.

World Bank (1983) 'Development Finance Companies, State and Privately Owned', World Bank Staff Working Paper no. 578 (Washington, DC: World Bank).

World Bank (1987) 'Twelfth Annual Review of Project Performance Results' (Washington, DC: World Bank).

World Bank (1988) 'Edited Excerpts on the Question of Net Transfers from Mr. Stern's Press Conference, Berlin, September 25, 1988', World Bank transcript (Washington, DC: World Bank).

World Bank (1990) *Evaluation Results for 1988: Issues in World Bank Lending over Two Decades* (Washington, DC: Operations Evaluation Department, World Bank).

World Bank (1992a) *Evaluation Results for 1990* (Washington, DC: Operations Evaluation Department, World Bank).

World Bank (1992b) 'Informal Board Seminar on the Status of the IBRD Portfolio', briefing notes, 6 March (Washington, DC: World Bank).

World Bank (1993a) *Evaluation Results for 1991* (Washington, DC: Operations Evaluation Department, World Bank).

World Bank (1993b) *The World Bank Annual Report 1993* (Washington, DC: World Bank).

World Bank (1993–94) *World Debt Tables: External Finance for Developing Countries* (Washington, DC: World Bank).

World Bank (1994) 'Debt, Net Transfers, and Forgiveness of World Bank Loans', no. 7, 'Setting The Record Straight...' (Washington, DC: External Affairs Department, World Bank). Material prepared in response to Rich, *Mortgaging the Earth* (1994).

World Bank (1995a) *Information Statement* (Washington, DC: World Bank, Financial Operations Department), 22 March.

World Bank (1995b) *The Multilateral Debt Facility for Heavily Indebted Poor Countries* (Washington, DC: Task Force of staff from Development Economics; Financial Policy and Resource Mobilization; Controller; Africa Region; Cofinancing and Advisory Services; Legal; and External Affairs, World Bank), 25 July.

Zagorin, A. (1994) 'Damning the World Bank', *Time*, 25 July.

11 Foreign Aid and the Erosion of Local Institutions: an Autopsy of Arun-3 from Inception to Abortion

Dipak Gyawali

AID: END OF AN AGE

Despite its noble sound, *we cannot assume that the practice of development is a benign social process*. Its arena is littered with oustees and relocatees, the coerced and the coercers, the winners and the losers. Development is a complex process with overlaps of contradictory certitudes regarding social justice, political harmony and environmental consequences.

The last forty years of development efforts teach us that *development is only secondarily about money* or the lack of it. Indeed, in Nepal, as in many countries of the South, there is almost three times more money chasing far fewer good projects than the other way around. Phrases have been coined to explain this phenomenon – low absorptive capacity, weak institutional base, lack of strong political commitment, etc. – but these hide more than they reveal. Such descriptions obscure the fact that capital shortage is obviously not the primary problem.

They fail to consider the *social climate in Southern societies which does not allow capital to function as it has done at the western end of the Eurasian peninsula* since the 1500s. These expressions do not shed light on the underlying dynamics of societal forces at work but, by implying that aid has nothing wrong with it except the recipient, suggest an incorrect policy message, Wappenhans notwithstanding.[1] Furthermore, the 'unseemly haste' with which Northern capital, in the form of what is termed official development assistance, seeks projects in Third World countries itself needs examining for the driving imperatives behind the phenomenon, and cannot be explained away as naive altruism. (For more on this, see Adams, Chapter 10, this volume.)

This chapter examines these imperatives by focusing on a major development project in Nepal, *the Arun-3 hydroelectric project*. It was promoted for ten years by seven donors and the Nepal Government with the World Bank in the lead (see Appendix, Table 11.1), and has now been ignominiously dropped by the Bank after opposition by groups espousing an alternative development paradigm. Many lessons can be drawn from the political dynamics between international donors and recipient societies from this single project in Nepal.

There are two reasons why one has to worry about foreign aid at the present historical juncture. First, the age of foreign aid is drawing to a close. It grew as an institution after the Second World War and behind its altruistic articulations lay the undercurrent of rivalries between the global power blocs of the First (Western) and Second (Communist) Worlds. After Gorbachev's *glasnost* and the admission that the Second World had basically become a part of the Third World, there emerged not only a plethora of new recipients in the former communist countries, but also the need among Western donors for fresh stock-taking. Subtle signals indicate that donor fatigue will be articulated more cleverly in the future.

Second, while donor fatigue itself may not be bad *per se*, the flip side of the coin is *aid addiction* among the recipients in the Third World; and this needs to be seriously addressed as it has severe implications for global governability. Sudden curtailment of aid may lead to acute withdrawal problems and accompanying social dislocations. Very few Third World countries thoroughly dependent on aid for their social and economic development are prepared to handle acute withdrawal syndromes. After the World Bank's new President withdrew funding for the controversial Arun-3 project in Nepal, the aftermath reactions from major political parties in Nepal vowing to 'return Arun-3' are an indicator of such an institutional syndrome.[2]

Foreign aid has been a major institutional force in the Third World for much of the last half of the twentieth century. On what is considered its benign side, it has introduced new technologies to the developing countries that they themselves would not have had access to otherwise. On the other hand, critiques of its malignant side assert that it works in collusion with the élites of the poor countries to maintain the status quo. Indeed, it has been critiqued in the Third World as a major distorter of national priorities, since *'development strategy has tended to follow aid rather than vice versa'* and that the main problem of foreign aid is that 'as long as it is "foreign", the recipient countries can be under the illusion that it does not have to be accepted metabolically by their socio- economic systems'.[3]

This pathological condition of an unassimilated foreign body within the body social becomes more pronounced as the size of the intrusion increases. A small thorn in the flesh is an irritant: an unadaptive heart, kidney or lung a life-threatening risk. Some of the development interventions and the technologies they have introduced have had major implications for the recipients. The opposition to such threats have also been unique in character as initiatives not previously seen by such societies. Nepal and its aid patrons had never experienced a history of opposition to externally introduced technology, as has happened in the case of Arun-3. The questions to be looked at are (1) whose decision was it to invite such risks; (2) how and why were such decisions taken; and (3) what are the driving imperatives behind decisions both to introduce as well as to oppose them? In this complex web of events, actors and goods, this chapter finds it helpful to adopt the perspective that politics, technology and social choice are an inchoate mass where conflicting perceptions regarding the risks involved, generated within particular social environments, vie with each other for acceptance, as Arun-3 demonstrates (Schwarz and Thompson, 1990).

ARUN-3 AND ITS PATHOLOGY

Arun-3 is a hydroelectric project on the Arun River which originates in Tibet and flows south into Nepal just east of two major peaks of over 8000 m, Everest and Makalu (salient features in the Appendix, Table 11.2). It joins other tributaries from the Nepali hills to form the Sapta Kosi, which in turn joins the Ganga in India, but not before being known as Bihar's 'river of sorrow' for frequently changing its course during floods. It was first identified as an attractive physical site for developing a hydro project, based on its flow and incline characteristics in a basin study financed by the Japanese International Cooperation Agency (JICA) between 1983 and 1985.

While this study was being conducted, another run-of-river hydroelectric project, the 69 MW Marsyangdi, was under construction in mid-west Nepal, with primarily World Bank funding. The Japanese, meanwhile, were busy constructing the 30 MW Kulekhani-2 and did not participate in the donor consortium for the Marsyangdi hydroelectric project, which was commissioned in 1989. At US$4000 per kW, the 69 MW Marsyangdi had been criticized as being outrageously expensive – almost four times what it was costing India to build hydro projects in the Indian Himalaya and in Bhutan. However, those in the hydropower business were already on the lookout for the next similarly profitable venture, and Arun-3 arrived on their doorsteps at the right time after much of the necessary institutional ground-breaking (or distortions, depending upon which paradigm one upholds) had been done by the Marsyangdi project.

As an example of local distortion, the power sector in Nepal was divided between the Electricity Department of the Ministry of Water Resources, which looked after construction of new projects, and the parastatal Nepal Electricity Corporation, which then owned and operated the plants and the transmission and distribution system. It was a clumsy but functioning institutional arrangement. *To justify returns from investment in such a large financial venture, the idea of one single electric utility for Nepal was pushed by the major lending banks such as the World Bank and the Asian Development Bank.* These two utilities were merged in 1985, as part of the conditionalities for the effectiveness of the loan for the Marsyangdi project, into what is now known as the Nepal Electricity Authority (NEA). The fact that such a merger was not desired by the recipient was highlighted by the transfer of almost a hundred experienced and senior engineers and other technical staff from the Electricity Department to the Ministry of Water Resources, effectively creating a virtual electricity department within the Ministry distinct from the NEA.[4]

Arun-3 was the logical culmination of this process of monism from the large multilateral donors' side, as opposed to institutional pluralism, a reality on the recipient's side, given its wide-ranging social diversity. It began to overtake the institutions that created it soon after it was identified. Indeed, questions are now being asked about whether it was identified primarily to cater to *external imperatives consisting of a certain electric utility philosophy which gave primacy to the principle of 'efficiency of size' rather than to 'local institutional needs*';[5] whether it was to serve the need of donors to push one large project for the whole country (more manageable from the donors' perspective) rather than smaller ones (more manageable from the recipient host society's perspective) for different regions of the country; and whether there were also *compulsions to market certain types of equipment* such as turbines, generators and services such as consultancies.

Even though the Japanese originally identified Arun-3 as an attractive site in their 1985 Kosi basin master plan study, they were more interested in pushing a 225 MW Sapta Gandaki hydroelectric project at a much more accessible site at about half the cost of Arun-3. Canadian consultants working in Nepal in conflicting roles, on the one hand as policy advisers to the Nepal Government through its Water and Energy Commission and on the other as contractors for an approximately $12 million feasibility study of the 10,800 MW Karnali project, helped other donors to pick up Arun-3 and eventually introduce it as a competitor to, and finally a winner over, Sapta Gandaki.[6]

In 1987, the Government of Nepal requested the World Bank to become a *'lead donor agency'* in mobilizing resources for Arun-3. Thus for *the first time in Nepal's development history, a ministry gave up its lead role to a foreign institution and authorized it to speak to other donors on its behalf.* At this point, on 19 July 1987, Chancellor Helmut Kohl of West Germany paid a state visit to Nepal. One of the gifts he left behind was a commitment on Germany's behalf to provide Nepal with a grant of 260 million Deutschmarks which was to be used for the feasibility and detailed engineering study of Arun-3. Thereupon, a German consultancy firm which had designed and supervised the expensive Marsyangdi hydroelectric project received the main contract to design the Arun-3. The same method had been used earlier in the Marsyangdi case to make sure that the consultancy contract went to a German firm. To quote an investigative journalist:

> Marsyangdi was among the least attractive projects identified in a UNDP-funded Gandak Basin Master Plan Study. This study done in the late Seventies had selected Kali Gandaki and Sapta Gandaki as the 'best' projects for taking up feasibility and pre-feasibility studies. An Australian firm is even said to have done a feasibility study of Kali Gandaki and a pre- feasibility of Sapta Gandaki, when a German hydropower mission landed in

Kathmandu and picked up the Kankai and the Bagmati multipurpose projects it would like to take up. Kankai was dropped because it was a multipurpose project and the financing arrangements could not come through. The government had requested the Asian Development Bank to support the irrigation component of this project. That did not happen. Among reasons for this was that the Indian director at the bank had maintained that financing this would need the approval of the lower riparian country and is said to have written a note of dissent on the vote. Following this, the 100 million Deutsche Marks which the Germans had committed for the Kankai project was transferred to fund the detailed engineering studies and the implementation of Marsyangdi. The Nepali government accepted the German marks even before an official decision to build or not build this project had been taken. The project for implementation at this stage was Sapta Gandaki. This was the one in which the Japanese were interested.

This German move on Marsyangdi (reportedly backed by the World Bank) knocked the Japanese off balance. This, experts said, was among the reasons why the latter stayed out of the project and it took about three years to find enough money (finally from the Middle East) to build it. The Arun detailed engineering grant, justified on grounds of possible power export to India, similarly served Germans to push the Arun project, experts added. It may be recalled that the three power generation units for Arun-3 will come from Germany. Japan – not by pure coincidence, perhaps – has yet to make a final commitment to finance the project (Bhattarai, 1993).

The manner in which a large project such as Arun-3 was selected, and competitors sidelined, highlights the fact that, subsequently, making this particular project 'feasible' became the paramount objective. This was primarily for the good of a monolithic monopolistic institution, as well as the monistic philosophy behind it, and only secondarily for the good of the Nepali industry or its consumers. *From its very inception, Arun-3 had many unanswered technical, economic and social anomalies which never featured in the official consideration of the project, either within the government of Nepal or within the World Bank* (see Appendix, Tables 11.1 and 11.2).

At *$1.1 billion, Baby Arun represented the largest investment ever made in Nepal* and hence also the investment with the largest attendant risks.

Out of a total annual budget of $1 billion, the internal revenue Nepal is able to raise is of the order of $300–$500 million, the rest coming as foreign aid in the form of grants, technical assistance or soft loans. The *risk of such a large project to an economy as small as that was never properly assessed by legitimate institutions such as the Water and Energy Commission and the National Planning Commission. Indeed, even the World Bank failed to conduct a proper macroeconomic impact assessment of this large investment prior to 1993.* Then it acted in response to pressure brought to bear upon it by Nepali and international environmental organizations. Even then, the Bank continued to maintain that social and other sectors would not suffer in Nepal as a result of this project until Mr Wolfensohn decreed otherwise in August 1995.

In fact, *several studies were conducted by the World Bank to justify Arun-3 and they did not really address the objections that had been raised.* In one expensive effort, the Bank hired Electricité de France to conduct a reconfirmation study of Arun-3. However, EdF states: 'During the screening analysis [March 1990], NEA and IDA imposed a number of conditions concerning the finalization of the study. One of these conditions is that none of the hydro projects selected would be able to be commissioned before 1998/1999' (i.e. before Arun-3). The other conditions required the consultant to apply cost-increase coefficients to alternative hydro projects up to 30 per cent with absolutely no rationale other than to make them less competitive than Arun-3 (Electricité de France, 1990).

Other planning defects were systematically ignored, for example: the need to have heavy infrastructure early on, such as a 118 km access road with additional side feeders in difficult Himalayan terrain; power for construction that would have to be ferried in by helicopters; idle Nepali manpower to the tune of 500 engineers and 10,000 employees, at best entrusted only with liaison duties to expatriate consultants, etc. Concerning the access road, the agency entrusted with overseeing the building of this road was not the Department of Roads, the legitimate road- building authority in Nepal, but the NEA, which has no experience of road building.

HISTORICAL FACTORS

The symptoms of today's sicknesses cannot be understood without examining the sins of yesteryear. Arun-3 pathology is the result of historical forces of the past still at work today and must be examined to gain insights into the nature of the problem.

Electricity was first generated in Nepal in 1911 from a 500 kW hydroelectric plant in Pharping at the southern end of Kathmandu Valley. The power was transmitted to the centre of Kathmandu and used to light the palaces of feudal rulers. A second 640 kW hydroelectric plant was constructed in Sundarijal only in 1936, representing an energy demand growth rate of just over 2 per cent per annum. A study of this phenomenon highlights two important points regarding technology and its social articulation. The first is that *demand for electricity (or any modern amenity) in a non-technical culture such as feudal Nepal is a function of the social worldview dominating the society at the particular point in time*; and the second is that *modern technology needs social carriers for its proper articulation.*

Electricity was seen as an item of luxury, an appendage to the exhibition of feudal power, rather than as a means to increasing productivity. Its demand was for the expensive comfort it provided (spending accumulated wealth) rather than for its ability to do things (creating wealth). This dominant streak in the worldview is still seen in village electrification works, when many hundreds of metres of conductors and several poles are used to supply domestic lighting to a powerful local politician rather than to the village school or an agroprocessing mill.

The people responsible for introducing this new technology were the feudal elements of society, and their objectives predominated in its use. If one examines the history of modern technology as it developed in Europe and America, the contrast is significant because, for the capitalist social framework therein, the social carriers of technology were the productive merchant and industrial classes (Stavrianos, 1981). *In Nepal, a dichotomy between the luxury class and the productive elements lies as the undercurrent in development intervention exercises* leading to its successful assimilation, an 'antibody' rejection or even an uncontrollable cancerous growth destroying the fabric of society as a whole.

Part of the problem with Arun-3 is the situation created by past dispensation which resulted in a *'no option trap'*. In a country like Nepal, so rich in water resources, it is ironic that every project from Kulekhani-1 in the early 1970s to Arun-3 today is being justified on the grounds that, because no other project has been adequately studied and that 'so much effort has already been spent on it', it must be picked up for public funding through loans from the banks. The costs of such projects have been some of the most expensive in the world. An international comparative study (Moore and Smith, 1990a and 1990b) shows the composite cost of power production per kW in 1989 US dollars (inclusive of generation, transmission, distribution and services) to be 1502 for China, 2061 for India and 4346 for Nepal. Even Papua New Guinea and Burma, which have predominantly hydro schemes, have not managed to go beyond 1925 and 2719 respectively, despite military dictatorships and general backwardness. Only Sri Lanka matches Nepal at 4451, but this has to be seen in the context of the widely criticized Mahaweli scheme.

This *overblowing of costs is a political–economic problem rather than a purely financial or administrative one* where an *'iron triangle' of vested interests are given a free hand to trap the country into a no-options scenario* and then escalate project costs, playing monopoly on the soft loans issued out of goodwill towards the Nepali poor. The *'iron triangle' in Nepal consists of three apexes – low-paid Nepali bureaucrats in very powerful positions who decide the fate of millions of rupees; donor agencies where promotion depends less on the success of projects than on success in getting projects; and loans through middleman 'commission agents' linking international manufacturers and servicing companies with local decision-makers.* Similar phenomena (described by the 'rent seeking' theory school in political economy) have also been observed in Africa and, indeed, even in the West, notably the scandalous Pentagon purchases in the US in the early 1980s.

Standard economics and rational management break down at this point because *the vested interests are not equity participants but 'rentiers' created by enjoying scarce access to decision-making; and the only remedy is institutional changes that provide for competition to break privileged access. Foreign aid, rather than changing this political economic framework, became a part itself of the neo-feudal order.*

Donor intervention into such a regime since the end of the Second World War has been characterized with frequent experimentation. This is in itself not a bad thing: regular monitoring and correction of course is essential in any development intervention. However, *when corrections become wholesale reversals of direction, especially in the basic philosophy, they entail severe institutional dislocation in poor societies which are already ill-equipped in this area.*[7] In the electricity sector, the focus of the Western donors in the past, ironically, had been the development and growth of the government-owned public sector. By this means it was easier to channel loans and assure, through iron-clad back-up of sovereign loans, a return on primary and ancillary investments. To this end, wholesale nationalization of small, private power-generating companies was encouraged in the 1970s with unshakeable belief in 'economy of scale'. Now, in the 1990s, the sins of 'inefficiency of size' have caught up with a society unprepared institutionally to handle the large scale; and leading donors are pushing for privatization as the simplistic panacea. It has confused the Nepali sociosystem not a little. Furthermore, *privatization is only one among many institutional possibilities, including means such as 'communitization' and 'municipalization', as intermediary solutions between the extremes of state control and* laissez-faire.

Because Arun-3 was ill-planned, the social and institutional cost of its implementation was bound to be very high. It was a project several times the size of the rest of NEA and was bound to raise the question: *'Are you putting Arun in NEA or NEA in Arun?'* The unidirectional focus of the Bank in massive tariff increase as the main solution to all the problems therein, and the pressure to include private-sector people on the board of directors of a wholly government-owned utility (without being shareholders responsible to their investments) are changing conditionalities that the sociosystem has not been able to digest.

A good and efficient technology, though feasible technically and financially, may not necessarily be feasible socially or politically. It may be putting strains on the social fabric – indeed insulting it immeasurably – with long-term costs that may far overshadow any perceived gains from efficiency. The current pressure from donors is to push the *Structural Adjustment Program* (SAP) as the simple solution to Third World institutional ills, and a major macroeconomic experiment such as Arun-3 was also bound to be tied to a SAP.

SAP programmes, their hidden agenda, development priorities or the risks inherent in pursuing such paths are rarely the subject of discourse in Third World societies. Elites operating the governmental levers have stopped actively questioning the philosophy of development (or lack of it) espoused in these programmes. There seems to be a fatalistic acceptance that the forces at work are so much more powerful that any chance of changing the future is beyond anything that can be attempted: some unseen hand in a faraway place, a good providence, will probably work, somehow, in their favour.[8]

The SAP, though formally introduced in the mid-1980s, has an earlier prehistory of foreign aid. Nepal's development efforts, with the help of foreign capital inflow, began in January 1951 with Nepal agreeing to be included in the Point IV Program of the Truman Administration. A few months later, India entered the donor game, followed by China in 1956, and eventually by other bilaterals. Nepal had adopted the mode of state planning in 1956 with the launching of the First Five-year Plan. Since Nepal had just seen the overthrow of the Rana Shogunate in 1951, which had ruled the country for the preceding 104 years, a period of interregnum was inevitable. In 1959 there was an exercise in parliamentary democracy. This was aborted by a royal coup in 1960, and rule by the Royal Palace (known as the Panchayat Raj) lasted till 1990.

During the Rana rule, when Nepal preserved its independence partly by isolating itself from world events and from markets, the idea of sovereign indebtedness was an anathema, except in times of war. The one well-recorded incidence was when Rana Prime Minister Chandra Sumshere borrowed money from the Pashupati Temple and used it to abolish slavery in 1924. The idea that sovereign loans could be used to usher in 'development' was formalized only in 1956 with the promulgation of the 'Development Board Act 2013 BS'. This act empowered the government of Nepal to take foreign money for purposes of development. Most major capital expenditure such as irrigation, hydropower or integrated rural development projects to date have been financed through empowerment by this Act.

Until the beginning of the 1970s foreign capital inflow was mostly in the form of grants by bilateral donors. Loans began to occupy a larger and alarming share of development efforts from the 1970s (coinciding with the Fourth Plan period) when the country launched major infrastructural projects. *Public debt as a share of the GDP was only 4.57 per cent in FY 1974/75 (with internal debt of the government being 2.48 per cent and external debt being 2.09 per cent), whereas it had risen to 40.51 per cent (internal 18.46 per cent and external 22.05 per cent) in FY 1984/85* (Integrated Development Systems, 1987).

To finance development, primarily to pay for local costs of development, the government began to borrow internally and to draw down reserves in the first half of the 1980s. Credit to private- and public-sector corporations to offset continuing losses began to expand very rapidly to the tune of 25 per cent per annum. Reserves fell to about three months of imports by 1984/85. In the face of such a deteriorating situation, the Government of Nepal adopted a stabilization programme in December 1985 and entered into a 14-month standby arrangement with the IMF (World Bank, 1987). This was the beginning of the Structural Adjustment Program in Nepal, through which several key areas of the economy were opened up to IMF intervention.[9] *Stringent austerity measures were expected to have minimal social impact, since 60 per cent of Nepal's population living below the poverty line 'engaged primarily in subsistence agriculture,* [and] are not closely linked with developments in the monetized sector of the economy'.

While the value of nitty-gritty financial and managerial measures cannot be disputed, it is the *very philosophy of the programme and the fatalistic submission to remote experts that is the question.* Although adjustment measures were decided upon without public debate or even knowledge, even now with democracy, let alone in 1985 under the autocratic Panchayat regime, they have not gone without some indigenous comment. An ex-finance secretary argued that

> this issue has two parts. One is the structural adjustment program, the other is the structural adjustment loan. The two are treated by the World Bank and the borrower as the same thing, but it does not have to be that way. My position is that Nepal needs the first but cannot afford the latter (Panday, 1987).

The charge made by him in the critique of the SAP was that the donor community was as much to be blamed for the mismanagement of the Nepalese economy and for its stagnation, as were the government authorities. It does not take further loans to seriously evaluate aid and development objectives, motives and performances. Structural adjustment has to transcend the economic field and capture the political, social and moral dimensions as well. Structural adjustment loans could have a role to play in economies of countries where the sources of structural problems are mainly economic. To break loose from these, they need additional external financing within a broader framework and a longer time-perspective than is the case with the use of the resources of the IMF alone.

Nepal's case was clearly different, he argued, because the need for adjustment was not precipitated by a change in the country's external economic environment. By and large, land-locked Nepal, which was very late in coming under international trade influences, continues to be relatively insulated against external shocks. Even the oil price increases of 1970s did not by themselves affect the country's external balance very much. *Whatever ills permeated the Nepali economy, they were the result of years of mismanagement, malpractice and malfunctioning of the country's planning and management system.* And there was no need to reward the government for such behaviour by giving it additional resources to play with.

In 1989, at the height of the Nepal–India trade and transit impasse – whereby India created an economic blockade – a second instalment of structural adjustment credit was made (World Bank, 1989).[10] As with the first SAL, SAL2 was also expected to have a positive impact on poverty. The programme was oriented towards growth facilitated by SAL/SAF resources, and was not constrained by fiscal austerity. In agriculture, the increase in the price of fertilizer meant this product would not be diverted to India, but would be available to smaller Nepali farmers. Adjustments in other sectors would only affect those with higher incomes who had been receiving economic rents.

At this point, Nepal entered a period of political upheavals related to deteriorating relations with India and lack of internal democracy. The impasse in both areas was resolved only in 1990 with the introduction of a multi-party democratic dispensation. The first year of democracy was steered by a coalition interim government of socialists, communists and the King's nominees, focusing only on drafting a new constitution and holding general elections. The general elections of 1991 brought to power the Nepali Congress, which professed a 'democratic socialist' agenda. The main opposition was the United Marxist–Leninist Communist Party of Nepal.

Strangely, the liberalization and privatization programme acquired a greater momentum under this new political stewardship. For example, while the previous autocratic Panchayat system had balked at privatizing public enterprises, the newly elected democratic government pushed it through with relatively little opposition or public debate.[11] The IMF praised the new government for moving away from a *dirigiste* approach to economic development and adopting, instead, a market-oriented strategy, aimed at encouraging a vigorous private sector. Praise was also forthcoming for achieving full convertibility 'a full year ahead of schedule' and for sacking over 3000 civil servants in 1992 (International Monetary Fund, 1993a and 1993b).

ARUN-3 AND STRUCTURAL ADJUSTMENT

The Enhanced Structural Adjustment Facility, the new incarnation of SAL, is a modified version of the strategy outlined in 1987. A major new addition is concentration on hydropower and the promotion of a large project (by Nepali standards) such as the Arun-3 which would double the generating capacity of the country in one go. *Although Nepal presents one of the more successful stories of small hydro generation in terms of both local manufacture, local capacity building and local construction skills, both the World Bank and the IMF have promoted Arun-3 which requires major involvement of international contractors and little use of local capacity.* They see the project as a major opportunity for fundamental structural changes within the Nepali economy. Yet they are not unaware of some potential problems. With Arun-3 foreign grants and loans of roughly $3/4 billion – that is, one quarter of the annual GDP – significant macro-economic and administrative uncertainties and challenges are posed. The risk of a large hydro development contributing to increased non-aid imports, balance-of-payments deficits and declining reserves is recognized by the IMF (see International Monetary Fund, 1993b), more readily perhaps than by the Nepali parliament. Also, concentration on this one large project would crowd out small and medium hydro programmes in the public sector, and decrease investments in hydropower in the private sector.[12]

As indicated in the 'grey literature', which the Supreme Court of Nepal has ordered to be placed in the public domain in a recent decision,[13] a major large hydroelectric project such as Arun-3 with significant impact on the country's macro- economic management seems to be a part of the SAP concept and philosophy of intervening in the heart of a country's economic management. A document recording the discussions between the representatives and the World Bank states:

IDA remains very concerned about the macroeconomic implications of a power investment program including even the scaled down version of the Arun Project. An up-date of IDA's previous affordability analysis of the power investment program concluded that a power investment program with the Arun Project as the next hydropower generation project to be added to Nepal's interconnected system could be manageable, provided the Government implements a set of significant macroeconomic and NEA reforms. In relation to NEA, the reforms included implementing tariff, institutional, labour and other financial policy reforms to enhance its operational efficiency and profitability so that it can finance an appropriate share of power investment program's local costs (World Bank, 1992).

In the covering letter of 10 August 1992 forwarding the above document to the State Minister of Finance, the Chief of the Energy and Infrastructure Operations, Country Department 1, South Asia Region warns:

the Government would need to adopt satisfactory macroeconomic and power sector institutional-financial reforms and initiate their implementation in parallel with the further processing of the hydroelectric project. Unless such steps are taken, IDA and other donors cannot be confident that the Government will be able to manage the implications of such a large power investment program. This is particularly important with regard to NEA. Unless significant steps have already been taken to convert this inefficient, loss-making utility into a more effective, autonomous, commercially oriented organization, IDA and other donors will simply not be able to support entrusting to it by far the largest project ever undertaken in Nepal.

Among the macroeconomic reforms demanded by the Bank to fund Arun-3 were:

* Satisfactory progress on implementing the requirements of the Enhanced Structural Adjustment Facility.
* Implementation of the reform proposals for revenue mobilization and tax reform in the FY 1994 budget.
* Adoption of a prioritized three-year rolling budget, including a core investment programme of expenditure reforms satisfactory to the IDA.
* Implementation of the Administration Reform Commission measures.

The micro-hydro industry in Nepal is one of the country's few success stories where, in just over a decade, over 800 small turbine units have been installed in areas of the country which would not see grid expansion in the foreseeable future. It has also developed national capacity in terms of manufacture, construction and installation leading to large secondary spin-offs beyond merely supplying electricity. Even regarding supply, recent analysis indicates that large-scale is not necessarily cheaper due to economy of scale:

> the energy from large hydropower schemes constructed by HMG/N using international contractors with minimal involvement of local industry and manpower is over 50 percent more expensive than Small Hydro and Mini/Micro hydro which use local industry extensively for its construction (Panday, 1994).

An examination of the cost of components of a turbine manufactured in Nepal and the impact due to SAP indicated that the cost of labour was more than half and the cost of material only about one-quarter of the total cost of the turbine in 1985 when SAP was implemented. Subsequently the cost of imported material increased very sharply till 1988, when it occupied a larger share of the total costs than labour, indicating that the value-added gains were shifting to imported items of trade rather than human resources skills (*Economic Review*, 1995).

Although more investigations are required to definitively establish the *negative interlinkage between SAP and the small hydro industry in Nepal*, the preliminary findings do indicate such a causal relationship. *The SAP measures have a negative impact on national industry and small turbine manufacturers by ignoring the small scale altogether, by favouring imports over import substitution, importing of skills over national capacity building, and by focusing on large and centrally managed SAP-friendly investments in the power sector over decentralized community managed schemes.*

IMPLICATIONS FOR DEVELOPMENT POLITICS

After four decades of development aid, the net flow of resources is from the South to the North, not the other way around. Today, at the tail end of the Age of Foreign Aid, there is fatigue in the North and institutional mayhem in the aftermath of aid in the South.

The SAP represents a type of fatalism in foreign aid and development thinking. Previous development philosophies, despite their shortcomings and contradictions, were essentially optimistic regarding the prospect for improving human welfare. By contrast, the SAP *is a pessimistic dead end whose primary concern is to protect the protectors — to assure that the development loans are paid even if development has not occurred and will probably never occur.* Indeed, one author has suggested that 'the imposition of a state of permanent stagnation was precisely the idea' of SAP (Bello *et al.*, 1994).

The fundamental message of the SAP to poor nations, the core philosophy, as it were, has been summarized as: earn more, spend less. On the face of it, it is sound advice, sound enough to be delivered not only to governments but also to ordinary households. It would also have been sound policy had the slate been blank to start with. Poor nations of the Third World getting poorer every day would be glad to follow the puritanical message of the SAP if only they had a fair chance.

There are questions regarding the very philosophy of national economic management which have to be seen within the context both of the historical evolution of the society in question and the international context within which this society finds itself. *In most Third World countries, a rent-seeking feudalistic society is the primary bane of development. Equally baneful is its other extreme — uncontrolled market forces and unchecked liberalization, disregard for welfare to the point of obdurateness and denial of any role for the state in development. A free hand for these forces will be tantamount to mass marginalization.*

Opposed to this fatalism is the activism of the new and alternative schools of development both in the North and the South. (For more on this, see Bello, Chapter 9, this volume.) Even though the defects of Arun-3 had been highlighted within the bureaucracy and publicly for quite some time, some mysterious institutional filter seemed to block their acceptance.[14] An explanation for this behaviour is provided by Cultural Theory which states that perceptions of reality are culturally determined, and that cultures are determined exhaustively by two parameters alone — grid ascription and the group affiliation — which are basically answers to two central questions: 'who am I?' and 'how should I behave?'. These give rise to four mutually exclusive and exhaustive social environments of the hierarchist, the egalitarian, the individualist and the conscripted fatalist (Thompson *et al.*, 1990). Arun-3 was essentially a fight between the hierarchists and the egalitarians. For the former, preservation of their legitimacy and structure was paramount. For them, facts which undermined the structure were more of a threat than the technical and economic risks. For the egalitarians, who had no commitment to uphold external grid control, those technical and economic risks were far more dangerous than the legitimacy of the structure and its gate-keeping functions which were so dear to the hierarchy.

The only way such clogged institutional filters have been penetrated is by the *national and international networks of activists who have effectively bypassed many of the sentry points set up by hierarchies.* Arun-3 is an excellent example of such a new method of international discourse. While the pyramidal thinking, on which international institutions such as the World Bank have been designed, envisages consensus within nations represented by governments and then a consensus at the international level between national governments, *the new reality is that activist groups cut across national boundaries and network all across the globe.* They are thus able to strongly influence the outcome of international negotiations.[15]

In the case of Arun-3, the objections raised within Nepal were systematically ignored until Nepali activists teamed up with international activists and conducted a sustained campaign from 1993 onwards.[16] Because of this linked network, decision-makers of the North were forced to re-examine the issues, and seek second opinions independent of Bank expertise such as the Lawrence Berkeley Lab and even Maurice Strong of Rio Earth Summit fame.[17] Evidence could no longer be denied and the best course to preserve the hierarchy was deemed to be an honourable retreat. *This battle and subsequent victory, brought about not on environmental issues but in the arena of the Bank's own economic theology, signals an assertion of the alternative school of development upholding Southern dignity over the fatalism of hierarchic donor fatigue.* It may creatively guide global politics well into the next century.

NOTES

1. Willi Wappenhans was the chairman of a Portfolio Management Task Force formed by Mr Lewis Preston, President of the World Bank, in 1992 to examine the problems bedevilling the Bank's loans to projects in the South. The output of his committee is known as the Wappenhans Report, which said that the number of Bank projects judged unsatisfactory at completion increased from 15 per cent in 1981 to 37.5 per cent in 1991. Among the primary reasons cited were the pervasive preoccupation in the Bank with new lending, no attention to macroeconomic risks for the countries concerned, and preoccupation of Bank

staff with procurement induced by an internal Bank incentive system that rewards its employees for executing loan agreements rather than for performance of projects.

2. The sound and fury in Nepal, after the announcement by the World Bank's new President James Wolfensohn of the Bank's withdrawal from the project in August 1995, are almost reminiscent of Zulfikar Ali Bhutto of Pakistan vowing, after India 'imploded' its 'peaceful nuclear device' in 1974: 'We will make the atomic bomb even if we have to eat grass.' Nepali Congress, the ruling party between 1991 and 1994 during which period Arun-3 was promoted with single-minded gusto, in a party publication dated 17 August 1995, swears to resurrect Arun-3 because it is a project 'important for national well-being and self-respect'.

3. Former finance secretary Devendra Raj Panday in Integrated Development Systems (IDS) (1983).

4. In fact, in 1993, during the height of tense negotiations on conditionalities for Arun-3, the Government of Nepal went ahead and formed an 'Electricity Development Centre (EDC)' under the Ministry of Water Resources, ostensibly to deal with 'multi-purpose' projects, but effectively resurrecting the construction-oriented Electricity Department. Within Nepali bureaucracy, a member of the regular civil service is considered superior (in terms of power to manipulate state machinery through their 'permanent' status and proximity to the minister) to an employee of a parastatal corporation, fully owned by the government though it may be. This power has been manifest in their ability to create an all-powerful EDC out of nothing.

5. The computer program WASP used by the World Bank to justify Arun-3 through what is called the Least Cost Generation Plan (LCGEP) exercise has been used in other countries too. In Sri Lanka, it has been criticized by their experts as inherently biased to select thermal over hydro and large hydro over smaller hydro (Ceylon Electricity Board planners, personnel communication).

6. The first analysis was done by Canadian International Water and Energy Consultants (CIWEC), a consortium of Canadian hydropower consulting firms led by Acres of Niagara Falls and financed by CIDA grants to Nepal, in a February 1987 report entitled 'Evaluation of Hydropower Projects for Generation Expansion Plan'. It was later enshrined in an official document (written by a CIWEC consultant, this time working not in WECS but in the NEA) that was to acquire the status of a Bible: 'Least Cost Generation Expansion Plan – 1987', published in April 1987 as Report No. PD/SP/431124/3-3 of the System Planning Department of the Planning Directorate of the Nepal Electricity Authority (NEA).

7. To repeat a point, the Bank saying constantly for 10 years, through about $25 million of expensive studies, that Arun-3 is the best thing for Nepal since the invention of the wheel and then suddenly reversing its position to say no to Arun-3 is driving societal leaders in Nepal, to use quaint Americanism, 'bananas'.

8. See the interview with Nepal's Minister of State for Finance where he is quoted as saying that the decision to sell shares in government-owned enterprises was not taken at the instance of donor agencies like the IMF, the World Bank, or the Asian Development Bank but was the conscious decision of the government: 'We see no harm in sharing the experience of multilateral agencies. They are

our friends. Even profit making public units must be privatized. Our banks are no longer being run as organizations for charity.' This from a minister from the ruling party whose professed main ideological plank on which they won the 1991 general elections was 'democratic socialism' (*Times of India Business Times*, 1993).

9. The government, through what is called Letter of Development Policy (LODP), opened up the following areas of the economy for IMF intervention:

1 Rural areas faced with environmental degradation as a result of a growing population and the uncertainties of monsoon agriculture.

2 Macroeconomic management to mobilize resources and control recurrent expenditure and inflationary financing.

3 Agricultural institutions which have been financially weak and thus a drain on public resources and which prevented private-sector initiatives.

4 Industrial and trade policies which have been inappropriate and have actually encouraged smuggling along the open Indo-Nepal border.

5 Poorly performing public enterprises.

6 Public administration which has been weak.

7 Management of development which has been poor, leading to low disbursement of committed aid.

Thus the entire economy was opened up to tutelage by external agencies. In response, the Bank defined the government's stabilization and structural adjustment programme in the following manner:

1 In macroeconomic management, devaluation with flexible exchange-rate management, tighter fiscal policies, controlled credit expansion, adjustment in administered prices, restraints on external borrowing and import liberalization were proposed to set the economy on a more sustainable path.

Domestic resource mobilization was to occur through increased taxes and a cut in the wage bill.

To strengthen the balance of payments, the expansion of carpets and garments for export would be encouraged.

2 Agriculture and forestry were to be reformed through improving production incentives, enhancing the availability of services and inputs, and providing incentives to private-sector entry.

Fertilizer imports would be strengthened but the monopoly of the parastatal would not be abolished immediately. Private-sector involvement in seed production, processing and marketing would be encouraged. In food grain, incentives to producers were to increase, with phasing-out of subsidized food-grain sales and levy procurement and the introduction of a market-oriented consumer price-stabilization system.

3 In forestry, the overall government monopoly was to be reduced by involving individuals and communities.

4 In trade and industry, realistic exchange rates were to be introduced, inputs were to be made available without price distortions, excess regulatory control would be reduced, and the government body's efficiency improved.

5 Public enterprises would be reduced through closure or divestiture. Specifically targeted were two in the agriculture sector – the Agriculture Inputs Corporation and the Nepal Food Corporation.

6 Since foreign aid was already accounting for over 60 per cent of development expenditure, the need to improve development implementation was acknowledged. It was to be done through a system known as programme budgeting, which was to have a controlling wing in every ministry and department concerned with foreign aid.

10. The continuing programme aimed at:

1 Rationalizing the revenue system by improving tax administration, broadening the tax base and streamlining and enhancing domestic indirect tax systems; and reducing the number of corporations eligible for tax holidays.

2 Continuing programme budgeting, strengthening the National Planning Commission and improving the auditing of the public sector, while categorizing projects as core (eligible for further support) and non-core.

3 Replacing rigid licensing of imports by more liberal import policies and diversifying Nepal's exports.

4 Targeting irrigation for turnover to farmer-managed systems.

5 Targeting the banking sector for reform.

11. See World Bank (1989): 'An action plan for public enterprise divestiture was prepared, but its subsequent implementation was side-tracked when the highest bidders for certain PEs were non-Nepalese, some of whom already had extensive industrial holdings in Nepal, and the Government was not prepared to proceed further.'

12. See newsletters published by Alliance for Energy (PO Box 3934, Baluwatar, Kathmandu), especially 'Arun Pushing Others Aside', 1, 1, July 1993, and 'How Arun Crowds Out the Smaller Schemes', 1, 3, 31 August 1993, as well as White Papers 2 and 3 of the Alliance.

13. Inhured International, a Nepali activist group opposed to Arun-3, had filed a case in the Supreme Court of Nepal challenging the NEA and Ministry of Water Resources for keeping information on Arun-3 secret. It based its petition on the provision in the new constitution of Nepal that guaranteed right to information. In a landmark judgement of 8 May 1994, the Supreme Court upheld the petitioner's claim and ordered the government to make complete disclosure of project documents and information.

14. New information emerging from the ruins of Arun-3 indicate that the Nepali professionals within the Water and Energy Commission of HMG had expressed severe internal criticisms regarding its assumptions and estimates in the Least Cost Generation Expansion Plan as early as 1987. These criticisms were suppressed within the Ministry. Publicly, the first criticisms to come out were after the advent of democracy in Nepal. See Gyawali (1990); *Himal* (1991) (a debate on the merits and demerits of Arun-3 between this author and the World Bank's deputy resident representative in Nepal); and Shrestha, 1991. Shrestha writes, 'The Arun-3 project promised to enrich a few powerful business interests, so propaganda and decisive lobbying were done in favour of the project by championing the Arun-3 as the least cost.... It is rather sad to note that a few people involved in the power sub-sector manipulated the real facts and misinformed high level decision makers.... The analysis of the data were manipulated and unfounded assumptions were made in support of Arun-3. Nothing can explain such motives except vested interests and greed.' Shrestha is a senior insider within the Nepali Ministry of Water Resources even today.

15. S. Rayner highlights this new approach, which was very effective in securing the Montreal Protocol on the Ozone Layer in 1987. He calls it the polycentric decision model (which is more real) as opposed to the realist model, based on the inviolable nation–state concept (which today is less real). See Rayner (1994).

16. In Nepal, the Anti-Arun 'Alliance for Energy' was set up in March 1993. It tried to preserve a national campaign to no avail: not only were their views ignored but the government (prodded by the World Bank, as government officials admit) threatened them with action for 'anti-Nepal activities'. When they finally teamed up with the International Rivers Network of the US, Intermediate Technology Development Group of the UK, Urgewald of Germany and other Northern NGOs, the Bank could no longer ignore them.

17. Besides the Lawrence Berkeley Review, a critical factor was the conclusion of the German Federal Audit Office 'Bundesrechnungshof', which reviewed the KfW staff appraisal report and came to the conclusion that the activists' perception of the high risks of Arun-3 for Nepal was justified and that the KfW and BMZ were wrong for not considering them (Urgewald-Kampagne für Regenwald, 1995).

APPENDIX

Table 11.1 Arun-3 – Donors and Funding ($ million)

Donor	Fund	%	For
World Bank	175.0	16.2	$C + Co + L^1$
ADB Manila	127.6	11.8	C^2
German KfW	124.4	11.5	$C + E + Co^3$
France	19.0	1.8	$E + Co^4$
Sweden BITS	17.0	1.6	E^5
Finland			
FINNIDA	10.0	0.9	E^6
HMG Nepal	155.0	14.3	L^7
NEA	290.7	26.8	I^8
Undetermined			
(Japan?)	163.3	15.1	$Ci + Co^9$
Total	1,082.3	100	

Key: C = Civil Works; Co = Consultancies; L = Local mitigative measures, compensation and other such costs; E = Electrical and Electromechanical Works; I = Interest During Construction.
Source: World Bank (1994).

NOTES

1. The lead donor which negotiated and organized the funding from various sources. This amount includes the proposed credit of $140.7 million as well as the leftover of $34.3 million from a previous credit approved on 30 May 1989 for the Arun Access Road, which could not materialize because of bids by contractors through the Department of Roads several times higher than the estimates. World Bank credit was to partially finance with ADB and KfW civil works bid package Lot C1 (dam and desanding basin), C3 (access road, camp facilities, surge tank and headrace tunnel, this last with KfW) and C2 (powerhouse and appurtenant structures with an undetermined co-financier). Land acquisition plus rehabilitation was also to be financed by the World Bank.
2. The Asian Development Bank (ADB) was to fund the civil works together with the World Bank, KfW and an undetermined co-financier. According to some informal agreement of donors defining their turf, ADB has been heavily involved with national grid transmission and distribution (especially rural) of electricity over the last 10 years through their 6th and 7th Power Projects, and the World Bank with generation only (viz. Kulekhani, Marsyangdi). ADB-led transmission and distribution have been ongoing mostly to plan and schedule but the World Bank's generation has slipped due to the singular focus on Arun-

3. As a result, ADB has been promoting the 144 MW Kali Gandaki separately as lead donor, much to the dislike and initial resistance of the World Bank.

3. The only grant portion among the large donors, of which $55 million was for tied procurement for electrical equipment from Germany and $35 million was for tied procurement with France for the transmission line, leaving about $24 million for untied international competitive bidding for civil works and tied procurement of consulting services for construction supervision (to be done by the German consulting firm which designed both the Marsyangdi as well as Arun-3 hydroelectric projects).

4. To finance with KfW the 220 kV transmission line from the powerhouse to Biratnagar in east Nepal as well as its construction supervision. This old commitment was reaffirmed by France during the visit of the Nepali finance minister to Paris in October 1995 *en route* to the IMF annual meeting. It must be remembered that the finance minister comes from the Nepali Congress in the coalition cabinet which has vowed to resurrect Arun-3 after World Bank President Wolfensohn withdrew support. Also it is the French–Italian consortium of contractors which had bid the lowest for, and was about to get, the approximately $300 million civil works contract for Lot C1/C3.

5. To fund Duhabi Sub-station on the 132 kV national grid at Biratnagar where the Arun-3-generated 201 MW is expected to evacuate. Because the current single circuit can only evacuate about 27 MW on a sustained basis, Sweden has been asked to examine the possibility of augmenting line capacity. 'Hot line' stringing of a second circuit would possibly cost another $9 million. As a result, Sweden has stated that it is willing to allocate up to $30 million towards the project. Even then the national grid would have the capability to absorb only half the Arun-3 power, assuming that, by the time Arun-3 comes on line, the Biratnagar area and the eastern districts of Nepal would have achieved a load demand of about 50 MW. It must be mentioned that Sweden withdrew from the aid business in Nepal in the 1960s after King Mahendra overthrew the elected government headed by B. P. Koirala in December 1960. Koirala was well acquainted with Olaf Palme through the Socialist International. Sweden entered the Nepal Aid Group consortium (NAG) only after the restoration of democracy in Nepal in 1990 and this aid commitment was its first major involvement in Nepal. Many Swedes are not happy about being a thin and influence-less spectrum in a large World Bank-led band and have felt that they could have done more rewarding work if they had entered another field, such as education, as single actors. What is difficult to understand about Swedish involvement is their apparent inability to question the main conductor orchestrating Arun-3, i.e. the World Bank. The Swedes had funded a power plant in Sri Lanka (the Kotmale hydropower project, a part of the Mahaweli scheme) of the exact size and type as Arun-3 – an underground powerhouse with three 67 MW units totalling 201 MW. Kotmale was completed in 1987 at a total cost of 11.75 billion Sri Lankan rupees (which is almost equivalent to the Nepali rupee today, even though the two have depreciated at different rates over the past decade). See Norpower and Swedish International Development Authority, 1989. This amount was criticized by Sri Lankan engineers as being too expensive, partly due to technical mistakes and partly due to the tied nature of the aid. In comparison, the costs for Arun-3 were about 52 billion Nepali rupees. Before agreeing to get into the Arun-3 funding consortium, the Swedes

do not seem to have examined this obvious anomaly. See also Gyawali (1994) for what Sri Lankan engineers had to say about Arun-3 and Kotmale.

6. Tied financing for the supply of construction power to be made through a diesel power plant for which, as the road does not exist, the fuel supply would have to be provided, together with other construction material, through (in the language of the World Bank) 'extended air support', i.e. helicopter lifting, for which almost $40 million was to be allocated in the Arun-3 project. Finns have in the past supplied the 26 MW multifuel (diesel) electric generating sets to Nepal, a land-locked country rich in unexploited hydropower but which is having to import all its fossil fuel requirements, expending in the process almost half its foreign exchange earnings.

7. This contribution of the Nepali Government was to meet part of the local cost for the project as well as its environmental mitigation plan and the creation of a 'hydro facility'. This latter fund was to be created to meet the objection of the alternative development community and environmentalists who argued that this large project would soak up all the funding for small-scale projects which have had a successful track record in Nepal. For this, HMG was to transfer the equivalent of about $6 million to the government-controlled Nepal Industrial Development Corporation, which is also managed by the Ministry of Water Resources, to which the private sector could apply for funding to prepare feasibility studies of mini hydro plants.

8. The Nepal Electricity Authority (NEA) was to finance the equivalent of $285 million interest during construction as well as $1.89 million for land acquisition, compensation and rehabilitation, and $3.76 million for NEA's project administration costs. Much of this was to come out of tariff increases which have already occurred through World Bank pressure: the first of over 60 per cent on 17 November 1991, the second of 25 per cent on 13 March 1993 and a third of 38 per cent in March 1994. This is only the first of the preconditions for considering Arun-3. Once its implementation began, there were to be further tariff increases of 26 per cent in FY 1996, 25 per cent in FY 1997, 4 per cent in FY 1998 and 13 per cent in FY 1999. All this would make electricity significantly more expensive in Nepal, one of the world's poorest countries with some of the richest hydropower potential, than in the US. Much of the revenue from these increases – estimated to amount to about 32 billion Nepali rupees (about Rs 50 to the dollar) was to be transferred to HMG to help the latter (eventually) finance priority investments in the social sector. Thus this would have made the government of Nepal rich, but its industry nor its people not necessarily dependent on electricity. Part of this covenant also meant that NEA would not invest in any other hydropower project without the World Bank's prior approval, thus leaving the Bank totally in control of the sector.

9. This is part of the infamous 'funding gap' which led the World Bank to pull out of the project. The World Bank did lobby strongly to get the Japanese to chip in through a tortuous break-up of construction bid lots, but to no avail. The Japanese would have been more interested had there been some possibility of contributing to the electromechanical works. The Nepali politicians expected that the Japanese would contribute this amount as grant; but the Japanese never gave any written commitment to this effect even though they did provide some technical assistance to fund the Arun-3 design consultancy. A heavyweight Japanese official delegation arrived in Nepal to review the project in October

1994 and left with a typically Japanese enigmatic-sounding announcement that 'it would not be issuing any written document regarding this review'. The signal was as obvious as a Zen haiku. The UK, another donor, did not commit any funds for the project even though they professed strong diplomatic support for it at the executive board level of the World Bank, primarily because they had been contributing to rural development in the area previously and because they had a UK consultant as a partner with the German consultant designing the Arun access road.

Table 11.2 Arun-3 – Salient Parameters and Problems

Feature	Size	Remarks
Capacity	201 MW	Originally thought of as a 268 MW run-of-river plant, optimized by Canadian consultants at 402 with the assumption of selling seasonal (flood) power to India at prime price. When that proved difficult (there only exists an agreement between Nepal and India to exchange 50 MW) and there did not seem that much money available, the plan was changed to a two-phase development with 'Baby Arun' initially with three 201 MW turbines with the remaining to be carried out sometime in the uncertain future. The cost in Table 11.1 is for Baby Arun (Phase I).
Energy (Baby phase)	1715 GWh	Of this, the 'firm energy' is 1513 GWh with the uncommitted as yet second phase adding only 45 GWh firm and 1131 GWh seasonal energy.
Average flow (estimated)	355 m³/s	Out of the drainage area of 26 747 km² at the dam site, 25 307 km² (or 95 per cent) lies in Tibet/China. China has now constructed the Pengchoe irrigation project in the Chongtsu area and has begun withdrawing water from the Arun river to irrigate about 9000 ha of land. There are indications it has plans to develop several such schemes upstream (which is a trans-Himalayan rainshadow 'desert' area) which would reduce the dry season flow of the Arun by perhaps a third, thus reducing power production at the Arun-3 dam site by some corresponding amount.

Flood flow (estimated)	7288m^3/s	Although said to be a flood with a one in 10,000 year recurrence and hence the design of Arun-3 structures for a probable maximum flood of 8100m^3/s, there are many doubts about the calculations. The actual measurements from which the calculations are made are scanty and thus prone to surprises; glacial lake outburst floods could have more severe peak volumes than those estimated by dam builders (only 4000m^3/s) and with tremendous debris flow even more damaging than water; and cloudbursts in the Himalaya in smaller rivers in drier zones such as the Bagmati, with an average flow of 260m^3/s at the dam site, resulted in a flood in 1993 that overtopped the barrage at 15 000m^3/s.
Dam	68 m height 155 m length	Rigid concrete gravity dam with a reservoir of only 4 m depth that has practically no storage capability (residence time of stock v. flow of about 70 minutes). Why this is such a high dam for a run-of-river project with no storage has never been answered. Suspicions remain that it is necessary to justify a particular type of turbine and higher energy per m^3/s of flow than other alternatives such as Sapta Gandaki.
Tunnel	11 km length 5.6 m width	One in the first phase and one in the second. Himalayan geology, which has arisen from the head-on collision of the Indic Gondwana and Laurasian continental plates, is full of surprises at every few metres. In some places the tunnel passes under ridges resulting in rock overburden depths of 1000–1500 m. At such depths, rock pressures, hydraulic pressure columns, etc. (which cannot be predicted a priori with a significant degree of certainty) can increase the nasty surprises. In the Alps (geologically much more stable than the Himalaya), the longest tunnel is about 6 km.

Transmission 220 kV 120 km length	For Baby Arun. The second (uncommitted) phase envisages 312 km of 220 kV transmission to Kathmandu as well as 100 km to India to sell seasonal energy. (On power evacuation difficulties, see Table 11.1, note 6.)

REFERENCES

Bello, W. *et al.* (1994) *Dark Victory: The United States, Structural Adjustment and Global Poverty* (London: Pluto with Food First and Transnational Institute).

Bhattarai, B. (1993) 'Hydropower – The Arun-3 Economics and Politics', *Spotlight National Newsmagazine* (Kathmandu), 17 December.

Economic Review (Colombo, Sri Lanka) (1995) 'Structural Adjustment – The Small Producer's Dilemma', January/February.

Electricité de France (1990) 'Reconfirmation of Arun-3 Hydroelectric Project (Update of the Least Cost Generation Expansion Plan)', First Draft Summary (Kathmandu: Nepal Electricity Authority Corporate Planning Department), May 1990.

Gyawali, D. (1990) 'Arun-3 Impasse – Is There an Escape from this Blind Alley?', *The Rising Nepal*, 13 July.

Gyawali, D. (1994) 'Water Resource in the Coming General Elections' (in Nepali), *Kantipur Daily*, 29 October.

Himal (Kathmandu) (1991) 4, 3, July/August.

Integrated Development Systems (IDS) (1983) 'Foreign Aid and Development in Nepal', Proceedings of a Seminar, 4–5 October, PO Box 2254, Kathmandu, Nepal.

Integrated Development Systems (IDS) (1987) *Financing Public Sector Expenditure in Nepal* (Kathmandu: IDS).

International Monetary Fund (1993a) 'Nepal – Staff Report for the 1993 Article IV Consultation and Mid-term Review under the First Annual Arrangement Under the Enhanced Structural Adjustment Facility' (Document EBS/93/128), 10 August.

International Monetary Fund (1993b) 'Nepal – Background Paper' (Document SM/93/193), 24 August.

Moore, E. A. (IENED) and Smith, G. (C.I. Power Services Ltd) (1990a) 'Capital Expenditures for Electric Power in Developing Countries in the 1990s' (Toronto, Ontario), February.

Moore, E. A. and Smith, G. (1990b) *Water Nepal* (Kathmandu), 3, 1.

Norpower and Swedish International Development Authority (1989) 'Kotmale Hydropower Project Sri Lanka – Evaluation Report', July.

Panday, B. (1994) 'Small Rather Than Big: The Case for Decentralized Power Development in Nepal', *Water Nepal* (Kathmandu), 4, 1, pp. 181–90.

212 Foreign Aid and the Erosion of Local Institutions

Panday, D. R. (1987) 'Structural Adjustment?', The Nepal Chronicle Weekly (Kathmandu).
Rayner, S. (1994) 'Governance and the Global Commons', Discussion Paper no. 8 (London: The Centre for the Study of Global Governance, London School of Economics).
Schwarz, M. and Thompson, M. (1990) Divided We Stand – Redefining Politics, Technology and Social Choice (London: Harvester Wheatsheaf).
Shrestha, A. (1991) Hydropower in Nepal – Issues and Concepts of Development (Kathmandu: Resources Nepal).
Stavrianos, L. S. (1981) Global Rift: The Third World Comes of Age (New York: William Morrow).
Thompson, M. et al. (1990) Cultural Theory (Boulder, CO: Westview).
Times of India Business Times (Ahmedabad, India) (1993), 17 December.
Urgewald-Kampagne für Regenwald (1995) Press Release, 14 February.
World Bank (1987) 'Report and Recommendation of the President of the International Bank for Reconstruction and Development to the Executive Directors on a Proposed First Structural Adjustment Credit in an Amount Equivalent to $50 Million to the Kingdom of Nepal' (Washington, DC: World Bank), 3 March.
World Bank (1989) 'Report and Recommendation of the President of the International Development Association to the Executive Directors on a Proposed Credit of SDR 46.2 Million to the Kingdom of Nepal for a Second Structural Adjustment Credit' (Washington, DC: World Bank), 5 June.
World Bank (1992) 'Nepal: Arun-3 Hydroelectric Project. World Bank Power Sector Mission: July/August 1992. Record of Discussions' (Washington, DC: World Bank).
World Bank (1994), 'Staff Appraisal Report – Arun-3 Hydroelectric Project', Report Number 12643–NEP (Washington, DC: Energy and Infrastructure Division, Country Department I, South Asia Region, World Bank), 29 August.

12 The Globalizers' Dilemma: Contention and Resistance in Intercultural Space

Larry Lohmann

INTRODUCTION

'To place the South at the heart of our understanding of the global order', as this book intends to do, can mean different things. One is to put the South in the centre of pictures Northerners sketch of the global order. Another is to ask how various groups in the South themselves sketch such pictures.

This chapter tries, in a rudimentary way, to do both. Its subject is *the ways in which different actors contend with and influence what is loosely called 'globalization'*. These actors include not only transnational corporations and political and technocratic élites – and their more telegenic opponents – but also figures who do not usually appear in headlines or political science textbooks. Constructive and engaged understanding of the power struggles of all these actors – and their resources, motivations, dynamics, strategies, effectiveness, and capacities for alliances – requires *coming to grips with the idioms in which they interpret and present their own struggles.*

These idioms are varied, flexible, and constantly shifting. For political purposes, there is little point in looking for some unitary, privileged essence of how any particular group in the South or elsewhere 'really understands itself' (Quine, 1960, 1969). At any particular time, *how people interpret and present themselves depends on where they are placed, and where they place themselves, in what is an increasingly broad intercultural landscape or field of action.* When on a 'protected site', as James C. Scott calls it, away from the eyes and ears of others, any particular group may interact with itself through one or another vernacular, 'local–friendly' social practice, developing solidarity, settling disputes, hatching schemes, and translating alien ideas it hopes to make use of into local idioms (Scott, 1990).[1] When aspiring to a more global reach, on the other hand, any such group is likely to find that its identity and actions are understood, and have an impact, mainly, as it were, in translation into other local idioms, in which other ways of resolving differences prevail. The result – what I will call the *'globalizers' dilemma'* – may not be to a group's liking or advantage, but it is a fact around which it must *build a political approach.*

THE GLOBALIZERS' DILEMMA

Petty merchants in peasant societies often face what Hans-Dieter Evers refers to as the 'traders' dilemma'. In their own villages, traders need to be ready to keep prices low to conform with the local moral sense that all residents have a right to subsistence security. Outside the village, on the other hand, traders must, in addition to building up solidarity and a distinct identity among themselves, buy and sell at prices which depend on supply and demand across a wide region. They are therefore caught between loss of cash on the one hand and ostracization in their own villages on the other – either of which can make their activities difficult. One solution is for traders to become a separate ethnic or cultural group with high internal solidarity but often with a lower moral or status position in the village. Another is to try to accumulate cultural capital through religious fervour or conspicuous generosity. Another is to migrate. Still another occurs when the cultural landscape across which traders operate is 'simplified' and centralized through the wholesale replacement, down to the village level, of 'fair' prices and wages with 'market' ones and the conversion of land and labour into quasi-commodities (Polanyi, 1944; Thompson, 1963). In this case, the traders' dilemma is shifted on to the shoulders of the state, which has to subsidize capitalist enterprises yet contain popular outrage about any resulting social and environmental problems (Evers and Schrader, 1994).

Generalizing Evers's analysis, we can say that a *'globalizers' dilemma' affects any group which seeks to act across many cultural arenas at once.* Bureaucrats, planners, and developers, for example, in their pursuit of revenue, resources, information, and clients, have no choice but, on the one hand, to attempt to recast diverse local social spaces into a recursive pattern legible at a distance to central authorities – a task requiring decontextualizing devices such as cadastral land surveys,[2] mapping of forest reserves, titling programmes, citizen registration, censuses, opinion polls, IQ tests, DNA tests, assessments of Gross National Product, cost-benefit analysis, supply/demand forecasts, population projections, formulations of 'sustainable yield', master plans, guaranteed 'human rights', parliamentary-style representation, and the remapping and rebuilding of gendered commons spaces as locations occupied by economic actors.

On the other hand – and one should never forget that this becomes a personal as well as an institutional problem for globalizers – *they must find their way through the blizzard of consequences which blows back at them from each local area as a result of this attempt to reduce unique spaces to locations on national or global grids.* Among these consequences are the institutional incoherence which results when local officials subvert central directives in order to preserve or enhance their position in local hierarchies; the difficulty of monitoring outcomes or gaining customers and clients at the grassroots without the detailed local knowledge that comes only through direct experience; the ecological changes which occur when highly-integrated local-friendly systems of subsistence and stewardship are split into manager-friendly systems of 'forestry', 'religion', 'hydrology', 'morality' and 'agriculture'; the frequent local irrelevance or triviality of the variables which, say, IQ or DNA tests, cost-benefit analyses, and GNP or 'human rights' assessments measure; and popular resistance to being deprived of what is 'lost in translation' from the local moral economy into an expert system, exchange mechanism, or supposedly 'neutral' imposed political structure or scientific framework.

Something like the 'globalizers' dilemma' is also a problem for humbler political actors – those who resist the centralizing, colonial efforts of, say, transnational corporations, states and international agencies and non-governmental organizations. Indeed, the dilemma tends in one sense to be even more severe for oppressed groups, in that typically they neither want, nor are in a position to demand, as a solution to the dilemma, that all public interaction among different groups takes place only in idioms and cultural arenas friendly to themselves. They thus have to be particularly alert to the structure of other idioms and arenas. Where oppressed groups are unwilling or unable to enter alien cultural forums, moreover, or have no credibility there, they may still want allies who are more comfortable in those forums to do so; and this too requires a consciousness of the diversity of such forums and their advantages and disadvantages. Subordinate groups, in short, must not only constantly be sensitive to, but also be prepared to use, in one sense or another, an increasingly wide palette of unfriendly discourses and cultural forums in order to seek alliances or blunt attempts at suppression.

An Algerian anti-fundamentalist activist describes how difficult the resulting dilemma can be:

> [T]he rise of the extreme Right in Europe – and the subsequent Islam-bashing – makes it hard for us to know quite how to denounce fundamentalism to foreign audiences without giving fuel to those who demonize Muslims. Inside Algeria we are able to wage a struggle against fundamentalists with great clarity of judgement. But as soon as we go abroad, whether as emigrants or political refugees, we experience a schizophrenic sense of betrayal of our own people and start defending some of the values and politics that we were fighting against within our own country (Mahl, 1995).

Outside the Algerian milieu, the task of reinforcing the anti-fundamentalist struggle within the country may involve, paradoxically, refusing to talk about anti-fundamentalism or even changing the subject entirely and presenting oneself simply as an Algerian Muslim, if that is what is necessary to defend self-determination or prevent foreign anti-fundamentalist 'sympathizers' from doing harm or drawing the conclusion that one's struggle is an endorsement of 'universal' Western values. By the same token, other grassroots Southern groups, though they would not normally do so among friends, sometimes adopt, when this is unavoidable, the centralizing languages of science, economics or 'development', trying to twist them to advantage or combine them with other, friendlier vocabularies. Social movements, similarly, may gain élite or Northern allies by occasionally adopting the appealing identity of, for example, offbeat 'environmentalist' or 'human rights' struggles. Whatever qualms a subordinate group may have about the resulting 'schizophrenia', the fact is that, with growing cross-global contacts and interdependence, pressures are especially strong not to view any identity as 'essential'; nor the strategy or analysis associated with any particular cultural arena (for example, the classroom, the office, the conference, or the published paper) as 'the strategy' or 'the analysis' to be followed; nor any one role as the only role one can play; nor any one set of actors as the only possible allies. *Strategy, analysis and identity cannot be effectively determined a priori outside intercultural space;* they must be open to being changed whenever one learns a new language or steps into a new cultural arena.

Even when oppressed groups use local idioms, they have to be sensitive to other vocabularies. They can use such idioms for concealment, for example, only if they know which outside groups can and cannot understand them. When, conversely, an oppressed group finds it possible and tactically useful to try to inveigle potential allies into a dialogue in cultural terms of its own choosing – as happened on an unusually wide scale during the Zapatista rebellion which was launched in southern Mexico in January 1994 – it needs to know which alien idioms it must translate most carefully in order to satisfy its interlocutors, and which concepts outsiders are least likely to grasp and thus require special efforts to be communicated.[3] At the same time, other things being equal, it must choose the discourse which will best block out or defang the practices it considers most dangerous. All these tactics, although they use local vocabularies, are hardly the result of atavistic, ignorant, doomed, aesthetic, heroic attachments to isolated, static, aboriginal cultural identities or 'traditions' suddenly buffeted by a bewildering whirlwind of 'modernity' from which they require paternalistic 'protection'. Rather, they are pragmatic and intercultural, revealing an acute grasp of incommensurable discourses and of their advantages and disadvantages, alone and in combination, for particular purposes. Even a fundamentalist refusal of dialogue may, in some sense, be considered a response to the existence of this intercultural space (Giddens, 1994).

The scope of this chapter is too limited for me to be able to illustrate more than a tiny fragment of the politics opened up by the globalizers' dilemma. In the pages remaining, I will confine myself to discussing a small handful of anecdotes which simultaneously reveal (1) a piece of the fine structure of some dilemmas facing economic globalizers in one Southern country, Thailand; and (2) local people's strategic use of local idioms to attempt to gain some hold over the intercultural space in which these globalizers seek to operate. Although this discussion will not even touch most of the topics raised above, I hope it calls attention to one or two often-overlooked dynamics of contention in a way in which, say, a list of 'resistance movements' categorized in conventional political-science terms could not do, and thus to call attention to the kind of *intercultural micropolitics* which, when not grasped, has so often led to disastrous misunderstandings of *global macropolitics*.

The Street Vendor and the Newspaper Office: Choice of Forum in Conflicts over 'Discipline'

Lek worked for a large daily newspaper in Bangkok. When Lek's mother, a street vendor and former farmer who had helped support her through school and university, wanted to see her, she would simply make her way to the newspaper office and wait. While Lek understood and was deeply sympathetic to this habit, it was also frustrating: Lek, of course, was often in a meeting, off on an assignment, or writing a story, and so unable to come out straightaway for a visit. 'Mother,' Lek said (I paraphrase), 'you have to understand, I can't just drop everything whenever you come in. I hate to see you have to waste time.' 'Never mind, daughter,' came the mother's response. 'Mother can wait.' 'But Mother, there are ways of avoiding this. You can call on the telephone before you come in to find out when I'll be free. Then you wouldn't have to wait.' But Lek's mother, although perfectly capable of using the telephone or making an appointment, continued to behave as she always had.

This example is about (among other things) *time, whose connections to the politics of centralization and globalization* have long been stressed by writers as diverse as Thompson (1967), Ong (1987), Giddens (1990), Harvey (1989) and McLuhan (1964). Lek, in so far as she sojourned in the newspaper world, had to abide by *decontextualized, 'public' time, which, for the convenience of centralized social organization, is the same everywhere and is therefore governed by the impersonal, globally-valid rhythm of the clock.* Lek's mother, on the other hand, chose in this instance to abide by what might be called a *'commons' time more strictly governed by informal, oral, face- to-face, flexible, non-contractual, locally-valid understandings to synchronize according to the life-rhythms of a particular small group* – comprehension of which is as critical to getting along in most parts of the world as obedience to the clock.[4] By treating Lek's schedule as a life-rhythm rather than a clock-rhythm, and signalling her willingness to adjust to it ('Mother can wait'), Lek's mother was putting implicit pressure on Lek to adjust to her personal rhythm as well, and thus to carry on their relationship in commons time rather than public time. This pressure helped to maintain a type of personalized power relation which would have been lost if Lek's mother had yielded to the seemingly 'rational' pressure to telephone, make appointments, and so on. Lek's mother, we may surmise, understood the culture of the office, and her potential place in it, rather better than most Western office-dwellers understand the culture in which she was choosing to attempt to conduct her relationships, or their place in it. The reality of millions of actions like that of Lek's mother, carried out daily in the streets and offices of cities like Bangkok, is one that transnational corporations and international agencies ignore only at the cost of hostility, losses, and costly restructuring.

It is fascinating to place such examples in the context of the evolving discourse of *'disciplining the Other'* which has accompanied capitalism and of modern imperialism, and which forms such a central part of national- and international-level politics today. Most past and present Northern elites would say that people like Lek's mother 'lack discipline', disagreeing only over whether this deficiency is permanent or not. For colonialists like Cromer and Kipling, Asiatics, bound by climate and geography, would never learn to look at clocks (Said, 1987). Hence the need both for imperialism and for Orientalists, specialists in Asiatics' eternal essences. For eighteenth- and nineteenth-century British capitalists, the incipient working class in their own country, too, 'lacked discipline', being noticeably reluctant to subject themselves to a wage-labour market. This deficiency, however, was held to be at least partly corrigible by means of expropriation of commons, attrition of poor relief, breaking up of trade unions, mechanization, establishment of workhouses, asylums, Sunday schools, and so forth (Thompson, 1963).

For the international development establishment of the last 40–odd years, similar 'lacks' in the 'Third World' have become, in theory, completely corrigible, justifying a wide range of capitalism-led attempts at social engineering ranging from structural adjustment and 'women's development' to 'empowerment' and population control. As Lawrence Summers, the young ex-Chief Economist of the World Bank and now a US Under-Secretary of the Treasury puts it, 'whenever anybody says "But economics works differently here", they're about to say something dumb' (cited in George and Sabelli, 1994). Not only must everyone have clocks, but everyone will learn to watch them. Summers's Orient, instead of being eternal, is simply past. Either way, of course, that Orient remains temporally Other. The one thing actions such as those of Lek's mother cannot be, on this view, is present (as opposed to a throwback to the past) – any more than they can reflect a presence (as opposed to an absence, or a lack) of discipline.[5]

Yet, as the example of the newspaper office suggests, if globalizers flatter themselves that they can 'contain' Lek's mother's actions by protesting that she is not 'keeping up with the times', she can also 'contain' them, in many social environments, through the application of a different kind of social pressure associated with a different discourse. Indeed, all such discourses provide a certain amount of political and economic dynamite enabling their users creatively to 'reduce the reductionism' associated with globalization. In rural Malaysia, to vary the example, villagers may mock neighbours who break 'implicit time codes' in order to rush around in pursuit of money (Ong, 1987); in Colombia, certain peasant groups may view the discipline associated with commoditization as mediated by the devil (Taussig, 1980); while in Brazil, personalistic or hierarchial cultural discipline is often used to 'encompass' individualistic or egalitarian discipline, as when the *jeitinho*, or art of 'institutional bypass', is brought into play to reshape supposedly universally valid bureaucratic procedures (Neves de H. Barbosa, 1995).

Understanding the relationship between globalization and various groups in the South entails learning to look at the office, the aeroplane, the classroom, and the doctrines of 'economic growth' or 'human rights' through the eyes of those who see and understand their significance but are able to insist on viewing them from their own angles.

Pronouns and Power: Digesting English, Processing Imperialism

In Thai, as in many other languages, pronouns translated indifferently into English as 'you' and 'I' signal status, age, occasion, friendship, hostility, gender and wealth. The pronouns *pii* and *nong*, indicating an older sibling–younger sibling type of relationship, are often used between seniors and juniors who are rough contemporaries, each element of the pair serviceable as either first- or second-person pronoun. A young couple teasingly deflating each other's pretensions may use the 'you'/'I' words *tuh* and *chan*. Toughs squaring off or drinking together may address each other aggressively as *mueng* and *koo*. Young women can cement their intimacy with *eng* and *khaa*. *Than* and *khaphajao* suggest that formal and elevated proceedings are under way. The first- or second-person child-designator *noo* is used among adults only of and by women. In dignified contrast are the first- person *dichan* or *chan* (*pome* for men), which insist on relations of greater equality, and which are all paired with the unigender second-person *khun*. Given names, nicknames, and a raft of other kinship and royal terms add to the pronominal repertoire.

The presence in Thailand of increasing numbers of English-speaking advisers, soldiers, tourists, businesspeople and bureaucrats posed a problem for this way of organizing relationships. What pronouns could be used to encapsulate, in indirect speech, relationships with these non-Thai-speaking intruders, with their money, hardware, tempting offers for the élite, get-rich-quick schemes, awkwardness, assertion, and lack of comprehension? Speaking as if foreigners had addressed you with (say) *khun* (or any other existing second-person Thai pronoun) would portray them as sensitive to status distinctions to which they were in fact oblivious. Portraying yourself as having addressing foreigners as *khun*, etc., by the same token, would leave out the fact that your feelings about them – which might include concealed contempt or amusement at the foreigners' pretensions or lack of subtlety, a sense of superiority to them combined with uneasy respect for their power, bashfulness, defensiveness, and a self-mocking awareness of the awkwardness of the encounter mixed with the desire to turn it to advantage – were quite different from those you would have in addressing a fellow Thai with the same pronoun.

The ingenious solution was to retool the English pronouns 'you' and 'I' and transplant them into the Thai language as *yoo* and *ai*, assigning them the function of symbolizing Thai–Western relationships or Western–Western relationships. Just as *koo* and *mueng* can instantly set the scene between two Thais about to come to blows, or *pii* and *nong* affirm a power hierarchy of age between two interlocutors, so, in reported speech, *yoo* and *ai* – whether appearing in the sly mockery of a Thai-language political cartoon or the sometimes satirical, sometimes straightforward after-hours conversation of Western embassy employees – came to denote a particular kind of intercultural and international relationship. The new pronoun pair, in short, was a way of containing, digesting, comprehending, calling attention to, and commenting on both the Thai–foreign relationship and the 'egalitarianism' and individualism of English-speaking societies. Even the smallest children came to understand the difference between a *yoo–ai* relationship and a *khun–dichan* or *eng–khaa* one. Although the pronouns used Western phonemes as raw material, the effect was the opposite of capitulation to Western ways. Keeping Thais and Westerners distinct within the Thai world, the new pronouns both shaped solidarity and resistance and sharpened the dilemma of globalizers hoping to integrate Thailand more closely within Western-dominated cultural and social systems.[6]

The point is hardly restricted to linguistics and manners. Ashis Nandy, for example, has noted that the 'placement' of some aspects of the West as a martial, violent, 'virile *Ksatriyahood*[7] which has run amuck [*sic*]' may have helped many Indians deal with, and survive under, colonialism. Even the *babu* or Brown Sahib, whom Westerners like to flatter themselves is a servile, second-rate imitator of their own mores, is, viewed from another angle,

> an interface who processes the West on behalf of his society and reduces it to a digestible bolus. Both his comical and dangerous selves protect his society against the White Sahib [who] turns out to be...not the conspiratorial dedicated oppressor that he is made out to be, but a self-destructive co-victim with a reified life style and a parochial culture, caught in the hinges of history he swears by.... What looks like Westernization is often only a means of domesticating the West (Nandy, 1983, xv, 108).

The Peruvian activist Eduardo Grillo Fernandez, in a somewhat different vein, speaks of how 'imperialism' is 'digested' in the Andes. 'Life and health in one's own culture', Grillo insists, can be maintained without

> accepting voluntary or imposed isolation. Only in this way does one have possibilities for decolonization, because one has a presence in each of the settings in which imperialism nests, and they are well-understood. The growth of the cities in the Andes...is mostly due to the affluence of individuals with Andean backgrounds who came to live in the city in order to experience this seductive phenomenon occurring within their environments which the official propaganda presents as desirable. These individuals, however, do not come to live in accordance with civic norms that claim to be universal, nor do they become part of an established order, but instead they do it

in their own communal way, Andeanizing the 'foreign' city. This allows them to rise above the crisis that they encounter there by confronting it as a collective solidarity and not as nuclear families or individuals ... barriadas ... sheltering migrants from separate rural communities, districts and provinces ... replicate their solidarity culture and fiestas in Lima ... side by side with colonial ways that began 500 years ago with the European invasion (Grillo Fernandez, 1993).

Here again, reality defeats globalizers' self-aggrandizing notion that vernacular practices belong to 'the past', while supposed 'universalizing' ways lie in 'the future'.

The Western Consultant and the Karen Villager

In the 1980s, Finland's Jaakko Poyry Oy, the largest forestry consulting firm in the world and a key force in globalization of the forestry and paper industry, contracted with Thailand's parastatal Forestry Industry Organization (FIO) to develop a locally-sensitive plan to exploit for lumber certain native pine forests used as sources of water and other subsistence goods by ethnic Karen villagers at Baan Wat Chan in Northern Thailand. At one point in the ensuing struggle over these forests, a Poyry consultant asked a villager how he thought they could best be managed under the plan. The consultant outlined three hypothetical choices. First, individual families in the area could be assigned rights to separate small forest plots to manage as they wished for an on-site sawmill. Second, sub-district or district-level officials could oversee the harvesting of larger areas. Third, management rights to such areas could be granted to separate communities.

The villager straightforwardly rejected all three alternatives. First, he objected to the manner in which the choice was put to him. If such matters were to be discussed and considered, they could only be discussed and considered in the community, not through approaches to separate individuals or opinion polling. Second, the villager said that each alternative would lead to destruction of the forest on which the villagers depended for water and other goods. Putting the forest in the hands of discrete individuals, he explained, would destroy the community and thus the forest. Putting the forest in the hands of government officials, on the other hand, would lead to power imbalances, corruption, and again forest destruction. And putting the forest in the hands of separate communities, while it would create more chances of checks and balances, would lead to inter- community conflict and could not succeed if commercial management were the goal. *The only way to preserve the forest, the villager maintained, was (roughly) to leave it defined as neither privately- nor publicly-owned, but as commons (The Ecologist, 1993), with local Karen maintaining authority over both the means and ends of its use.*

Such a thoroughgoing rejection not only of an official initiative, but also of the terms in which it is advanced, is, however often it is wished for by local groups, unusual in a popular struggle – as is the implicit demand that a local debate take place entirely in a local-friendly vocabulary. What made it possible in this case was not an attitude of heroic defiance on the part of the villager, but rather the fact that *a recent, popularly-supported national logging ban had ensured the local Karen of national-level allies in any anti-logging struggle* – allies who were able to carry the struggle into other cultural forums as well.

In the course of the battle against Jaakko Poyry's plan, the villagers also did not hesitate to avail themselves of the élite-sanctioned discourse of Buddhism – holding elaborate 'tree-ordaining' ceremonies in which the pines were wrapped in, and thus symbolically protected by, orange robes like those worn by monks – and of widespread urban middle-class and journalistic concern about the area's rare pine forests. In the context of this intercultural politics, the instrument of brute force on which officials fell back in order to suppress meetings and marches proved weak and clumsy. The Jaakko Poyry project was suspended in 1993. This victory – though it is unlikely it will ever be acknowledged as such in any United Nations document or political science textbook – added weight to an *accretion of local resistance which continues to constrict and channel attempts to centralize and globalize control of Thailand's resources.*

CONCLUSION

In an era of increasing global contact and interdependence, there exists no single local perspective – including that of those local traditions that describe themselves collectively as 'modernity' – which can by itself reveal all of the springs or potential of any particular movement contesting imperialism, development, centralized planning, or the spread of global capitalism. Nor does there exist any single cultural arena within which alone the resulting struggles can be played out. In this chapter I have tried to challenge both what Dean MacCannell (1993) calls the 'White Culture' idea that politics can or should be housed in a single forum or language and the 'traditionalist' idea that resistance flows outward from an isolated cultural identity which predates or floats free from intercultural space and time. *Inhabiting a particular cultural system, even a familiar one, need not mean that it is permanently central to one's identity, merely that it has its own advantages, satisfactions, or strategic uses as a 'playing field' at certain times of struggle.*

These conclusions allow us to gain a certain sociological distance from a number of classical political strategists' dichotomies: for example, reform v. revolution, co-operation v. non-cooperation, and 'being co-opted' v. 'proper resistance' (cf. Foucault, 1980). A movement which, to ease its 'globalizers' dilemma', needs to operate in many different forums at the same time, may acquiesce in the translation of its struggle into the terms of neo-classical economics in one forum while (perhaps through allies) criticizing the entire framework of economics elsewhere; may support steps toward reform in one cultural forum while, through allies, actively pursuing revolutionary change in another; and may co-operate with the authorities where unavoidable while (again, perhaps through allies) defying them elsewhere. The frequent impossibility or irrelevance of programmes of liberal 'compromise', and the need to fight in many arenas at once without being sucked into any single 'approved' version of resistance, are, paradoxically, two sides of the same coin of intercultural struggle. As Nandy observes, resisters must remain aware of the West's skills at producing 'not only its servile imitators and admirers but also its circus-tamed opponents and its tragic counterplayers performing their last gladiator-like acts of courage in front of appreciative Caesars' (1983: xiv).

Also brought into question by the conclusions of this chapter is a cluster of views according to which social change (or at least 'damage control') is necessarily above all else a matter of pressuring or massaging 'the powerful' in their preferred idioms; re-educating 'world leaders'; 'changing society's paradigm'; carefully formulating a utopian 'blueprint for change' and then 'implementing' it; 'determining concrete goals and then convincing others to act on them'; 'seizing the state apparatus'; 'influencing the UN'; 'taking control of the media'; 'attempting to overturn the world system'; and the like. This cluster of views assumes that power and thus social change must always be primarily a matter of acting within, or expanding, a single cultural forum, consciousness, or 'paradigm', outside of which power is sometimes held not even to exist. Little attention is given to *strategies for acting interculturally,* and without a single guiding or co-ordinating 'subject', in a many- centred mosaic of overlapping forums, each with its own forms of power and possibilities of change. Because they fail to take full account of what I have called the globalizers' dilemma, groups whose resistance strategies are guided by one or another of this cluster of views become exceptionally vulnerable to it (Ferguson, 1994).

In its emphasis on the *radical diversity of sources, resources, and limitations of resistance,* this chapter has picked out threads which tend to run across boundaries between North and South (see Wilkins and Gills, chapters 2 and 3, this volume). The intercultural nature of struggle against oppression, for example, is hardly news to North American or European women of any colour, who daily have to operate in a space consisting of a variety of contrasting webs of power both on and off 'protected sites', in the office, the street, and the household, using both 'men's' and 'women's' dialects (Gilligan, 1976; Tannen, 1992). Nor will it be unfamiliar to many local environmental activists in the North who, at least on their own 'protected sites', use languages and other social practices of the commons in opposition to those of economics, planning, and the public/private dichotomy (*The Ecologist,* 1993, 1995).

On the whole, however, it is not unfair to say that *Southerners are more versed than Northerners in intercultural politics,* partly because of the greater current prevalence in the South of clashes between subsistence and capitalist economies, orality- and literacy-based cultures, personalistic and impersonalistic social structures, communal and individualistic styles of action, and so on. In a Southern country, to make just one comparison, if a consultant undertakes a cost-benefit analysis of a controversial hydroelectric dam, or conducts an opinion poll in a remote rural village containing questions like 'Would you like to have a washing machine in your house or not? Please answer yes or no', the choice of these techniques is in itself likely to be treated by local people as political and cultural aggression on the part of central authorities. In the North, by contrast, such techniques are more easily mystified as 'unbiased aids to rational decision-making' or a 'democratic sounding of popular opinion'.

Awareness of the globalizers' dilemma, too, tends for obvious reasons to be sharper in the South than in the North. *On the ground in Chiapas or Chiang Mai, it is simply common sense that what 'Third World development' (for example) claims to do and what it really winds up doing have little to do with each other.* In the high-rise meeting-rooms of London or Washington, this is still an atrocious, intolerable paradox, open discussion of which is barred not because it is taboo, but because it is nearly inconceivable. A diplomat based in Zaire recently remarked sardonically that according to World Bank statistical indicators of economic welfare, most people in the country should be dead by now. It would hardly be surprising if, being alive, such people had learned to take a critical and watchful stance toward the categories in which they are placed by others.[8]

NOTES

1. The multiplicity of such 'local–friendly' or 'protected-site' idioms is likely to persist and to continue to figure in the way Southerners interpret themselves to themselves and to others. While the last few centuries have eroded the boundaries around many former 'protected sites' by eliminating languages, turning land and labour into quasi-commodities under more centralized control, and spreading 'development' (Polanyi 1944, Thompson 1963, and see Chapter 12), divisions of labour, differences in class and interests, and other forms of social diversity show little inclination to wither away, and new boundaries and sites are constantly being formed. Detailed, uniform responses, moreover, will never be elicitable over wide areas, even in cooperative subjects, from a distant central location through sets of decontextualized rules (Wittgenstein 1953; Collins 1987, 1990), and it will continue to be difficult to replace highly-localized commons with 'universal' public or private goods without massive damage and disruption resulting. Rural Southerners and the shrewder variety of capitalist planner alike have learned, moreover, that the supposedly universal logic of 'economics' and of 'development' not only cannot deliver the goods it promises but is, if pushed too far, counterproductive (*The Ecologist*, 1993 and 1995; Illich, 1981 and 1982; Norgaard, 1994; Sachs, 1992; Escobar, 1995; Ferguson, 1994). Even multinational businesses, once optimistic that cultural homogenization would provide an outlet for the large-scale production of uniform commodities in which they specialized, have come to the realization that the 'apparent convergence between different cultures has not gone as far as they thought' and are shifting their production and marketing strategies accordingly (*The Economist*, 1995).
2. Revealing the extent, value and ownership of land for taxation purposes.

3. When, two hours after the North American Free Trade Agreement came into force on 1 January 1994, thousands of Indians occupied four of the main towns in Chiapas and declared war on the Mexican government, their rebellion was immediately and deliberately portrayed from high levels as a lack of either rationality or of development. On the one hand, President Salinas's categorization of the event as a foreign-led communist insurrection, plus the call of the international financial community to wipe out the Zapatistas, gave sanction to military suppression. On the other, institutions such as *The Economist* lost little time in reinterpreting the Chiapas uprising as a sign of 'underdevelopment' and 'overpopulation' – i.e. a sign that yet more economic integration and foreign investment was required. Such attempts to 'mute' resisting voices have the effect – and to some extent are meant to – of making events such as the Chiapas revolt look bewildering, alien and inexcusable to Northern publics. The Zapatistas' intercultural tactical skills, however – including their humour, openness to dialogue, and talent for flouting the expectations of outsiders – helped make them capable of insisting on being treated as a presence rather than an absence to be filled. By prolonging the dance of interpretation and counter-interpretation, they gained both time and bargaining power, and succeeded in communicating at least a few of their aims to a wide Mexican and international public, among them an end to 500 years of oppression and 40 years of 'development' and a chance to reclaim their own 'art of living and dying' and foster post-economic forms of social life (Esteva, 1994; EZLN, 1994).

4. What counts as 'late' or as 'wasting time' in the framework of public time is determined by the clock (and, of course, by the political interests clustered around it) and can be corrected by adjusting one's rhythms more closely to it. What counts as 'late' in commons time, on the other hand, is determined by the feelings and actions of others one knows personally and can be corrected by adjusting one's rhythms more closely to theirs, whether those rhythms coincide with clock time or not. If every participant at a meeting shows up an hour after the agreed-upon time, they are all 'late' in the framework of public time, but not necessarily 'late' in a commons time framework. Conversely, someone who is 'on time' according to a public conception may, under certain circumstances, be 'late' according to commons time. Commons time is hardly confined to the Asian continent. In Brazil, for example, competitive swimmers tend to measure themselves not against 'the clock', or against some impersonal programme of self-improvement, but against whoever is competing against them at a particular time; while at meetings, as in Thailand, 'the clock waits for people instead of people waiting for the clock' (Kottak, 1995). As Subcomandante Marcos has noted of the 2.00 a.m. start of the Chiapas revolt, 'as usual, we were late'.

5. This attitude is, of course, not confined to the North. At a meeting in March 1995, the head of one of Thailand's leading conservation organizations asked a village leader how, if local people remained in control of a local community forest, they could possibly prevent the area from being overrun by outside mushroom-gatherers. Although he was striving to be sympathetic to her defence of grassroots forest conservation, her answer – that local villagers would exclude outsiders who planned to market their gatherings but would allow others in, provided no damage was done, if their aim was subsistence –

clearly surprised him in its cogency. He was conceptually unprepared for a 'discipline' which was neither public nor private, depending neither on the state nor on business.

6. As Edmund Leach (1954) wrote of Northern Burma, long before 'globalization' became a buzzword:

In any geographical area which lacks fundamental natural frontiers, the human beings in adjacent areas of the map are likely to have relations with one another – at least to some extent – no matter what their cultural attributes may be...But...if social structures are expressed in cultural symbols, how can the structural relations between groups of different culture be expressed at all? My answer to this is that the maintenance and insistence upon cultural difference can itself become a ritual action expressive of social relations. (p. 17)

Or as Nandy (1983) puts it, 'familiarity can breed distance, too'.

7. *Ksatriya* refers to a member of the second of the four great Hindu castes, the military caste.

8. Thanks to Sarah Sexton and Nicholas Hildyard for helpful editorial advice and to Heinrich-Böll-Stiftung for financial support.

REFERENCES

Collins, H. M. (1987) *Changing Order: Replication and Induction in Scientific Practice* (London: Sage).

Collins, H. M. (1990) *Artificial Experts: Social Knowledge and Intelligent Machines* (Cambridge, MA: MIT Press).

The Ecologist (1993) *Whose Common Future?: Reclaiming the Commons* (London: Earthscan).

The Ecologist (1995) 'Overfishing: Causes and Consequences', 25, 4, special issue, May/June.

The Economist (1995) 'Big is Back: A Survey of Multinationals', 24 June.

Escobar, A. (1995) *Encountering Development* (Princeton: Princeton University Press).

Esteva, G. (1994) 'Basta! Mexican Indians Say "Enough!"', *The Ecologist*, 24, 3, May/June, pp. 83–5.

Evers, H.-D. and Schrader, H. (eds) (1994) *The Moral Economy of Trade: Ethnicity and Developing Markets* (London: Routledge).

EZLN (Ejército Zapatista de Liberación Nacional (or Zapatista National Liberation Army)) (1994) *Zapatistas: Documents of the New Mexican Revolution* (Mexico City: Autonomedia Press).

Ferguson, J. (1994) *The Anti-Politics Machine: Development and Bureaucratic Power in Lesotho* (Minneapolis, MN: University of Minnesota Press).

Foucault, M. (1980) *Power/Knowledge*, ed. Colin Gordon (New York: Pantheon).

George, S. and Sabelli, F. (1994) *Faith and Credit: The World Bank's Secular Empire* (Harmondsworth: Penguin).

Giddens, A. (1990) *The Consequences of Modernity* (Cambridge: Polity).

Giddens, A. (1994) *Beyond Left and Right: The Future of Radical Politics* (London: Polity).

Gilligan, C. (1976) *In Another Voice* (Cambridge, MA: Harvard University).

Grillo Fernandez, E. (1993) 'Cultural Affirmation: Digestion of Imperialism in the Andes', in F. Apffel-Marglin and S. A. Marglin (eds) (1993) *Decolonizing Knowledge* (Oxford: Clarendon).

Harvey, D. (1989) *The Condition of Postmodernism* (Oxford: Blackwell).

Illich, I. (1981) *Shadow Work* (London: Marion Boyars).

Illich, I. (1982) *Gender* (New York: Pantheon).

Kottak, C. (1995) 'Swimming in Cross-Cultural Currents', in D. J. Hess and R. A. Da Matta (1995) *The Brazilian Puzzle: Culture on the Borderlands of the Western World* (New York: Columbia University Press), pp. 49–58.

Leach, E. R. (1954) *Political Systems of Highland Burma: A Study of Kachin Social Structure* (London and Cambridge, MA: LSE and Harvard University Press).

MacCannell, D. (1993) *Empty Meeting Grounds* (London: Routledge).

McLuhan, M. (1964) *Understanding Media* (London: Routledge).

Mahl (pseudonym) (1995), 'Women on the Edge of Time', *New Internationalist*, 14, August.

Nandy, A. (1983) *The Intimate Enemy: Loss and Recovery of Self under Colonialism* (Delhi: Oxford University Press).

Neves de H. Barbosa, L., 'The Brazilian Jetinho: An Exercise in National Identity', in D. J. Hess and R. A. Da Matta (1995) *The Brazilian Puzzle: Culture on the Borderlands of the Western World* (New York: Columbia University Press), pp. 35–46.

Norgaard, R. (1994) *Development Betrayed* (London: Routledge).

Ong, A. (1987) *Spirits of Resistance and Capitalist Discipline* (Albany, NY: State University of New York).

Polanyi, K. (1944) *The Great Transformation* (Boston, MA: Beacon).

Quine, W. V. O. (1960) *Word and Object* (Cambridge, MA: MIT Press).

Quine, W. V. O. (1969) *Ontological Relativity* (New York: Columbia University Press).

Sachs, W. (1992) *The Development Dictionary* (London: Zed).

Said, E. (1987) 'Introduction' to Rudyard Kipling, *Kim* (London: Penguin.)

Scott, J. C. (1990) *Domination and The Arts of Resistance: Hidden Transcripts* (New Haven, CT: Yale University Press).

Tannen, D. (1992) *You Just Don't Understand* (London: Virago).

Taussig, M. (1980) *The Devil and Commodity Fetishism* (Chapel Hill, NC: University of North Carolina Press).

Thompson, E. P. (1963) *The Making of the English Working Class* (London: Penguin).

Thompson, E. P. (1967) 'Time, Work-Discipline and Industrial Capitalism', *Past and Present*, 38, pp. 56–97.

Wittgenstein, L. (1953) *Philosophical Investigations* (Cambridge: Cambridge University Press).

Index